Automating Excel with P

Processing Spreadsheets with OpenPyXL

Michael Driscoll

Automating Excel with Python

Processing Spreadsheets with OpenPyXL

Michael Driscoll

Leanpub

This is a Leanpub book. Leanpub empowers authors and publishers with the Lean Publishing process. Lean Publishing is the act of publishing an in-progress ebook using lightweight tools and many iterations to get reader feedback, pivot until you have the right book and build traction once you do.

Also By Michael Driscoll

Python 201

ReportLab - PDF Processing with Python

Jupyter Notebook 101

Creating GUI Applications with wxPython

Python 101

Pillow: Image Processing with Python

Contents

About the Technical Reviewer

Ethan Furman

Ethan, a largely self-taught programmer, discovered Python around the turn of the century, but wasn't able to explore it for nearly a decade. When he finally did, he fell in love with its simple syntax, lack of boiler-plate, and the ease with which one can express one's ideas in code. After writing a dbf library to aid in switching his company's code over to Python, he authored PEP 409, wrote the Enum implementation for PEP 435, and authored PEP 461. He was invited to be a core developer after PEP 435, which he happily accepted.

He thanks his wife for choosing to join him in life's great adventure – without her he would be a much poorer man.

Acknowledgments

Learning and writing about OpenPyXL and how to use Python to automate Excel was a lot of fun. However, it wouldn't have been as good a book as it is without Ethan Furman returning as my technical reviewer and editor. Thank you so much!

Steve Barnes is a long time reader and friend of mine who helped out by reviewing a few chapters here and there. Steve gave me some great feedback that helped make the book better.

Special thanks goes out to the folks who wrote OpenPyXL, XslxWriter, Pandas and all the other great Python packages you can use to work with Microsoft Excel.

And to anyone that I am forgetting and to you, thank you too!

Thank you for reading this book!

Mike

Introduction

Welcome to **Automating Excel with Python**! Microsoft Excel is one of the most popular spreadsheet programs in the world. Most businesses use Excel for something in their work. Many businesses will add onto Excel using macros or Visual Basic for Applications.

The purpose of this book is to help you learn how to use Python to work with Excel. You will be using a package called **OpenPyXL** to create, read, and edit Excel documents with Python. While the focus of this book will be on OpenPyXL, you will also learn about other Python packages that you can use to interact with Excel using the Python programming language.

By the time you have finished this book, you will have learned the following:

- Opening and Saving Workbooks
- Reading Cells and Sheets
- Creating a Spreadsheet
- Working with Formulas
- Cell Styling
- Conditional Formatting
- Charts
- Pivot Tables
- and more!

OpenPyXL is a versatile Python package that will allow you to automate Excel using Python. You will be able to enhance your knowledge of Python and Excel by reading this book. If you have only dabbled in programming before, then you will find that Python can really expand your knowledge and abilities.

This book will be using **Python 3.8** or newer.

Who is this book for?

This book is targeted at intermediate level developers. The ideal person reading this book will know the Python language already and understand how to install 3rd party packages. However, if you are new to Python, the examples in this book should still be easy to follow. If you need to know more about the Python programming language, there are many free resources.

About the Author

Mike Driscoll has been programming with the Python language for more than a decade. When Mike isn't programming for work, he writes about Python on his blog[1] and contributes to Real Python. He has worked with Packt Publishing and No Starch Press as a technical reviewer. Mike has also written several books.

You can see a full listing of Mike's books on his blog[2].

Conventions

This book doesn't have a lot of conventions. However, there are a few small ones. The first convention is how a code block is formatted:

```
# open_workbook.py

from openpyxl import load_workbook

def open_workbook(path):
    workbook = load_workbook(filename=path)
    print(f'Worksheet names: {workbook.sheetnames}')
    sheet = workbook.active
    print(sheet)
    print(f'The title of the Worksheet is: {sheet.title}')

if __name__ == '__main__':
    open_workbook('books.xlsx')
```

You may also see tip blocks that look like this:

> # This is a tip block
>
> Lorem ipsum

Other than that, there are no other conventions you need to know about.

[1] https://www.blog.pythonlibrary.org/
[2] https://www.blog.pythonlibrary.org/books/

Book Source Code

The book's source code can be found on Github:

- https://github.com/driscollis/automating_excel_with_python

The book's code is under the MIT license, which is very permissive and allows you to do almost anything with the code.

Reader Feedback

I welcome feedback about my writings. If you'd like to let me know what you thought of the book, you can send comments to the following address:

- comments@pythonlibrary.org

Errata

I try my best not to publish errors in my writings, but it happens from time to time. If you happen to see an error in this book, feel free to let me know by emailing me at the following:

- errata@pythonlibrary.org

Cover Art

The cover art was created by Nisa Tokmak.

Now let's get started!

Chapter 1 - Setting Up Your Machine

Automating Microsoft Excel with Python requires that you have a few dependencies installed. The purpose of this chapter is to get your computer configured so that you can work with Microsoft Excel files using the Python programming language.

In this chapter, you will cover the following:

- Dependencies
- Installing OpenPyXL with pip
- Installing OpenPyXL with conda
- Using OpenPyXL in a Python Virtual Environment

Let's get started!

Dependencies

To be able to use this book, you will need to have the Python programming language installed. If you are on Mac or Linux, you may have Python already installed. If you want to, you can install the latest version of Python from their website[3].

You will also need some kind of spreadsheet software. You will be reading and writing XLSX documents. These documents are a special type of XML. They can be read by other spreadsheet programs besides Microsoft Excel.

While this book will focus on using Microsoft Excel and Python, you can use Apple's **Numbers** application, **LibreOffice** or any other spreadsheet software that supports creating and reading XSLX files. However, a spreadsheet program is technically not required at all to use OpenPyXL. OpenPyXL can create, read and edit Excel files without needing any spreadsheet applications installed.

The reason you may want to have a spreadsheet program installed is for you to be able to open the spreadsheets yourself.

The other tool you will need is the **OpenPyXL** package. This package does not come pre-installed in Python. There are multiple ways you can install OpenPyXL. These will be covered in the next couple of sections.

---

[3]https://www.python.org/

Installing OpenPyXL with pip

You can install OpenPyXL by using `pip`. This will install the package to your system Python. If you'd rather not install OpenPyXL into your system Python, you should use Anaconda or a virtual environment (see following sections).

Here is the command you should run on your machine to install OpenPyXL to your system Python:

```
python -m pip install openpyxl
```

If you have Python 2 on your machine in addition to Python 3, then you will need to modify the command to run it like this:

```
python3 -m pip install openpyxl
```

Now your Python installation should be ready to go!

If you use Anaconda instead of Python, then you will want to see the next section.

Installing OpenPyXL with conda

Anaconda is an alternate Python distribution that is used often by data scientists. If you have Anaconda, then you should use `conda` instead of `pip` to install OpenPyXL.

Here is the command to use:

```
conda install -c anaconda openpyxl
```

Once `conda` is finished, you should be ready to use OpenPyXL with your Anaconda distribution.

Using OpenPyXL in a Python Virtual Environment

Python comes with a library named `venv` that you can use to create a Python virtual environment. What that means, is that you can create a self-contained folder to test out Python packages in. This allows you to install packages in a folder instead of your system Python installation. Using virtual Python environments is a great way to try out a new version of a package to compare it with an old version.

Here is how you create a new virtual environment in your terminal or console:

Chapter 2 - Reading Spreadsheets with OpenPyXL

There are a couple of fundamental actions that you will do with Microsoft Excel documents. One of the most basic is the act of reading data from an Excel file. You will be learning how to get data from your Excel spreadsheets.

Before you dive into automating Excel with Python, you should understand some of the common terminologies:

- Spreadsheet or Workbook – The file itself (.xls or .xlsx).
- Worksheet or Sheet – A single sheet of content within a Workbook. Spreadsheets can contain multiple Worksheets.
- Column – A vertical line of data labeled with letters, starting with "A".
- Row – A horizontal line of data labeled with numbers, starting with 1.
- Cell – A combination of Column and Row, like "A1".

Now that you have some basic understanding of the vocabulary, you can move on.

In this chapter, you will learn how to do the following tasks:

- Open a spreadsheet
- Read specific cells
- Read cells from a specific row
- Read cells from a specific column
- Read cells from multiple rows or columns
- Read cells from a range
- Read all cells in all sheets

You can get started by learning how to open a workbook in the next section!

Open a Spreadsheet

The first item that you need is a Microsoft Excel file. You can use the file that is in this book's GitHub code repository[4]. There is a file in the chapter 2 folder called `books.xlsx` that you will use here.

It has two sheets in it. Here is a screenshot of the first sheet:

[4]https://github.com/driscollis/automating_excel_with_python

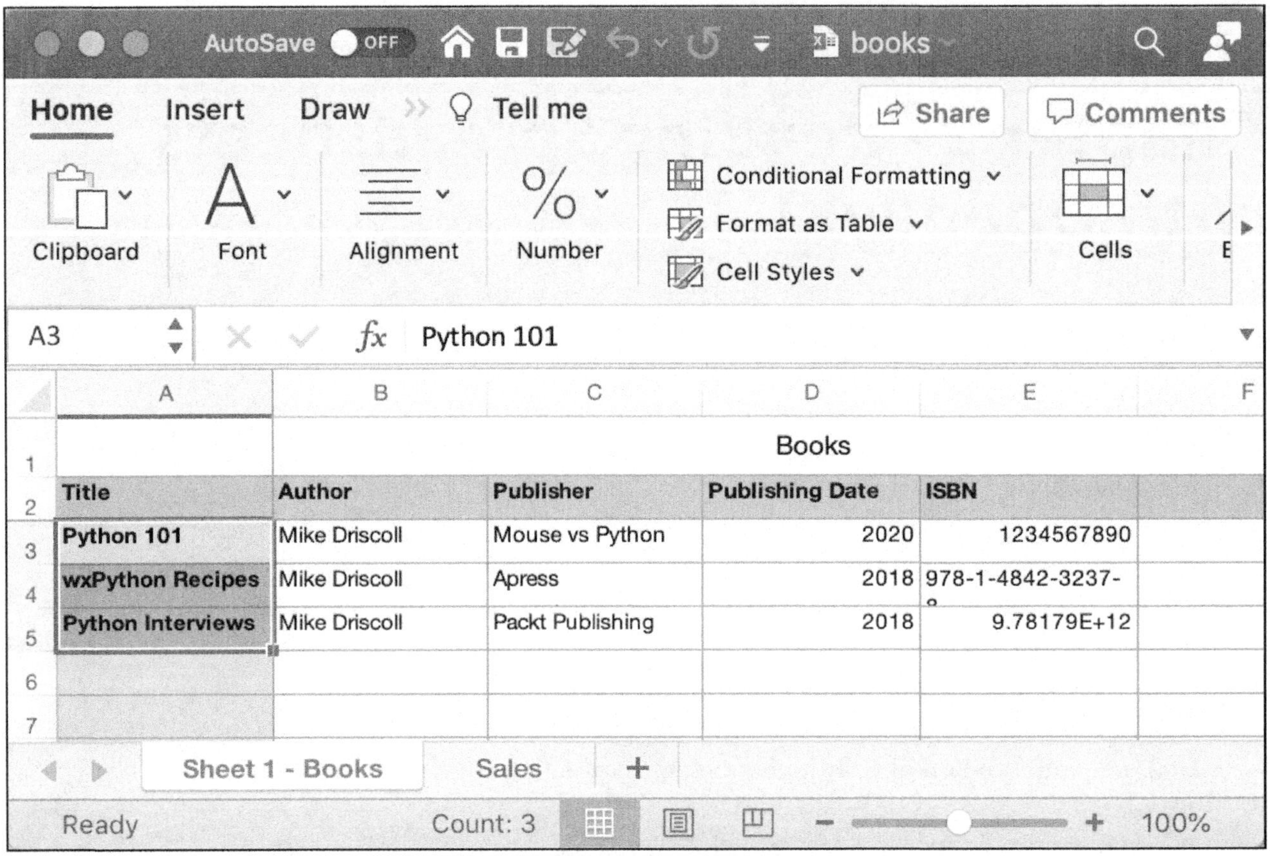

Fig. 2-1: The "Sheet 1 - Books" Worksheet

For completeness, here is a screenshot of the second sheet:

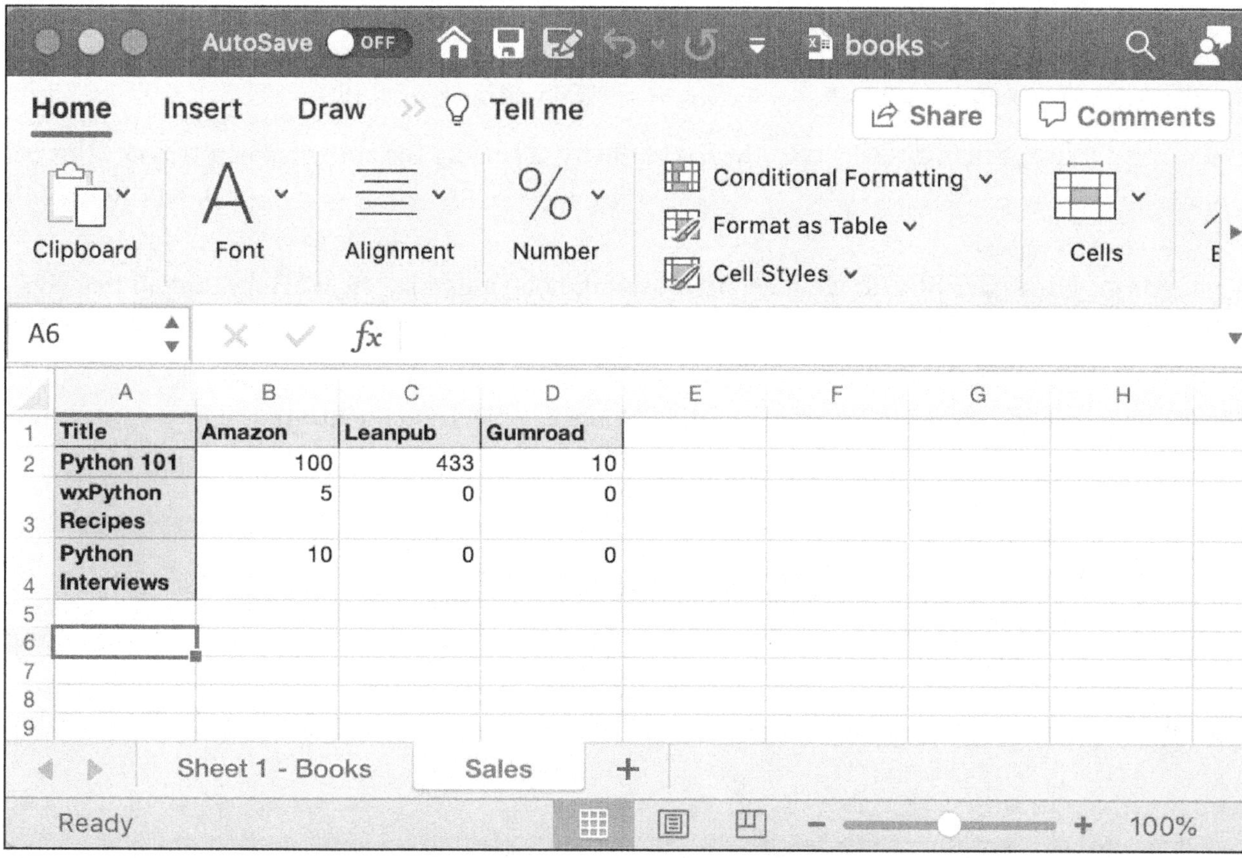

Fig. 2-1: The "Sheet 1 - Books" Worksheet

Note: The data in these sheets are inaccurate, but they help learn how to use OpenPyXL.

Now you're ready to start coding! Open up your favorite Python editor and create a new file named `open_workbook.py`. Then add the following code to your file:

```
# open_workbook.py

from openpyxl import load_workbook


def open_workbook(path):
    workbook = load_workbook(filename=path)
    print(f"Worksheet names: {workbook.sheetnames}")
    sheet = workbook.active
    print(sheet)
    print(f"The title of the Worksheet is: {sheet.title}")


if __name__ == "__main__":
    open_workbook("books.xlsx")
```

The first step in this code is to import `load_workbook()` from the `openpyxl` package. The `load_workbook()` function will load up your Excel file and return it as a Python object. You can then interact with that Python object like you would any other object in Python.

You can get a list of the worksheets in the Excel file by accessing the `sheetnames` attribute. This list contains the titles of the worksheets from left to right in your Excel file. Your code will print out this list.

Next, you grab the currently active sheet. If your workbook only has one worksheet, then that sheet will be the active one. If your workbook has multiple worksheets, as this one does, then the last worksheet will be the active one.

The last two lines of your function print out the `Worksheet` object and the title of the active worksheet.

What if you want to select a specific worksheet to work on, though? To learn how to accomplish that, create a new file and name it `read_specific_sheet.py`.

Then enter the following code:

```
# read_specific_sheet.py

from openpyxl import load_workbook


def open_workbook(path, sheet_name):
    workbook = load_workbook(filename=path)
    if sheet_name in workbook.sheetnames:
        sheet = workbook[sheet_name]
        print(f"The title of the Worksheet is: {sheet.title}")
        print(f"Cells that contain data: {sheet.calculate_dimension()}")


if __name__ == "__main__":
    open_workbook("books.xlsx", sheet_name="Sales")
```

Your function, `open_workbook()` now accepts a `sheet_name`. `sheet_name` is a string that matches the title of the worksheet that you want to read. You check to see if the `sheet_name` is in the `workbook.sheetnames` in your code. If it is, you select that sheet by accessing it using `workbook[sheet_name]`.

Then you print out the sheet's title to verify that you have the right sheet. You also call something new: `calculate_dimension()`. That method returns the cells that contain data in the worksheet. In this case, it will print out that "A1:D4" has data in them.

Now you are ready to move on and learn how to read data from the cells themselves.

Read Specific Cells

There are a lot of different ways to read cells using OpenPyXL. To start things off, you will learn how to read the contents of specific cells.

Create a new file in your Python editor and name it `reading_specific_cells.py`. Then enter the following code:

```
# reading_specific_cells.py

from openpyxl import load_workbook


def get_cell_info(path):
    workbook = load_workbook(filename=path)
    sheet = workbook.active
    print(sheet)
    print(f'The title of the Worksheet is: {sheet.title}')
    print(f'The value of A2 is {sheet["A2"].value}')
    print(f'The value of A3 is {sheet["A3"].value}')
    cell = sheet['B3']
    print(f'The variable "cell" is {cell.value}')

if __name__ == '__main__':
    get_cell_info('books.xlsx')
```

In this example, there are three hard-coded cells: A2, A3 and B3. You can access their values by using dictionary-like access: `sheet["A2"].value`. Alternatively, you can assign `sheet["A2"]` to a variable and then do something like `cell.value` to get the cell's value.

You can see both of these methods demonstrated in your code above.

When you run this code, you should see the following output:

```
<Worksheet "Sales">
The title of the Worksheet is: Sales
The value of A2 is 'Python 101'
The value of A3 is 'wxPython Recipes'
The variable "cell" is 5
```

This output shows how you can easily extract specific cell values from Excel using Python.

Now you're ready to learn how you can read the data from a specific row of cells!

Read Cells From Specific Row

In most cases, you will want to read more than a single cell in a worksheet at a time. OpenPyXL provides a way to get an entire row at once, too.

Go ahead and create a new file. You can name it `reading_row_cells.py`. Then add the following code to your program:

```
# reading_row_cells.py

from openpyxl import load_workbook


def iterating_row(path, sheet_name, row):
    workbook = load_workbook(filename=path)
    if sheet_name not in workbook.sheetnames:
        print(f"'{sheet_name}' not found. Quitting.")
        return

    sheet = workbook[sheet_name]
    for cell in sheet[row]:
        print(f"{cell.column_letter}{cell.row} = {cell.value}")


if __name__ == "__main__":
    iterating_row("books.xlsx", sheet_name="Sheet 1 - Books",
                  row=2)
```

In this example, you pass in the row number 2. You can iterate over the values in the row like this:

```
for cell in sheet[row]:
    ...
```

That makes grabbing the values from a row pretty straightforward. When you run this code, you'll get the following output:

```
A2 = Title
B2 = Author
C2 = Publisher
D2 = Publishing Date
E2 = ISBN
F2 = None
G2 = None
```

Those last two values are both **None**. If you don't want to get values that are None, you should add some extra processing to check if the value is None before printing it out. You can try to figure that out yourself as an exercise.

You are now ready to learn how to get cells from a specific column!

Read Cells From Specific Column

Reading the data from a specific column is also a frequent use case that you should know how to accomplish. For example, you might have a column that contains only totals, and you need to extract only that specific column.

To see how you can do that, create a new file and name it `reading_column_cells.py`. Then enter this code:

```
# reading_column_cells.py

from openpyxl import load_workbook


def iterating_column(path, sheet_name, col):
    workbook = load_workbook(filename=path)
    if sheet_name not in workbook.sheetnames:
        print(f"'{sheet_name}' not found. Quitting.")
        return

    sheet = workbook[sheet_name]
    for cell in sheet[col]:
        print(f"{cell.column_letter}{cell.row} = {cell.value}")


if __name__ == "__main__":
    iterating_column("books.xlsx", sheet_name="Sheet 1 - Books",
                     col="A")
```

This code is very similar to the code in the previous section. The difference here is that you are replacing `sheet[row]` with `sheet[col]` and iterating on that instead.

In this example, you set the column to "A". When you run this code, you will get the following output:

```
A1 = Books
A2 = Title
A3 = Python 101
A4 = wxPython Recipes
A5 = Python Interviews
A6 = None
A7 = None
A8 = None
A9 = None
A10 = None
A11 = None
A12 = None
A13 = None
A14 = None
A15 = None
A16 = None
A17 = None
A18 = None
A19 = None
A20 = None
A21 = None
A22 = None
A23 = None
```

Once again, some columns have no data (i.e., "None"). You can edit this code to ignore empty cells and only process cells that have contents.

Now let's discover how to iterate over multiple columns or rows!

Read Cells from Multiple Rows or Columns

There are two methods that OpenPyXL's worksheet objects give you for iterating over rows and columns. These are the two methods:

- `iter_rows()`
- `iter_cols()`

These methods are documented[5] fairly well in OpenPyXL's documentation. Both methods take the

[5]https://openpyxl.readthedocs.io/en/stable/api/openpyxl.worksheet.worksheet.html

following parameters:

- min_col (int) – smallest column index (1-based index)
- min_row (int) – smallest row index (1-based index)
- max_col (int) – largest column index (1-based index)
- max_row (int) – largest row index (1-based index)
- values_only (bool) – whether only cell values should be returned

You use the min and max rows and column parameters to tell OpenPyXL which rows and columns to iterate over. You can have OpenPyXL return the data from the cells by setting values_only to True. If you set it to False, iter_rows() and iter_cols() will return cell objects instead.

It's always good to see how this works with actual code. With that in mind, create a new file named iterating_over_cells_in_rows.py and add this code to it:

```
# iterating_over_cells_in_rows.py

from openpyxl import load_workbook


def iterating_over_values(path, sheet_name):
    workbook = load_workbook(filename=path)
    if sheet_name not in workbook.sheetnames:
        print(f"'{sheet_name}' not found. Quitting.")
        return

    sheet = workbook[sheet_name]
    for value in sheet.iter_rows(
        min_row=1, max_row=3, min_col=1, max_col=3,
        values only=True):
        print(value)


if __name__ == "__main__":
    iterating_over_values("books.xlsx", sheet_name="Sheet 1 - Books")
```

Here you load up the workbook as you have in the previous examples. You get the sheet name that you want to extract data from and then use iter_rows() to get the rows of data. In this example, you set the minimum row to 1 and the maximum row to 3. That means that you will grab the first three rows in the Excel sheet you have specified.

Then you also set the columns to be 1 (minimum) to 3 (maximum). Finally, you set values_only to True.

When you run this code, you will get the following output:

```
('Books', None, None)
('Title', 'Author', 'Publisher')
('Python 101', 'Mike Driscoll', 'Mouse vs Python')
```

Your program will print out the first three columns of the first three rows in your Excel spreadsheet. Your program prints the rows as tuples with three items in them. You are using `iter_rows()` as a quick way to iterate over rows and columns in an Excel spreadsheet using Python.

Now you're ready to learn how to read cells in a specific range.

Read Cells from a Range

Excel lets you specify a range of cells using the following format: (col)(row):(col)(row). In other words, you can say that you want to start in column A, row 1, using **A1**. If you wanted to specify a range, you would use something like this: **A1:B6**. That tells Excel that you are selecting the cells starting at **A1** and going to **B6**.

Go ahead and create a new file named `read_cells_from_range.py`. Then add this code to it:

```
# read_cells_from_range.py

import openpyxl
from openpyxl import load_workbook


def iterating_over_values(path, sheet_name, cell_range):
    workbook = load_workbook(filename=path)
    if sheet_name not in workbook.sheetnames:
        print(f"'{sheet_name}' not found. Quitting.")
        return

    sheet = workbook[sheet_name]
    for column in sheet[cell_range]:
        for cell in column:
            if isinstance(cell, openpyxl.cell.cell.MergedCell):
                # Skip this cell
                continue
            print(f"{cell.column_letter}{cell.row} = {cell.value}")


if __name__ == "__main__":
    iterating_over_values("books.xlsx", sheet_name="Sheet 1 - Books",
                          cell_range="A1:B6")
```

Here you pass in your `cell_range` and iterate over that range using the following nested `for` loop:

```
for column in sheet[cell_range]:
    for cell in column:
```

You check to see if the cell that you are extracting is a `MergedCell`. If it is, you skip it. Otherwise, you print out the cell name and its value.

When you run this code, you should see the following output:

```
A1 = Books
A2 = Title
B2 = Author
A3 = Python 101
B3 = Mike Driscoll
A4 = wxPython Recipes
B4 = Mike Driscoll
A5 = Python Interviews
B5 = Mike Driscoll
A6 = None
B6 = None
```

That worked quite well. You should take a moment and try out a few other range variations to see how it changes the output.

Note: while the image of "Sheet 1 - Books" looks like cell A1 is distinct from the merged cell B1-G1, A1 is actually part of that merged cell.

The last code example that you'll create will read all the data in your Excel document!

Read All Cells in All Sheets

Microsoft Excel isn't as simple to read as a CSV file, or a regular text file. That is because Excel needs to store each cell's data, which includes its location, formatting, and value, and that value could be a number, a date, an image, a link, etc. Consequently, reading an Excel file is a lot more work! openpyxl does all that hard work for us, though.

The natural way to iterate through an Excel file is to read the sheets from left to right, and within each sheet, you would read it row by row, from top to bottom. That is what you will learn how to do in this section.

You will take what you have learned in the previous sections and apply it here. Create a new file and name it `read_all_data.py`. Then enter the following code:

```
# read_all_data.py

import openpyxl
from openpyxl import load_workbook


def read_all_data(path):
    workbook = load_workbook(filename=path)
    for sheet_name in workbook.sheetnames:
        sheet = workbook[sheet_name]
        print(f"Title = {sheet.title}")
        for row in sheet.rows:
            for cell in row:
                if isinstance(cell, openpyxl.cell.cell.MergedCell):
                    # Skip this cell
                    continue

                print(f"{cell.column_letter}{cell.row} = {cell.value}")


if __name__ == "__main__":
    read_all_data("books.xlsx")
```

Here you load up the workbook as before, but this time you loop over the `sheetnames`. You print out each sheet name as you select it. You use a nested `for` loop to loop over the rows and cells to extract the data from your spreadsheet.

Once again, you skip `MergedCells` because their value is `None` – the actual value is in the normal cell that the `MergedCell` is merged with. If you run this code, you will see that it prints out all the data from the two worksheets.

You can simplify this code a bit by using `iter_rows()`. Open up a new file and name it `read_all_data_values.py`. Then enter the following:

```
# read_all_data_values.py

import openpyxl
from openpyxl import load_workbook


def read_all_data(path):
    workbook = load_workbook(filename=path)
    for sheet_name in workbook.sheetnames:
        sheet = workbook[sheet_name]
```

```
        print(f"Title = {sheet.title}")
        for value in sheet.iter_rows(values_only=True):
            print(value)


if __name__ == "__main__":
    read_all_data("books.xlsx")
```

In this code, you once again loop over the sheet names in the Excel document. However, rather than looping over the rows and columns, you use `iter_rows()` to loop over only the rows. You set `values_only` to `True` which will return a tuple of values for each row. You also do not set the minimum and maximum rows or columns for `iter_rows()` because you want to get all the data.

When you run this code, you will see it print out the name of each sheet, then all the data in that sheet, row-by-row. Give it a try on your own Excel worksheets and see what this code can do!

Wrapping Up

OpenPyXL lets you read an Excel Worksheet and its data in many different ways. You can extract values from your spreadsheets quickly with a minimal amount of code.

In this chapter, you learned how to do the following:

- Open a spreadsheet
- Read specific cells
- Read cells from a specific row
- Read cells from a specific column
- Read cells from multiple rows or columns
- Read cells from a range
- Read all cells in all sheets

Now you are ready to learn how to create an Excel spreadsheet using OpenPyXL. That is the subject of the next chapter!

Chapter 3 - Creating a Spreadsheet with OpenPyXL

Reading Excel spreadsheets is all well and good. However, you also need to be able to create or edit a spreadsheet. The focus of this chapter will be on learning how to do that! OpenPyXL lets you create Microsoft Excel spreadsheets with a minimum of fuss.

Creating Excel spreadsheets using Python allows you to generate a new type of report that your users will use. For example, you might receive your data from a client in the form of JSON or XML. These data formats are not something that most accountants or business people are used to reading.

Once you learn how to create Excel spreadsheets with Python, you can leverage that knowledge to transform other data into Excel spreadsheets. This knowledge also allows you to do the reverse, taking in an Excel spreadsheet and output a different format, such as JSON or XML.

In this chapter, you will learn how to use OpenPyXL to do the following:

- Create a spreadsheet
- Write to a spreadsheet
- Add and remove sheets
- Insert and delete rows and columns
- Edit cell data
- Create merged cells
- Fold rows and columns

Let's get started by creating a brand new spreadsheet!

Creating a Spreadsheet

Creating an empty spreadsheet using OpenPyXL doesn't take much code. Open up your Python editor and create a new file. Name it `creating_spreadsheet.py`.

Now add the following code to your file:

```
# creating_spreadsheet.py

from openpyxl import Workbook


def create_workbook(path):
    workbook = Workbook()
    workbook.save(path)


if __name__ == "__main__":
    create_workbook("hello.xlsx")
```

The critical piece here is that you need to import the `Workbook` class. This class allows you to instantiate a `workbook` object that you can then save. All this code does is create the file that you pass to it and save it.

Your new spreadsheet will look like this:

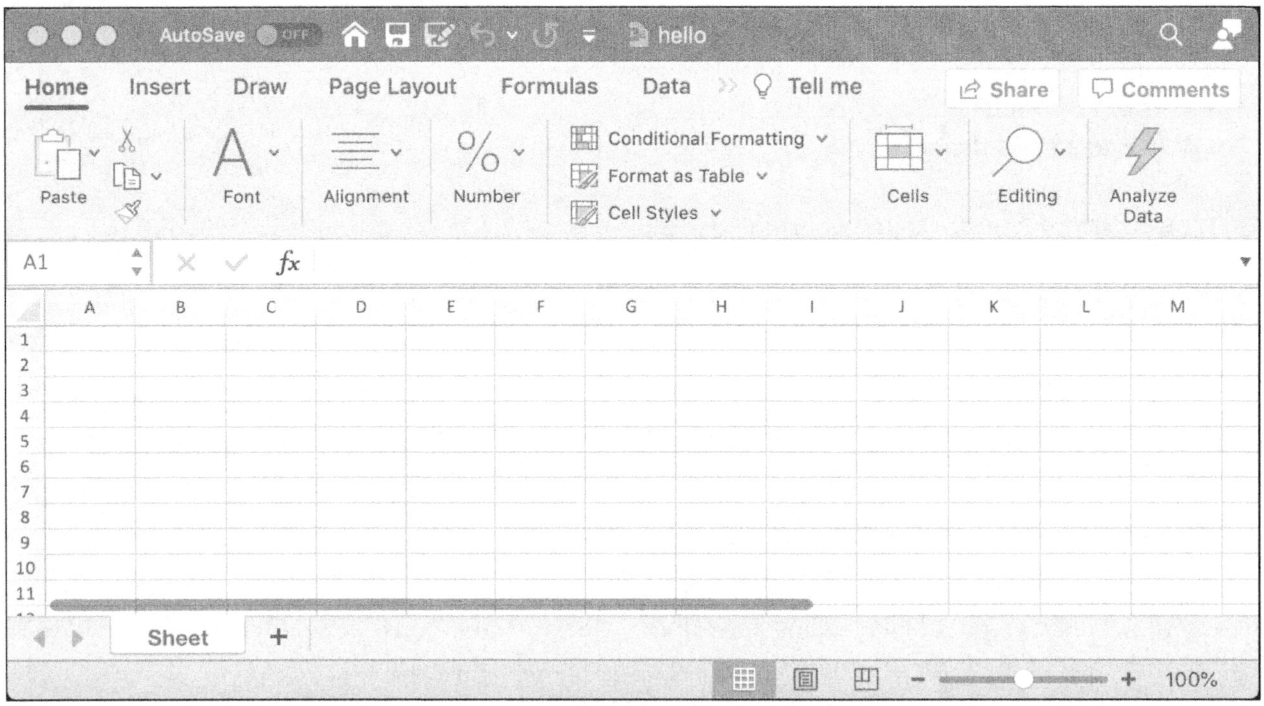

Fig. 3-1: A Newly Created Empty Spreadsheet

Now you're ready to learn how to add some data to the cells in your spreadsheet.

Writing to a Spreadsheet

When writing data in a spreadsheet, you need to get the "sheet" object. You learned how to do that in the previous chapter using `workbook.active`, which gives you the active or currently visible sheet. You could also explicitly tell OpenPyXL which sheet you want to access by passing it a sheet title.

For this example, you will create another new program and then use the active sheet. Open up a new file and name it `adding_data.py`. Now add this code to your file:

```
# adding_data.py

from openpyxl import Workbook


def create_workbook(path):
    workbook = Workbook()
    sheet = workbook.active
    sheet["A1"] = "Hello"
    sheet["A2"] = "from"
    sheet["A3"] = "OpenPyXL"
    workbook.save(path)


if __name__ == "__main__":
    create_workbook("hello.xlsx")
```

This code will overwrite the previous example's Excel spreadsheet. After you create the `Workbook()` object, you grab the active Worksheet. Then you add text strings to the cells: A1, A2, and A3. The last step is to save your new spreadsheet.

When you run this code, your new spreadsheet will look like this:

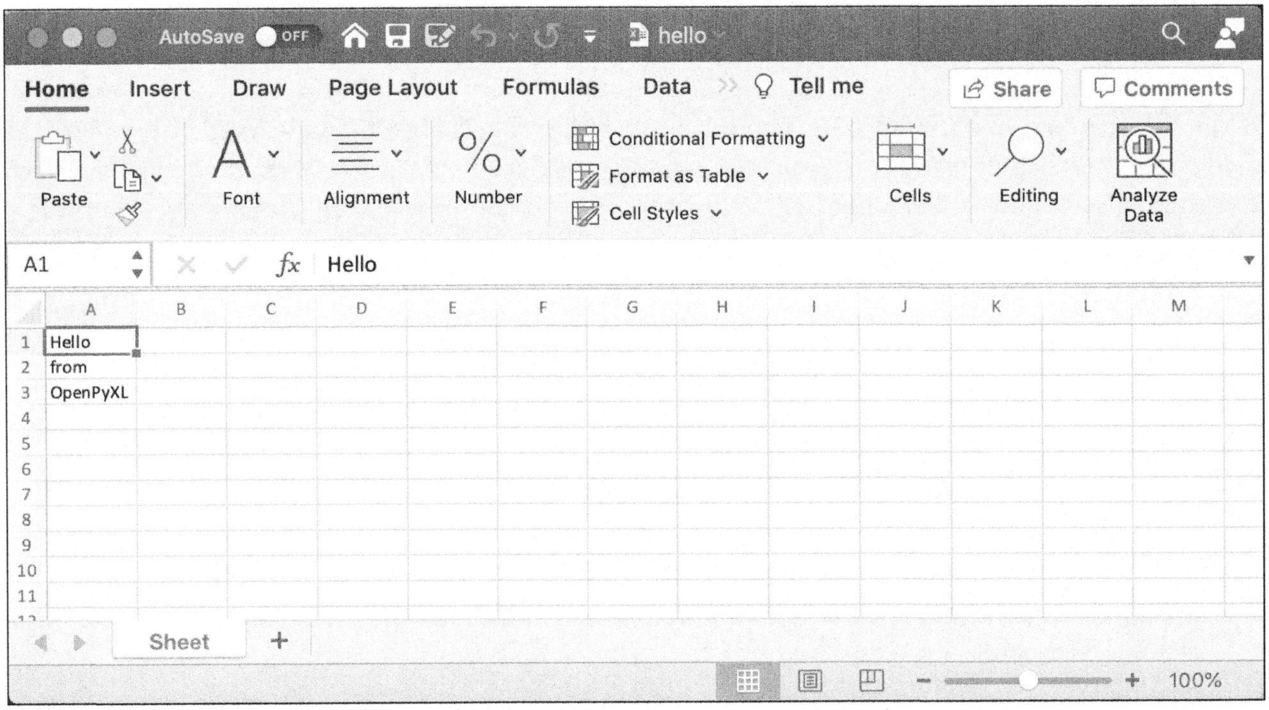

Fig. 3-2: A Spreadsheet with Data

You can use this technique to write data to any cell in your spreadsheet.

What if you need to add rows of data? You can use the worksheet's `append()` method for that! To see how that might work, create a new file named `adding_data_rows.py` and add the following code:

```
# adding_data_rows.py

from openpyxl import Workbook


def create_workbook(path):
    workbook = Workbook()
    sheet = workbook.active
    data = [[1, 2, 3],
            ["a", "b", "c"],
            [44, 55, 66]]
    for row in data:
        sheet.append(row)
    workbook.save(path)


if __name__ == "__main__":
    create_workbook("write_rows.xlsx")
```

In this example, you create a list of lists that represents three rows of data. Then you iterate over your list of lists, calling `append()` each time. The `append()` method will add data to each row in your Excel spreadsheet starting at A1.

After running this code, your new spreadsheet will look like this:

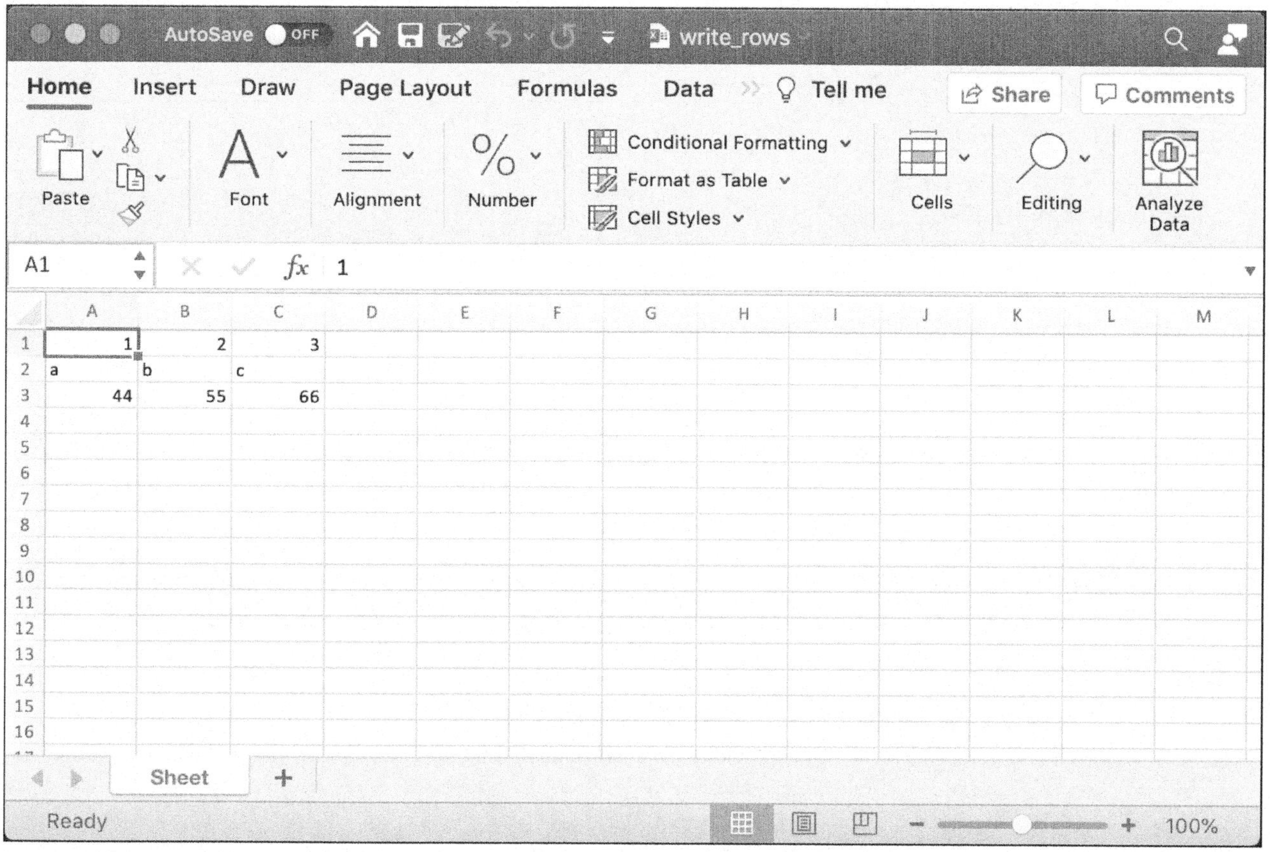

Fig. 3-3: Adding Rows of Data

Now let's find out how to add and remove a worksheet!

Adding and Removing Sheets

Adding a worksheet to a workbook happens automatically when you create a new Workbook. The Worksheet will be named "Sheet" by default. If you want, you can set the name of the sheet yourself.

To see how this works, create a new file named `creating_sheet_title.py` and add the following code:

```
# creating_sheet_title.py

from openpyxl import Workbook


def create_sheets(path):
    workbook = Workbook()
    sheet = workbook.active
    sheet.title = "Hello"
    sheet2 = workbook.create_sheet(title="World")
    workbook.save(path)


if __name__ == "__main__":
    create_sheets("hello_sheets.xlsx")
```

Here you create the `Workbook` and then grab the active Worksheet. You can then set the Worksheet's title using the `title` attribute. The following line of code adds a new worksheet to the Workbook by calling `create_sheet()`.

The `create_sheet()` method takes two parameters: `title` and `index`. The `title` attribute gives a title to the Worksheet. The `index` tells the `Workbook` where to insert the Worksheet, from left to right. If you specify zero, your Worksheet gets inserted at the beginning.

If you run this code, your new spreadsheet will look like this:

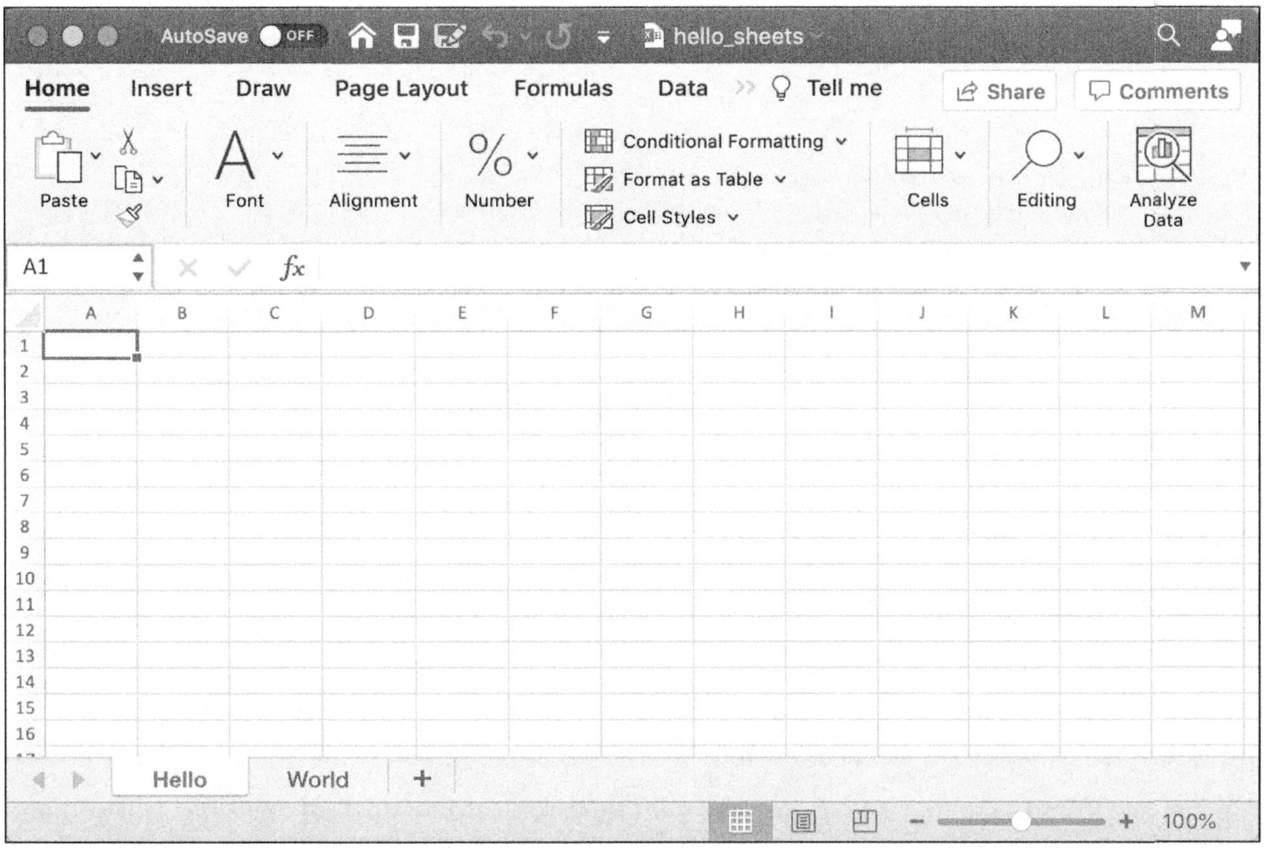

Fig. 3-4: A Spreadsheet with Two Worksheets

Sometimes you will need to delete a worksheet. Perhaps that sheet no longer has valid information, or it was created by accident.

To see how to delete a worksheet, create another new file and name it `delete_sheets.py`. Then add this code:

```
# delete_sheets.py

import openpyxl


def create_worksheets(path):
    workbook = openpyxl.Workbook()
    workbook.create_sheet()
    print(workbook.sheetnames)
    # Insert a worksheet
    workbook.create_sheet(index=1, title="Second sheet")
    print(workbook.sheetnames)
    del workbook["Second sheet"]
    print(workbook.sheetnames)
```

```
    workbook.save(path)


if __name__ == "__main__":
    create_worksheets("del_sheets.xlsx")
```

In this example, you create two new sheets. The first Worksheet has no title specified, so it defaults to "Sheet1". You supply a title to the second sheet, and then you print out all the current worksheet titles.

Next, you use Python's `del` keyword to delete the Worksheet's name from the workbook, which removes the sheet. Then you print out the current worksheet titles again.

Here is the output from running the code:

```
['Sheet', 'Sheet1']
['Sheet', 'Second sheet', 'Sheet1']
['Sheet', 'Sheet1']
```

The first Worksheet gets created automatically when you instantiate the `Workbook`. The Worksheet is named "Sheet". Then you make "Sheet1". Lastly, you create "Second sheet", but you insert it at position 1, which tells the Workbook to shift 'Sheet1' to the right by one position.

You can see from the output above how the worksheets are ordered before and after you add and delete the "Second sheet".

Now let's learn about inserting and removing rows and columns!

Inserting and Deleting Rows and Columns

The OpenPyXL package provides you with several methods that you can use to insert or delete rows and columns. These methods are a part of the `Worksheet` object.

You will learn about the following four methods:

- `.insert_rows()`
- `.delete_rows()`
- `.insert_cols()`
- `.delete_cols()`

Each of these methods can take these two arguments:

- `idx` – The index to insert into (or delete from)
- `amount` – The number of rows or columns to add (or delete)

You can use the insert methods to insert rows or columns at the specified index.

Open up a new file and name it `insert_demo.py`. Then enter this code in your new file:

```python
# insert_demo.py

from openpyxl import Workbook


def inserting_cols_rows(path):
    workbook = Workbook()
    sheet = workbook.active
    sheet["A1"] = "Hello"
    sheet["A2"] = "from"
    sheet["A3"] = "OpenPyXL"
    # insert a column before A
    sheet.insert_cols(idx=1)
    # insert 2 rows starting on the second row
    sheet.insert_rows(idx=2, amount=2)
    workbook.save(path)


if __name__ == "__main__":
    inserting_cols_rows("inserting.xlsx")
```

Here you create another new Spreadsheet. In this case, you add text to the first three cells in the "A" column. Then you insert one column at index one. That means you inserted a single column before "A", which causes the cells in column "A" to shift to column "B".

Next, you insert two new rows starting at index two. This code will insert two rows between the first and second rows.

You can see how this changes things by taking a look at the following screenshot:

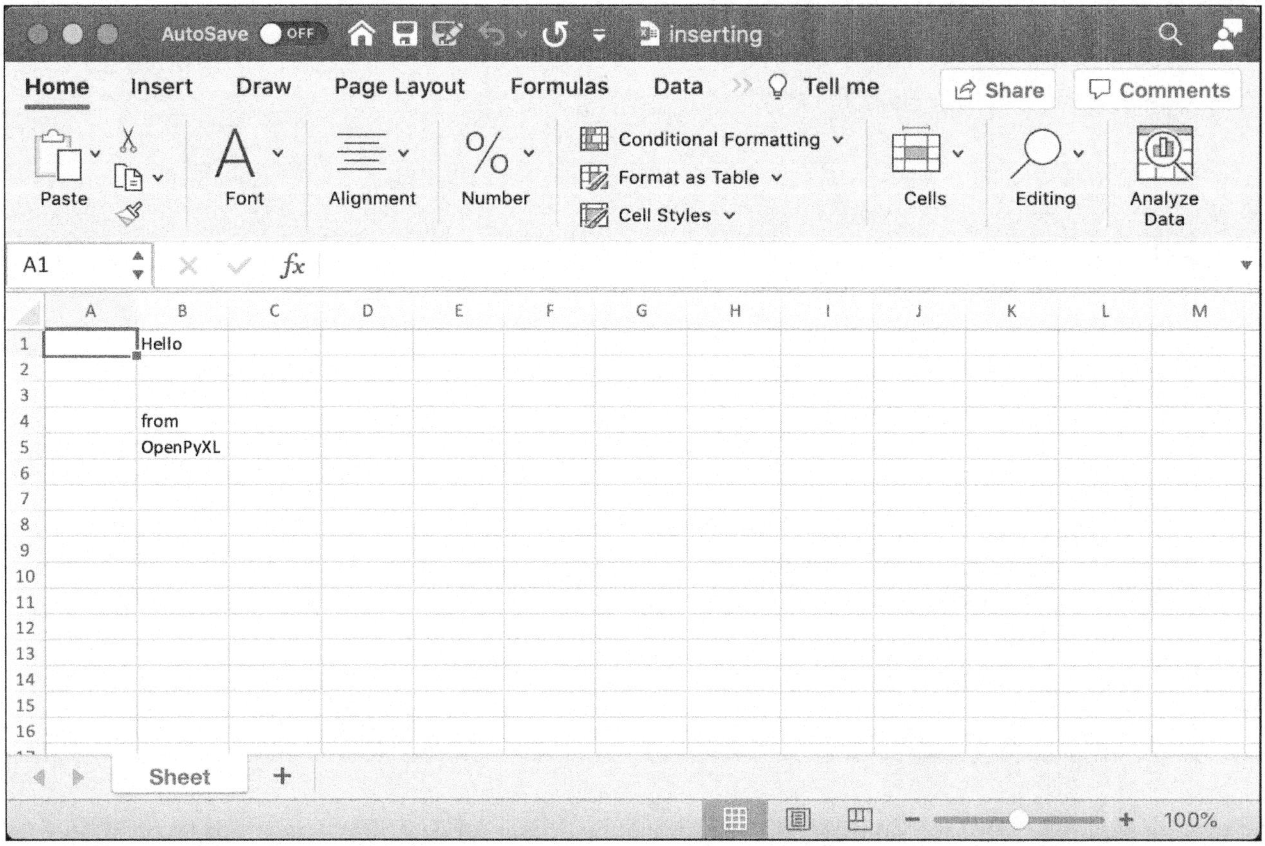

Fig. 3-5: Inserting Rows and Columns

Try changing the indexes or number of rows and columns that you want to insert and see how it works.

You will also need to delete columns and rows from time to time. To do that you will use `.delete_rows()` and `.delete_cols()`.

Open up a new file and name it `delete_demo.py`. Then add this code:

```
# delete_demo.py

from openpyxl import Workbook


def deleting_cols_rows(path):
    workbook = Workbook()
    sheet = workbook.active
    sheet["A1"] = "Hello"
    sheet["B1"] = "from"
    sheet["C1"] = "OpenPyXL"
    sheet["A2"] = "row 2"
```

```
    sheet["A3"] = "row 3"
    sheet["A4"] = "row 4"
    # Delete column A
    sheet.delete_cols(idx=1)
    # delete 2 rows starting on the second row
    sheet.delete_rows(idx=2, amount=2)
    workbook.save(path)


if __name__ == "__main__":
    deleting_cols_rows("deleting.xlsx")
```

In this example, you add text to six different cells. Four of those cells are in column "A". Then you use `delete_cols()` to delete column "A"! That means you got rid of four values. Next, you delete two rows, starting at row number two.

When you run this code, your result should look like this:

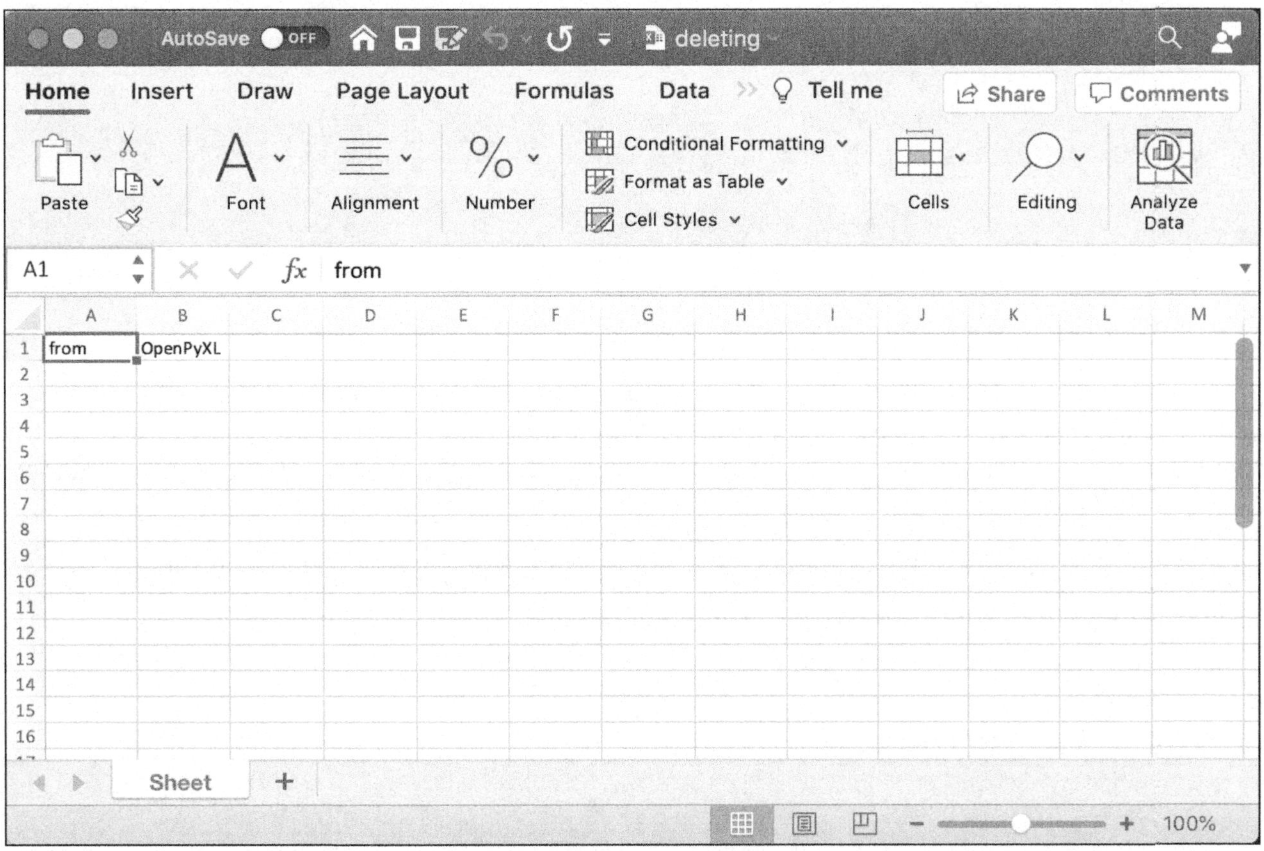

Fig. 3-6: Deleting Rows and Columns

Try editing the index or amount values to get familiar with deleting rows and columns.

Now you are ready to learn about editing a spreadsheet's values!

Editing Cell Data

You can use OpenPyXL to change the values in a pre-existing Excel spreadsheet. You can do that by specifying the cell you want to change and then setting it to a new value.

For this example, you will use the `inserting.xlsx` file you created in the previous section. Now create a new Python file named `editing_demo.py`. Then add the following code:

```
# editing_demo.py

from openpyxl import load_workbook


def edit(path, data):
    workbook = load_workbook(filename=path)
    sheet = workbook.active
    for cell in data:
        current_value = sheet[cell].value
        sheet[cell] = data[cell]
        print(f'Changing {cell} from {current_value} to {data[cell]}')
    workbook.save(path)

if __name__ == "__main__":
    data = {"B1": "Hi", "B5": "Python"}
    edit("inserting.xlsx", data)
```

This code loads up the Excel file that you created in the previous section. It then loops over each value in the `data` dictionary that you passed to the `edit()` function. You get the current value for the cell using a key in the dictionary. Then you change that cell's value to match the value in the dictionary.

To make it more obvious what is going on, you print out the old and new values of the cell.

When you run this code, you will see the following output:

```
Changing B1 from Hello to Hi
Changing B5 from OpenPyXL to Python
```

Open up the new version of the `inserting.xlsx` file, and it should now look like this:

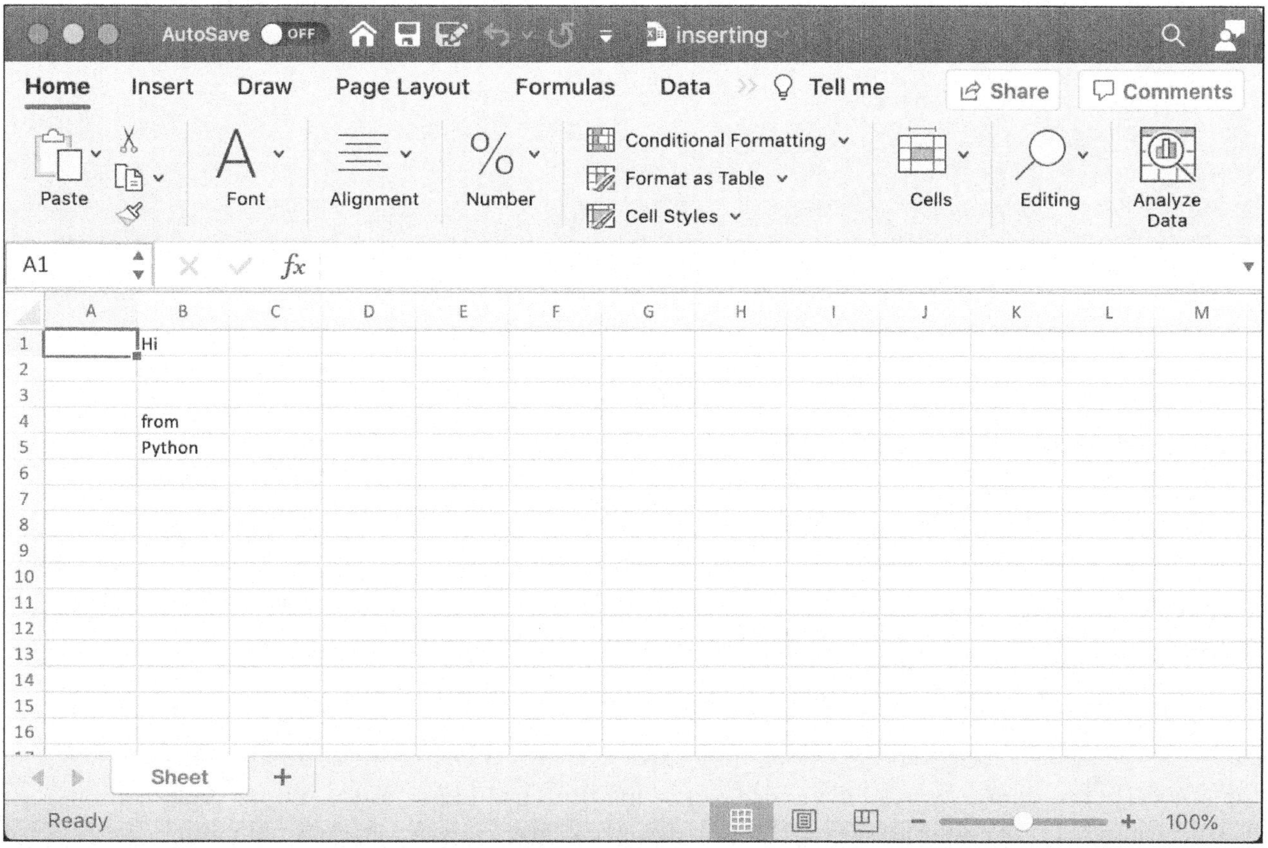

Fig. 3-7: Editing Cells

Here you can see how the cell values have changed to match the one specified in the `data` dictionary.

Now you can move on and learn how to create merged cells!

Creating Merged Cells

A merged cell is where two or more cells get merged into one. To set a MergedCell's value, you have to use the top-left-most cell. For example, if you merge "A2:E2", you would set the value of cell "A2" for the merged cells.

To see how this works in practice, create a file called `merged_cells.py` and add this code to it:

```
# merged_cells.py

from openpyxl import Workbook
from openpyxl.styles import Alignment


def create_merged_cells(path, value):
    workbook = Workbook()
    sheet = workbook.active
    sheet.merge_cells("A2:E2")
    top_left_cell = sheet["A2"]
    top_left_cell.alignment = Alignment(horizontal="center",
                                        vertical="center")
    sheet["A2"] = value
    workbook.save(path)


if __name__ == "__main__":
    create_merged_cells("merged.xlsx", "Hello World")
```

OpenPyXL has many ways to style cells. In this example, you import `Alignment` from `openpyxl.styles`. You will learn more about styles and formatting cells in a later chapter.

Here you merge the cells "A2:E2" and set the alignment to the center of the cell. Then you set the value of "A2" to a string that you passed to the `create_merged_cells()` function.

When you run this example, your new Excel spreadsheet will look like this:

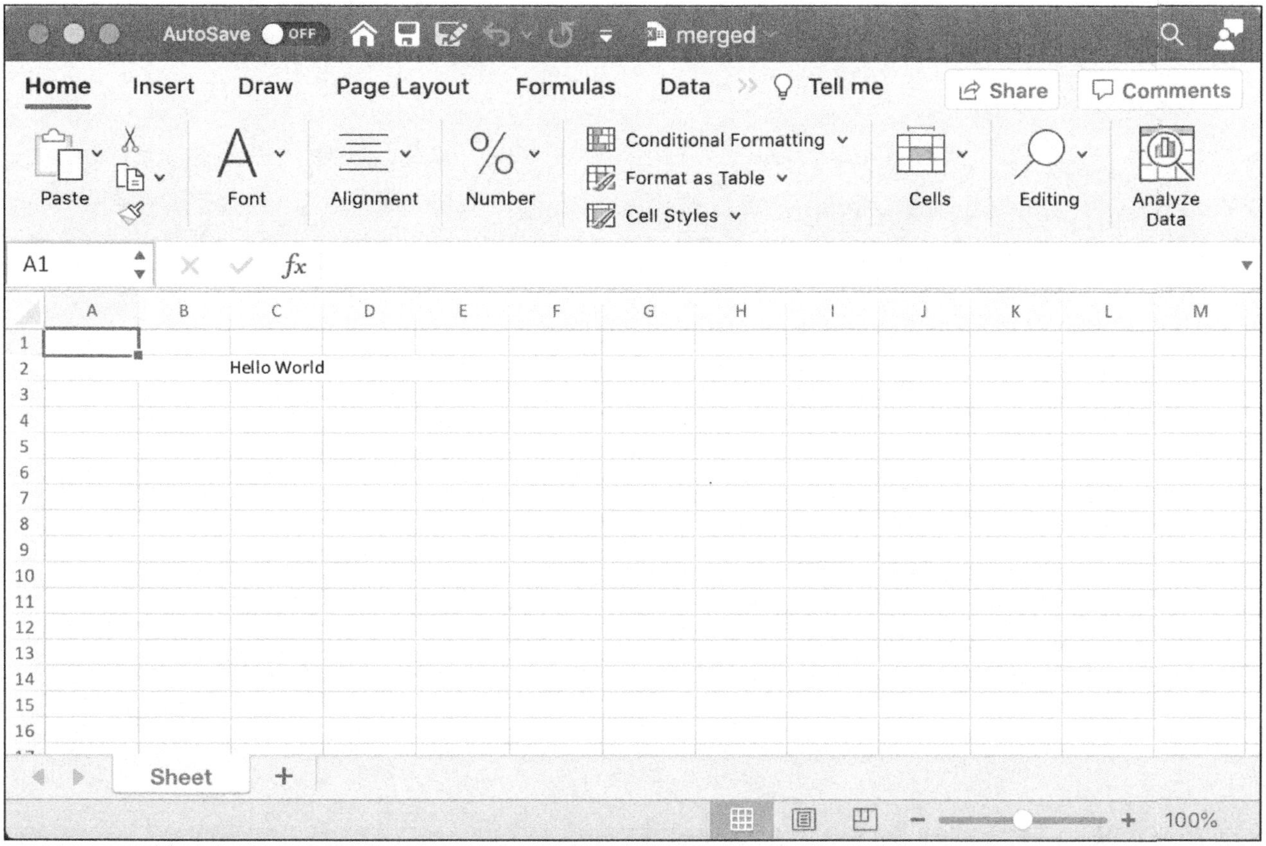

Fig. 3-8: Merged Cells

To get some hands-on experience, change the range of cells you want to merge and try it with and without the alignment set.

Now you are ready to learn about folding columns or rows!

Folding Rows and Columns

Microsoft Excel supports the folding of rows and columns. The term “folding” is also called “hiding” or creating an “outline”. The rows or columns that get folded can be unfolded (or expanded) to make them visible again. You can use this functionality to make a spreadsheet briefer. For example, you might want to only show the sub-totals or the results of equations rather than all of the data at once.

OpenPyXL supports folding too. To see how this works, create a new file named `folding.py` and enter the following code:

```python
# folding.py

import openpyxl


def folding(path, rows=None, cols=None, hidden=True):
    workbook = openpyxl.Workbook()
    sheet = workbook.active

    if rows:
        begin_row, end_row = rows
        sheet.row_dimensions.group(begin_row, end_row, hidden=hidden)

    if cols:
        begin_col, end_col = cols
        sheet.column_dimensions.group(begin_col, end_col, hidden=hidden)

    workbook.save(path)


if __name__ == "__main__":
    folding("folded.xlsx", rows=(1, 5), cols=("C", "F"))
```

Your `folding()` function accepts a tuple of rows or columns or both. You can tell OpenPyXL whether or not you want those rows and columns to be hidden, or folded. In this example, you fold rows 1-5 and columns C-F. To cause the folding to occur, you need to call `sheet.row_dimensions.group()`.

When you run this code, your spreadsheet will look like this:

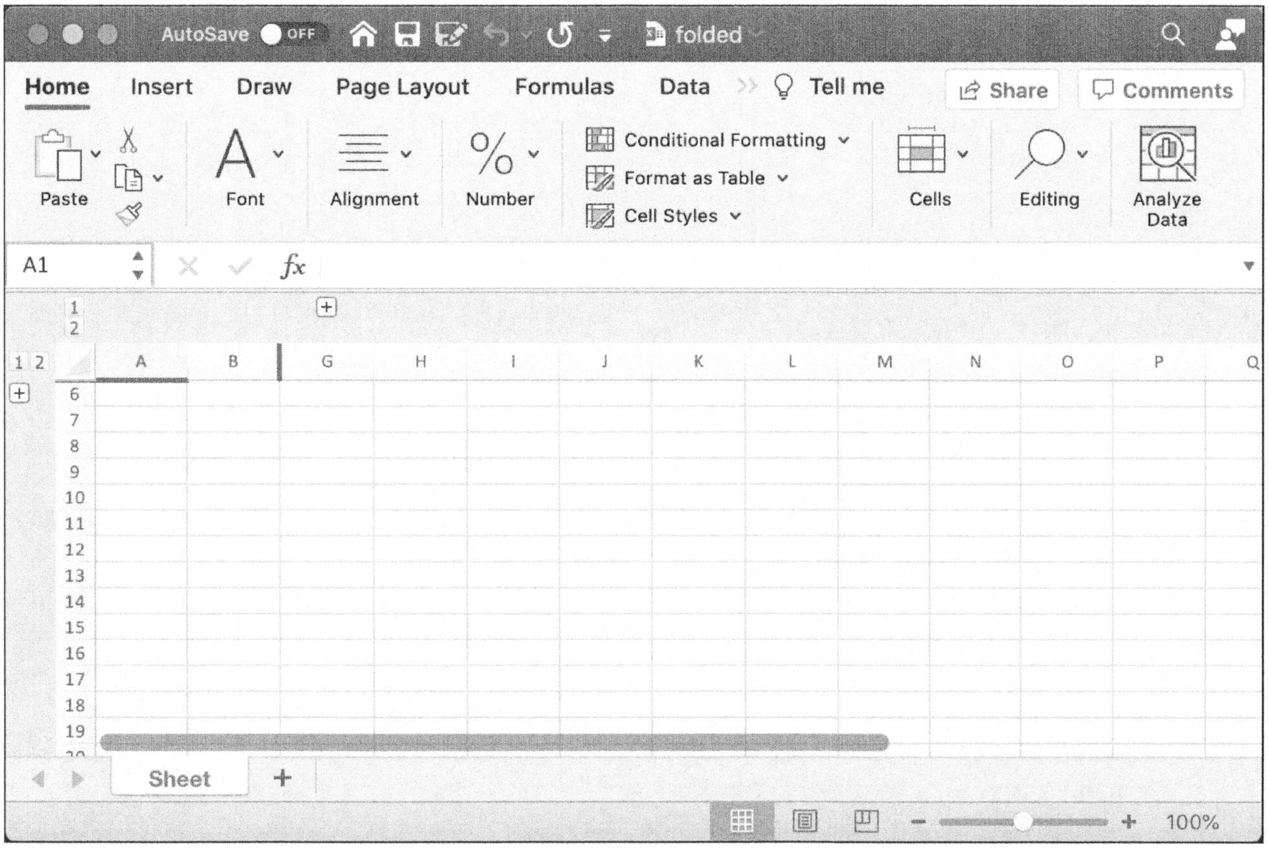

Fig. 3-9: Folding Cells

You can see in this spreadsheet that some of the rows and columns are folded or hidden. There is a "+" symbol next to row 6 and another "+" symbol above column "G". If you click on either of those buttons, it will expand the folded rows or columns.

Give this code a try. You can also experiment with different row or column ranges.

Now you are ready to learn how to freeze a pane!

Freezing Panes

Microsoft Excel allows you to freeze panes. What that means is that you can freeze one or more columns or rows. One popular use case is to freeze a row of headers so that the headers are always visible while scrolling through a lot of data.

OpenPyXL provides a `freeze_panes` attribute on the Worksheet object that you can set. You need to select a cell below and to the right of the columns that you want to freeze. For example, if you want to freeze the first row in your spreadsheet, then you would select cell at "A2" to apply the freeze to that row.

You can see how this works by writing some code. Open up a new file and name it `freezing_panes.py`. Then enter the following into it:

```python
# freezing_panes.py

from openpyxl import Workbook


def freeze(path, row_to_freeze):
    workbook = Workbook()
    sheet = workbook.active
    sheet.title = "Freeze"
    sheet.freeze_panes = row_to_freeze
    headers = ["Name", "Address", "State", "Zip"]
    sheet["A1"] = headers[0]
    sheet["B1"] = headers[1]
    sheet["C1"] = headers[2]
    sheet["D1"] = headers[3]
    data = [dict(zip(headers, ("Mike", "123 Storm Dr", "IA", "50000"))),
            dict(zip(headers, ("Ted", "555 Tornado Alley", "OK", "90000")))]
    row = 2
    for d in data:
        sheet[f'A{row}'] = d["Name"]
        sheet[f'B{row}'] = d["Address"]
        sheet[f'C{row}'] = d["State"]
        sheet[f'D{row}'] = d["Zip"]
        row += 1
    workbook.save(path)


if __name__ == "__main__":
    freeze("freeze.xlsx", row_to_freeze="A2")
```

Here you create a new `Workbook` and set the active sheet's title to "Freeze". Then you set the `freeze_panes` attribute to "A2". The rest of the code in the function adds a couple of rows of data to the Worksheet.

When you run this code, the spreadsheet that you create will look like this:

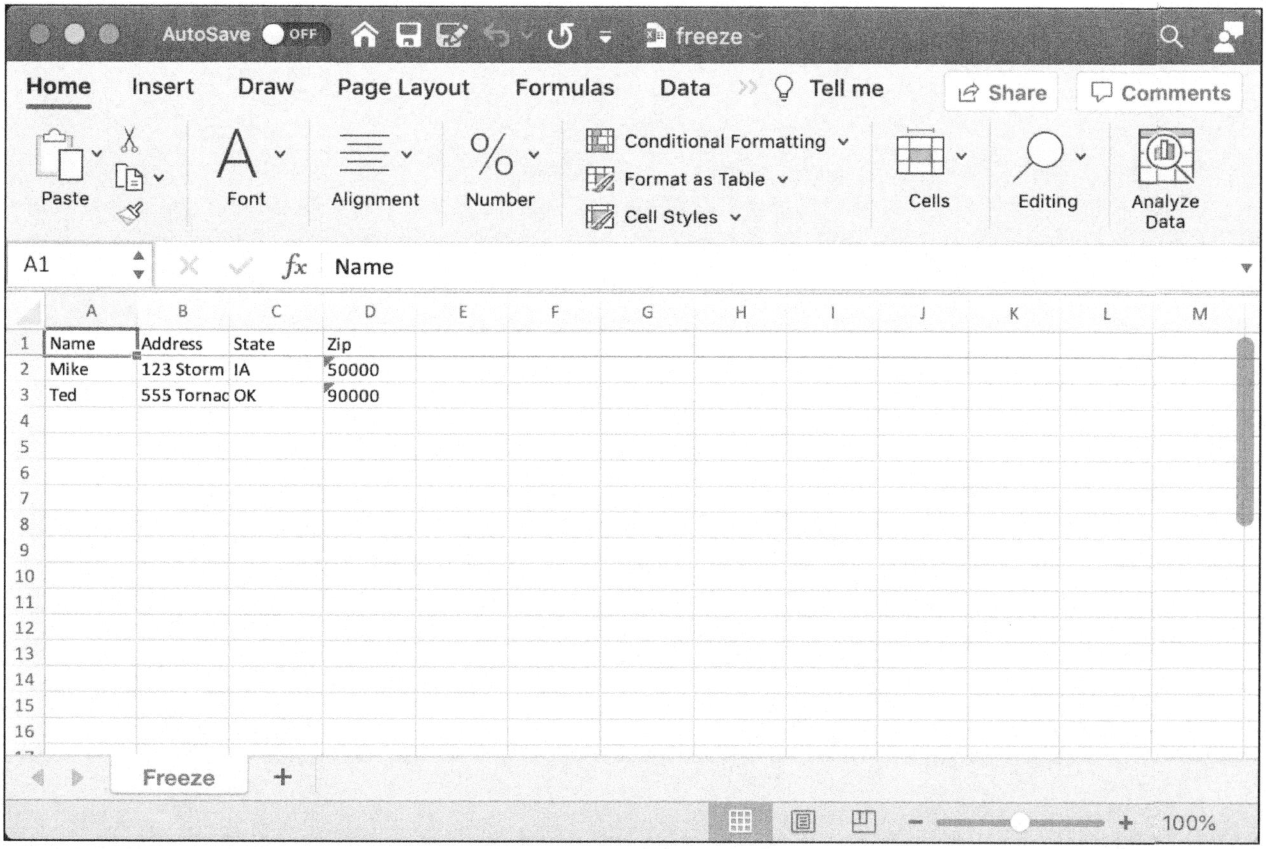

Fig. 3-10: Freeze Panes

Try scrolling down through some rows in the spreadsheet. The top row should always remain visible because it has been "frozen".

Wrapping Up

You can use OpenPyXL not only to create an Excel spreadsheet, but modify a pre-existing one. In this chapter, you learned how to do the following:

- Create a spreadsheet
- Write to a spreadsheet
- Add and remove sheets
- Insert and delete rows and columns
- Edit cell data
- Create merged cells
- Freeze panes

Give the examples in this chapter a try. Then modify them a bit to see what else you can do on your own. When you're ready, go on to the next chapter!

Chapter 4 - Styling Cells

OpenPyXL gives you the ability to style your cells in many different ways. Styling cells will give your spreadsheets pizazz! Your spreadsheets can have some pop and zing to them that will help differentiate them from others. However, don't go overboard! If every cell had a different font and color, your spreadsheet would look like a mess.

You should use the skills that you learn in this chapter sparingly. You'll still have beautiful spreadsheets that you can share with your colleagues. If you would like to learn more about what styles OpenPyXL supports, you should check out their documentation[6].

In this chapter, you will learn about the following:

- Working with fonts
- Setting the alignment
- Adding a border
- Changing the cell background-color
- Inserting images into cells
- Styling merged cells
- Using a built-in style
- Creating a custom named style

Now that you know what you're going to learn, it's time to get started by discovering how to work with fonts using OpenPyXL!

Working with Fonts

You use fonts to style your text on a computer. A font controls the size, weight, color, and style of the text you see on-screen or in print. There are thousands of fonts that your computer can use. Microsoft includes many fonts with its Office products.

When you want to set a font with OpenPyXL, you will need to import the `Font` class from `openpyxl.styles`. Here is how you would do the import:

```
from openpyxl.styles import Font
```

The `Font` class takes many parameters. Here is the `Font` class's full list of parameters according to OpenPyXL's documentation:

[6]https://openpyxl.readthedocs.io/en/stable/styles.html

```
class openpyxl.styles.fonts.Font(name=None, sz=None, b=None, i=None, charset=None,
    u=None, strike=None, color=None, scheme=None, family=None, size=None,
    bold=None, italic=None, strikethrough=None, underline=None, vertAlign=None,
    outline=None, shadow=None, condense=None, extend=None)
```

The following list shows the parameters you are most likely to use and their defaults:

- name='Calibri'
- size=11
- bold=False
- italic=False
- vertAlign=None
- underline='none'
- strike=False
- color='FF000000'

These settings allow you to set most of the things you'll need to make your text look nice. Note that the color names in OpenPyXL use hexadecimal values to represent RGB (red, green, blue) color values. You can set whether or not the text should be bold, italic, underlined, or struck-through.

To see how you can use fonts in OpenPyXL, create a new file named `font_sizes.py` and add the following code to it:

```
# font_sizes.py

import openpyxl
from openpyxl.styles import Font


def font_demo(path):
    workbook = openpyxl.Workbook()
    sheet = workbook.active
    cell = sheet["A1"]
    cell.font = Font(size=12)
    cell.value = "Hello"

    cell2 = sheet["A2"]
    cell2.font = Font(name="Arial", size=14, color="00FF0000")
    sheet["A2"] = "from"

    cell2 = sheet["A3"]
    cell2.font = Font(name="Tahoma", size=16, color="00339966")
    sheet["A3"] = "OpenPyXL"
```

```
    workbook.save(path)


if __name__ == "__main__":
    font_demo("font_demo.xlsx")
```

This code uses three different fonts in three different cells. In **A1**, you use the default, which is Calibri. Then in **A2**, you set the font size to Arial and increase the size to 14 points. Finally, in **A3**, you change the font to Tahoma and the font size to 16 points.

For the second and third fonts, you also change the text color. In **A2**, you set the color to red, and in **A3**, you set the color to green.

When you run this code, your output will look like this:

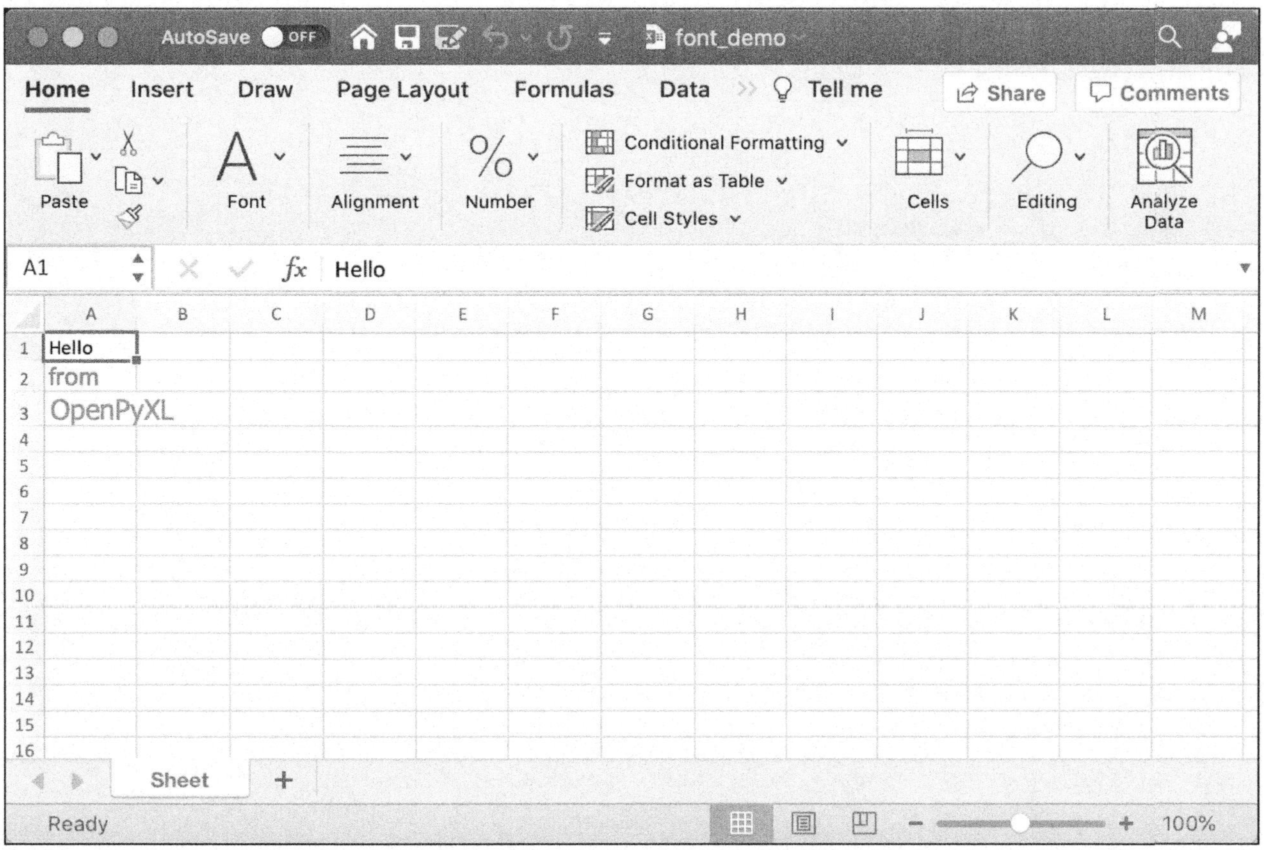

Fig. 4-1: Using Different Fonts in OpenPyXL

Try changing the code to use other fonts or colors. If you want to get adventurous, you should try to make your text bold or italicized.

Now you're ready to learn about text alignment.

Setting the Alignment

You can set alignment in OpenPyXL by using `openpyxl.styles.Alignment`. You use this class to rotate the text, set text wrapping, and for indentation.

Here are the defaults that the `Alignment` class uses:

- horizontal='general'
- vertical='bottom'
- text_rotation=0
- wrap_text=False
- shrink_to_fit=False
- indent=0

It's time for you to get some practice in. Open up your Python editor and create a new file named `alignment.py`. Then add this code to it:

```
# alignment.py

from openpyxl import Workbook
from openpyxl.styles import Alignment


def center_text(path, horizontal="center", vertical="center"):
    workbook = Workbook()
    sheet = workbook.active
    sheet["A1"] = "Hello"
    sheet["A1"].alignment = Alignment(horizontal=horizontal,
                                      vertical=vertical)
    sheet["A2"] = "from"
    sheet["A3"] = "OpenPyXL"
    sheet["A3"].alignment = Alignment(text_rotation=90)
    workbook.save(path)


if __name__ == "__main__":
    center_text("alignment.xlsx")
```

You will center the string both horizontally and vertically in **A1** when you run this code. Then you use the defaults for **A2**. Finally, for **A3**, you rotate the text 90 degrees.

Try running this code, and you will see something like the following:

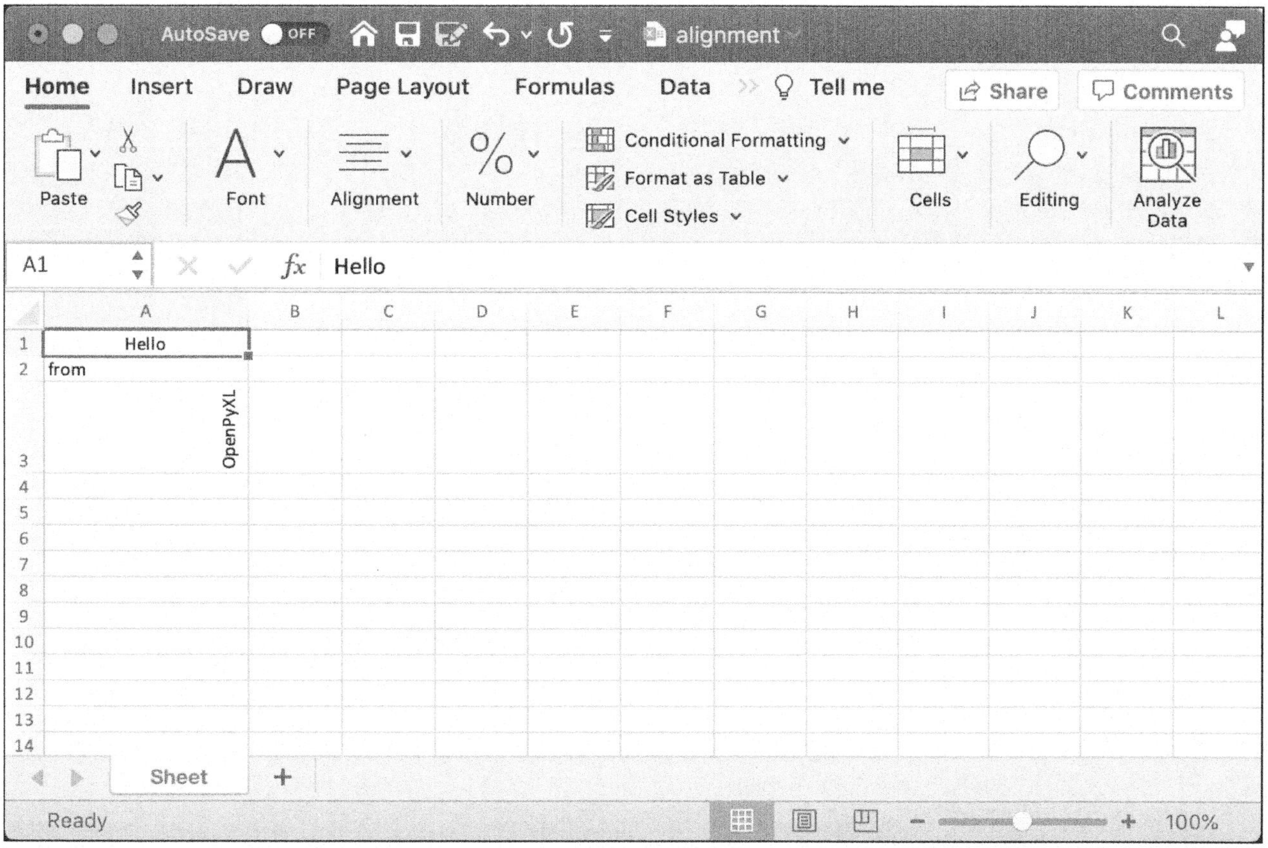

Fig. 4-2: Changing Text Alignment in OpenPyXL

That looks nice! It would be best if you took the time to try out different `text_rotation` values. Then try changing the `horizontal` and `vertical` parameters with different values. Pretty soon, you will be able to align your text like a pro!

Now you're ready to learn about adding borders to your cells!

Adding a Border

OpenPyXL gives you the ability to style the borders on your cell. You can specify a different border style for each of the four sides of a cell.

You can use any of the following border styles:

- 'dashDot'
- 'dashDotDot'
- 'dashed'
- 'dotted'
- 'double'
- 'hair'

- 'medium'
- 'mediumDashDot'
- 'mediumDashDotDot',
- 'mediumDashed'
- 'slantDashDot'
- 'thick'
- 'thin'

Open your Python editor and create a new file named `border.py`. Then enter the following code in your file:

```
# border.py

from openpyxl import Workbook
from openpyxl.styles import Border, Side


def border(path):
    pink = "00FF00FF"
    green = "00008000"
    thin = Side(border_style="thin", color=pink)
    double = Side(border_style="double", color=green)

    workbook = Workbook()
    sheet = workbook.active

    sheet["A1"] = "Hello"
    sheet["A1"].border = Border(top=double, left=thin, right=thin, bottom=double)
    sheet["A2"] = "from"
    sheet["A3"] = "OpenPyXL"
    sheet["A3"].border = Border(top=thin, left=double, right=double, bottom=thin)
    workbook.save(path)


if __name__ == "__main__":
    border("border.xlsx")
```

This code will add a border to cell **A1** and **A3**. The top and bottom of **A1** use a "double" border style and are green, while the cell sides are using a "thin" border style and are colored pink.

Cell **A3** uses the same borders but swaps them so that the sides are now green and the top and bottom are pink.

You get this effect by creating `Side` objects in the `border_style` and the `color` to be used. Then you pass those `Side` objects to a `Border` class, which allows you to set each of the four sides of a cell individually. To apply the `Border` to a cell, you must set the cell's `border` attribute.

When you run this code, you will see the following result:

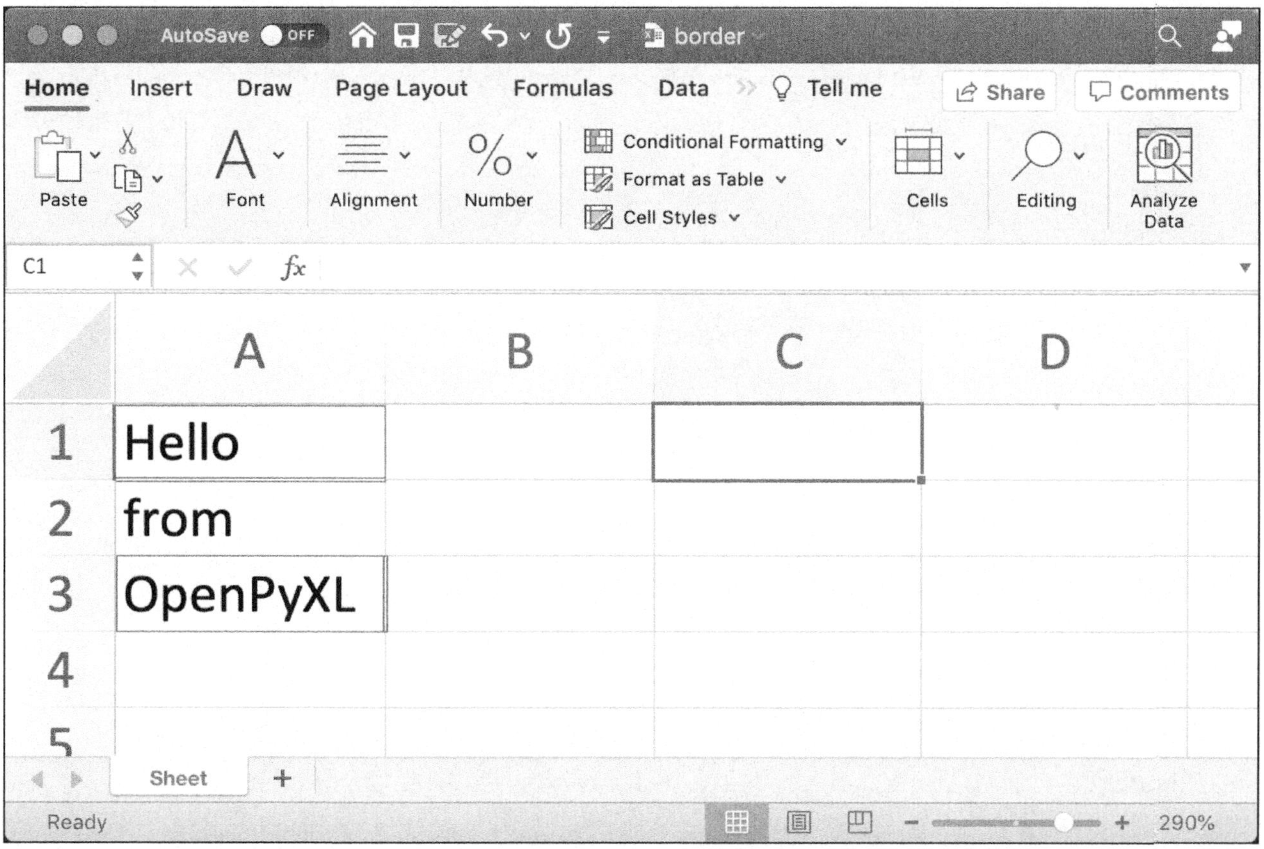

Fig. 4-3: Changing the Border in OpenPyXL

This image is zoomed in a lot so that you can easily see the borders of the cells. It would be best if you tried modifying this code with some of the other border styles mentioned at the beginning of this section so that you can see what else you can do.

Changing the Cell Background Color

You can highlight a cell or a range of cells by changing its background color. Highlighting a cell is more eye-catching than changing the text's font or color in most cases. OpenPyXL gives you a class called `PatternFill` that you can use to change a cell's background color.

The `PatternFill` class takes in the following arguments (defaults included below):

- patternType=None

- fgColor=Color()
- bgColor=Color()
- fill_type=None
- start_color=None
- end_color=None

There are several different fill types you can use. Here is a list of currently supported fill types:

- 'none'
- 'solid'
- 'darkDown'
- 'darkGray'
- 'darkGrid'
- 'darkHorizontal'
- 'darkTrellis'
- 'darkUp'
- 'darkVertical'
- 'gray0625'
- 'gray125'
- 'lightDown'
- 'lightGray'
- 'lightGrid'
- 'lightHorizontal'
- 'lightTrellis'
- 'lightUp'
- 'lightVertical'
- 'mediumGray'

Now you have enough information to try setting the background color of a cell using OpenPyXL. Open up a new file in your Python editor and name it `background_colors.py`. Then add this code to your new file:

```
# background_colors.py

from openpyxl import Workbook
from openpyxl.styles import PatternFill


def background_colors(path):
    workbook = Workbook()
    sheet = workbook.active
    yellow = "00FFFF00"
```

```
    for rows in sheet.iter_rows(min_row=1, max_row=10, min_col=1, max_col=12):
        for cell in rows:
            if cell.row % 2:
                cell.fill = PatternFill(start_color=yellow, end_color=yellow,
                                        fill_type = "solid")
    workbook.save(path)


if __name__ == "__main__":
    background_colors("bg.xlsx")
```

This example will iterate over nine rows and 12 columns. It will set every cell's background color to yellow if that cell is in an odd-numbered row. The cells with their background color changes will be from column **A** through column **L**.

When you want to set the cell's background color, you set the cell's `fill` attribute to an instance of `PatternFill`. In this example, you specify a `start_color` and an `end_color`. You also set the `fill_type` to "solid". OpenPyXL also supports using a `GradientFill` for the background.

Try running this code. After it runs, you will have a new Excel document that looks like this:

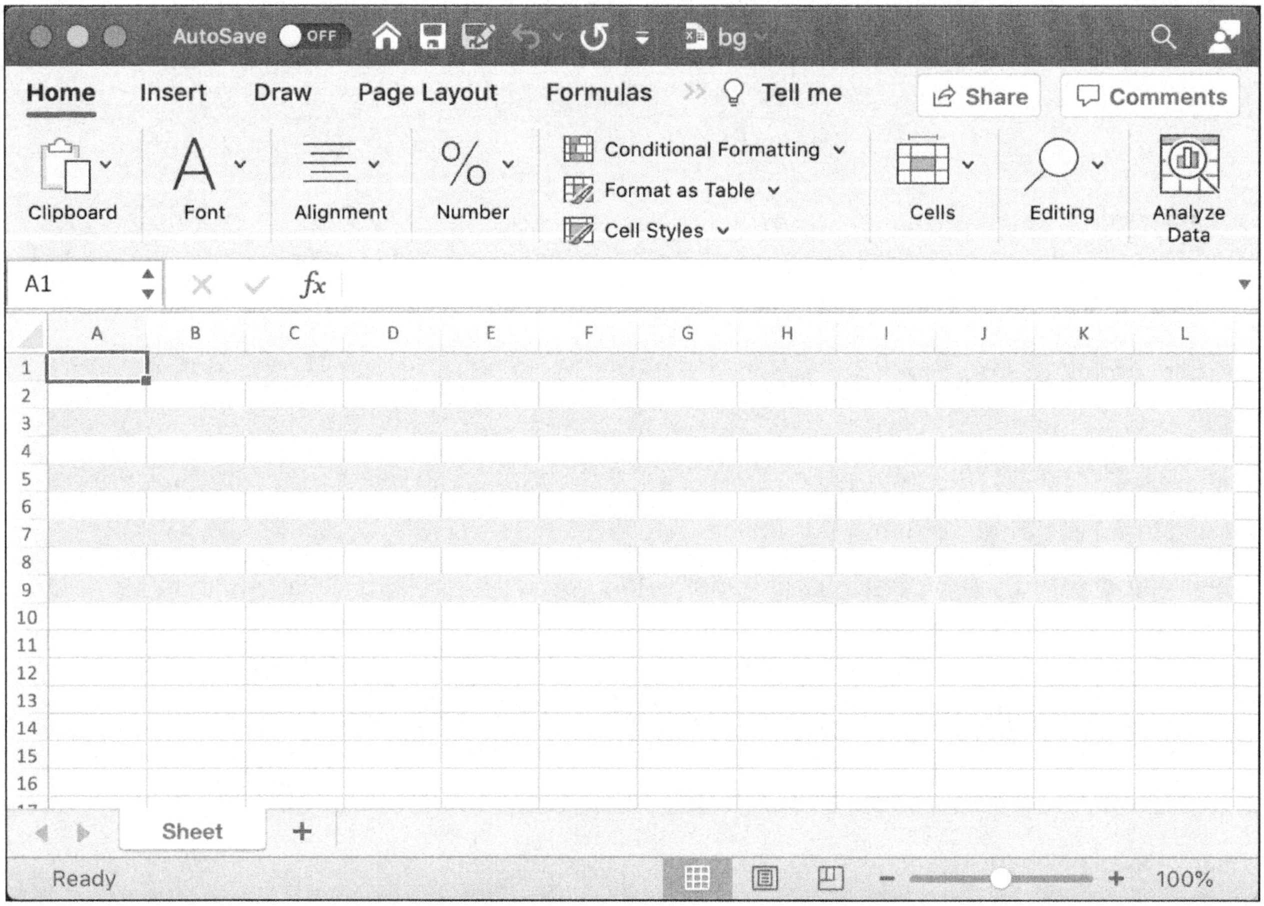

Fig. 4-4: Changing the Background Color in OpenPyXL

Here are some ideas that you can try out with this code:

- Change the number of rows or columns that are affected
- Change the color that you are changing to
- Update the code to color the even rows with a different color
- Try out other fill types

Once you are done experimenting with background colors, you can learn about inserting images in your cells!

Inserting Images into Cells

OpenPyXL makes inserting an image into your Excel spreadsheets nice and straightforward. To make this magic happen, you use the `Worksheet` object's `add_image()` method. This method takes in two arguments:

- `img` - The path to the image file that you are inserting

- `anchor` - Provide a cell as a top-left anchor of the image (optional)

For this example, you will be using the Mouse vs. Python logo:

Fig. 4-5: Mouse vs. Python Logo

The GitHub repository[7] for this book has the image for you to use.

Once you have the image downloaded, create a new Python file and name it `insert_image.py`. Then add the following:

```
# insert_image.py

from openpyxl import Workbook
from openpyxl.drawing.image import Image


def insert_image(path, image_path):
    workbook = Workbook()
    sheet = workbook.active
    img = Image("logo.png")
    sheet.add_image(img, "B1")
    workbook.save(path)


if __name__ == "__main__":
    insert_image("logo.xlsx", "logo.png")
```

Here you pass in the path to the image that you wish to insert. To insert the image, you call `add_image()`. In this example, you are hard-coding to use cell **B1** as the anchor cell. Then you save your Excel spreadsheet.

If you open up your spreadsheet, you will see that it looks like this:

[7] https://github.com/driscollis/automating_excel_with_python

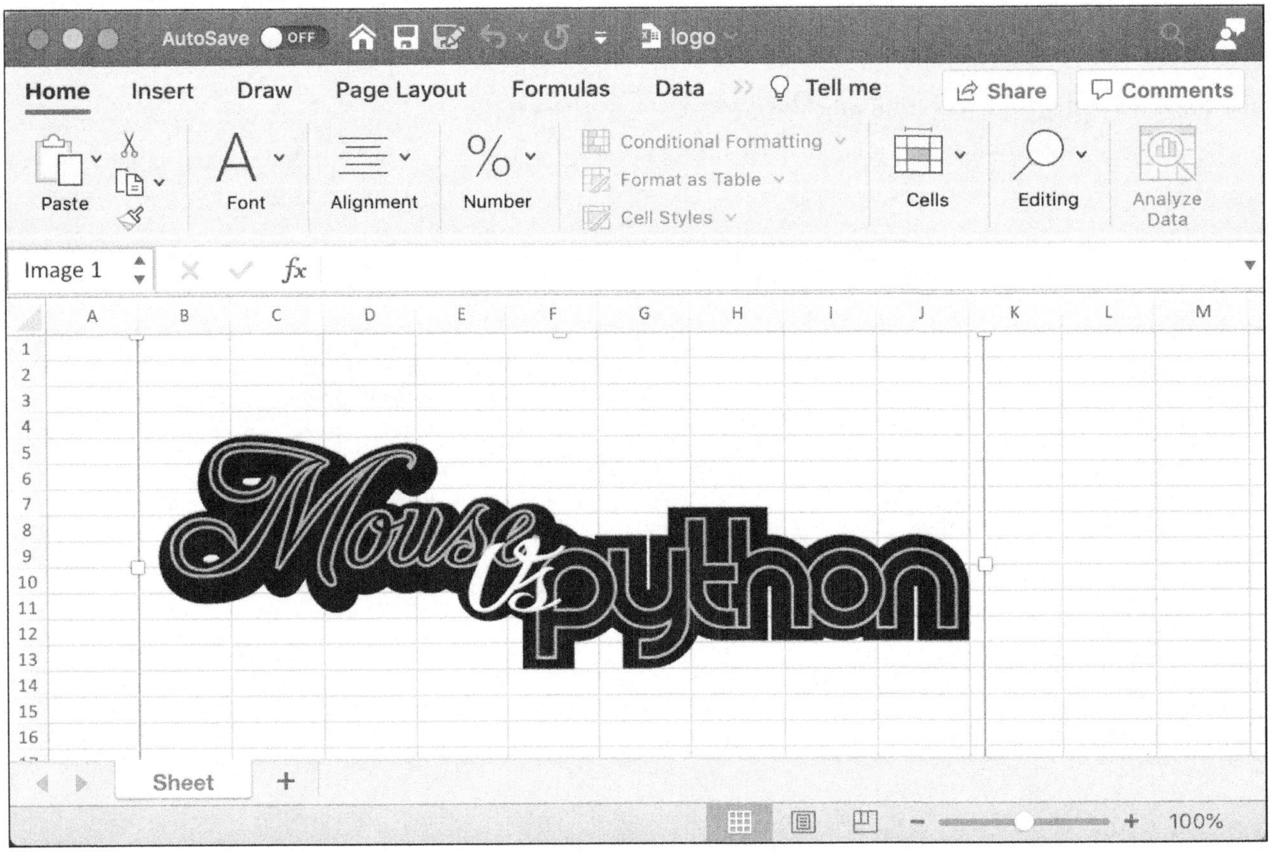

Fig. 4-6: Inserting an Image

You probably won't need to insert an image into an Excel spreadsheet all that often, but it's an excellent skill to have.

Styling Merged Cells

Merged cells are cells where you have two or more adjacent cells merged into one. If you want to set the value of a merged cell with OpenPyXL, you must use the top left-most cell of the merged cells.

You also must use this particular cell to set the style for the merged cell as a whole. You can use all the styles and font settings you used on an individual cell with the merged cell. However, you must apply the style to the top-left cell for it to apply to the entire merged cell.

You will understand how this works if you see some code. Go ahead and create a new file named `style_merged_cell.py`. Now enter this code in your file:

```
# style_merged_cell.py

from openpyxl import Workbook
from openpyxl.styles import Font, Border, Side, GradientFill, Alignment


def merge_style(path):
    workbook = Workbook()
    sheet = workbook.active
    cell_range = "A2:G4"
    sheet.merge_cells(cell_range)
    top_left_cell = sheet["A2"]

    light_purple = "00CC99FF"
    green = "00008000"
    thin = Side(border_style="thin", color=light_purple)
    double = Side(border_style="double", color=green)

    top_left_cell.value = "Hello from PyOpenXL"
    for column in sheet[cell_range]:
        for cell in column:
            cell.border = Border(top=double, left=thin, right=thin,
                                 bottom=double)
    top_left_cell.fill = GradientFill(stop=("000000", "FFFFFF"))
    top_left_cell.font  = Font(b=True, color="FF0000", size=16)
    top_left_cell.alignment = Alignment(horizontal="center",
                                        vertical="center")
    workbook.save(path)


if __name__ == "__main__":
    merge_style("merged_style.xlsx")
```

Here you create a merged cell that starts at **A2** (the top-left cell) through **G4**. Then you set the cell's value, border, fill, font and alignment. You will need to loop over the `cell_range` and apply the border to each of those cells for the border to be applied correctly to the entirety of the merged cell.

When you run this code, your new spreadsheet will look like this:

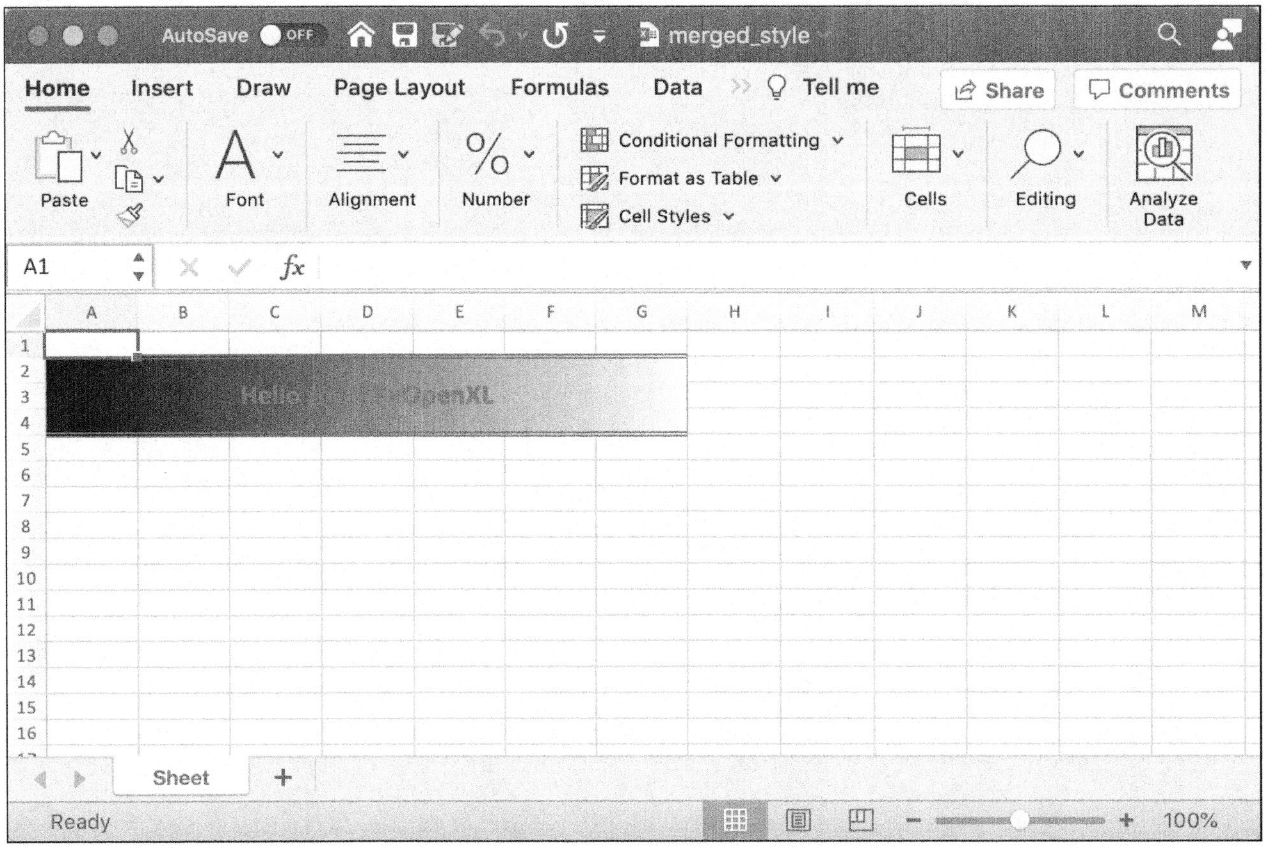

Fig. 4-7: Styling a Merged Cell

Doesn't that look nice? You should take some time and try out some different styles on your merged cell. Maybe come up with a better gradient than the gray one used here, for example.

Now you're ready to learn about OpenPyXL's built-in styles!

Using a Built-in Style

OpenPyXL comes with multiple built-in styles that you can use as well. Rather than reproducing the entire list of built-in styles in this book, you should go to the official documentation[8] as it will be the most up-to-date source for the style names.

However, it is worth noting some of the styles. For example, here are the number format styles you can use:

- 'Comma'
- 'Comma [0]'
- 'Currency'
- 'Currency [0]'

[8]https://openpyxl.readthedocs.io/en/stable/styles.html#using-builtin-styles

- 'Percent'

You can also apply text styles. Here is a listing of those styles:

- 'Title'
- 'Headline 1'
- 'Headline 2'
- 'Headline 3'
- 'Headline 4'
- 'Hyperlink'
- 'Followed Hyperlink'
- 'Linked Cell'

OpenPyXL has several other built-in style groups. You should check out the documentation to learn about all the different styles that are supported.

Now that you know about some of the built-in styles you can use, it's time to write some code! Create a new file and name it `builtin_styls.py`. Then enter the following code:

```
# builtin_styles.py

from openpyxl import Workbook


def builtin_styles(path):
    workbook = Workbook()
    sheet = workbook.active
    sheet["A1"].value = "Hello"
    sheet["A1"].style = "Title"

    sheet["A2"].value = "from"
    sheet["A2"].style = "Headline 1"

    sheet["A3"].value = "OpenPyXL"
    sheet["A3"].style = "Headline 2"

    workbook.save(path)


if __name__ == "__main__":
    builtin_styles("builtin_styles.xlsx")
```

Here you apply three different styles to three different cells. You use "Title", "Headline 1" and "Headline 2", specifically.

When you run this code, you will end up having a spreadsheet that looks like this:

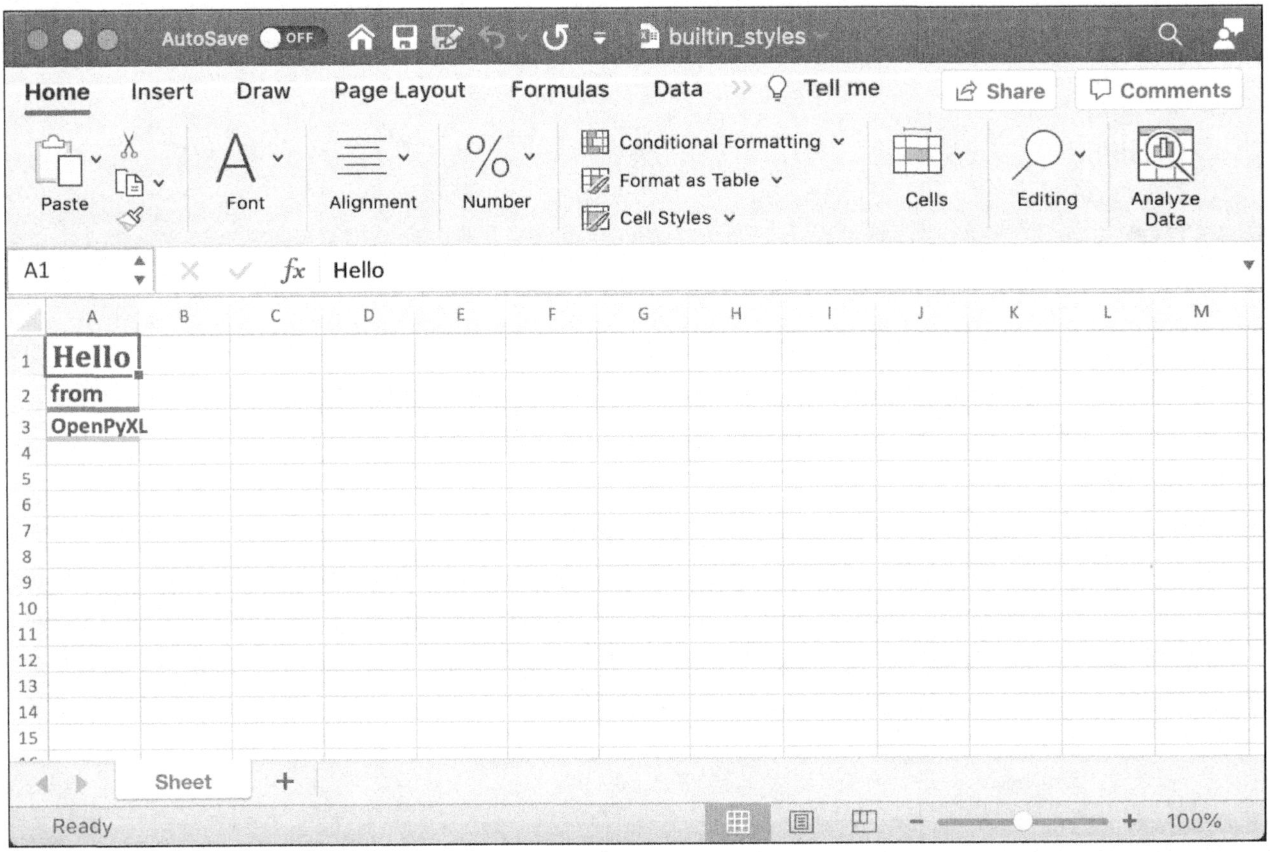

Fig. 4-7: Inserting an Image

As always, you should try out some of the other built-in styles. Trying them out is the only way to determine what they do and if they will work for you.

But wait! What if you wanted to create your style? That's what you will cover in the next section!

Creating a Custom Named Style

You can create custom styles of your design using OpenPyXL as well. To create your style, you must use the `NamedStyle` class.

The `NamedStyle` class takes the following arguments (defaults are included too):

- name="Normal"
- font=Font()
- fill=PatternFill()

- border=Border()
- alignment=Alignment()
- number_format=None
- protection=Protection()
- builtinId=None
- hidden=False
- xfId=None

You should always provide your own `name` to your `NamedStyle` to keep it unique. Go ahead and create a new file and call it `named_style.py`. Then add this code to it:

```
# named_style.py

from openpyxl import Workbook
from openpyxl.styles import Font, Border, Side, NamedStyle


def named_style(path):
    workbook = Workbook()
    sheet = workbook.active

    red = "00FF0000"
    font = Font(bold=True, size=22)
    thick = Side(style="thick", color=red)
    border = Border(left=thick, right=thick, top=thick, bottom=thick)
    named_style = NamedStyle(name="highlight", font=font, border=border)

    sheet["A1"].value = "Hello"
    sheet["A1"].style = named_style

    sheet["A2"].value = "from"
    sheet["A3"].value = "OpenPyXL"

    workbook.save(path)


if __name__ == "__main__":
    named_style("named_style.xlsx")
```

Here you create a `Font()`, `Side()`, and `Border()` instance to pass to your `NamedStyle()`. Once you have your custom style created, you can apply it to a cell by setting the cell's `style` attribute. Applying a custom style is done in the same way as you applied built-in styles!

You applied the custom style to the cell, **A1**.

When you run this code, you will get a spreadsheet that looks like this:

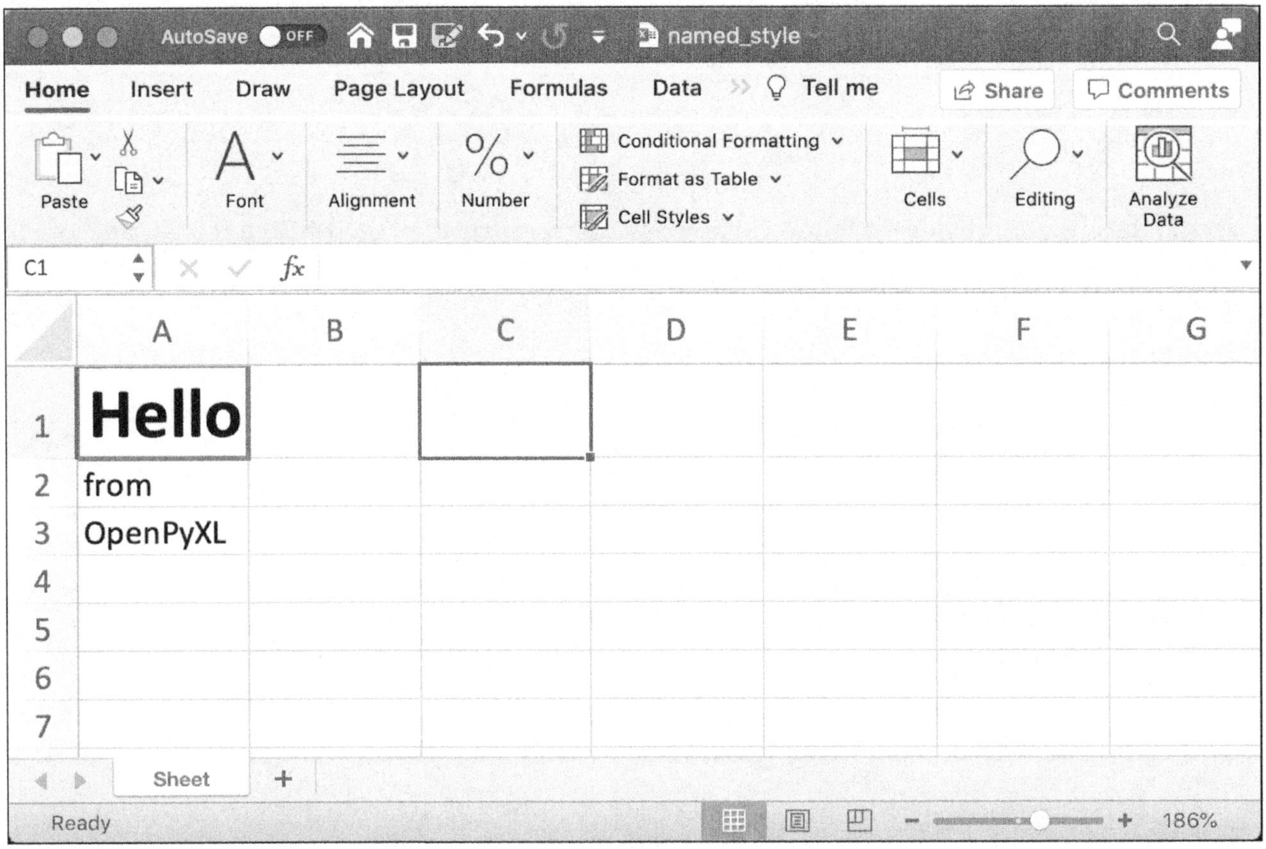

Fig. 4-8: Using a Named Style

Now it's your turn! Edit the code to use a `Side` style, which will change your border. Or create multiple `Side` instances so you can make each side of the cell unique. Play around with different fonts or add a custom background color!

Wrapping Up

You can do a lot of different things with cells using OpenPyXL. The information in this chapter gives you the ability to format your data in beautiful ways.

In this chapter, you learned about the following topics:

- Working with fonts
- Setting the alignment
- Adding a border
- Changing the cell background-color

- Inserting images into cells
- Styling merged cells
- Using a built-in style
- Creating a custom named style

You can take the information that you learned in this chapter to make beautiful spreadsheets. You can highlight exciting data by changing the cell's background color or font. You can also change the cell's format by using a built-in style. Go ahead and give it a try.

Experiment with the code in this chapter and see how powerful and valuable OpenPyXL is when working with cells.

Chapter 5 - Conditional Formatting

Microsoft Excel has the concept of **conditional formatting**. You apply conditional formatting to a range of cells. You can set up rules for the formatting, such as change the background color of a row if it contains a specific string. You can also set cell formatting based on a formula-type condition. There are many different ways to set up conditional formatting using OpenPyXL.

Microsoft Excel supports three different types of conditional formatting:

- Builtins - combines specific rules with predefined cell styles
- Standard - combines specific rules with custom formatting
- Custom - uses custom formulae to apply custom formats using different styles.

This chapter will focus on built-in formats. You can read more about OpenPyXL's support for Excel's conditional formatting in the package's documentation[9].

You will learn about the following in this chapter:

- Builtin formats
- Working with `ColorScales`
- Adding `IconSets`
- Creating a `DataBar`
- Using `DifferentialStyles`

Let's get started by learning about built-in formats!

Builtin Formats

OpenPyXL has three built-in formats that you can use. They are as follows:

- `ColorScale`
- `IconSet`
- `DataBar`

These built-in formats allow you to format your data dynamically. You will start by learning how to use a `ColorScale` first!

[9]https://openpyxl.readthedocs.io/en/stable/formatting.html

Working with `ColorScales`

A `ColorScale` lets you set 2 or 3 colors. These colors allow you to put a gradient from one color to the other. You could use a `ColorScale` to add a range of colors to a column based on the data within the column. The third color gives you an additional color for your two gradients to use.

The `ColorScale` class takes two arguments:

- `cfvo` - A list of `FormatObjects`
- `color` - A list of `Color` objects

The `FormatObject` can use any of the following settings: 'num', 'percent', 'max', 'min', 'formula', and 'percentile'. The `FormatObject` tells OpenPyXL how to apply the `ColorScale` to your data. The `Color` objects define the two or three colors that you will use on your data.

To get started, you will need some data. You can use the **ratings.xslx** spreadsheet provided in the book's source code repository on GitHub[10] for this chapter.

It looks like this:

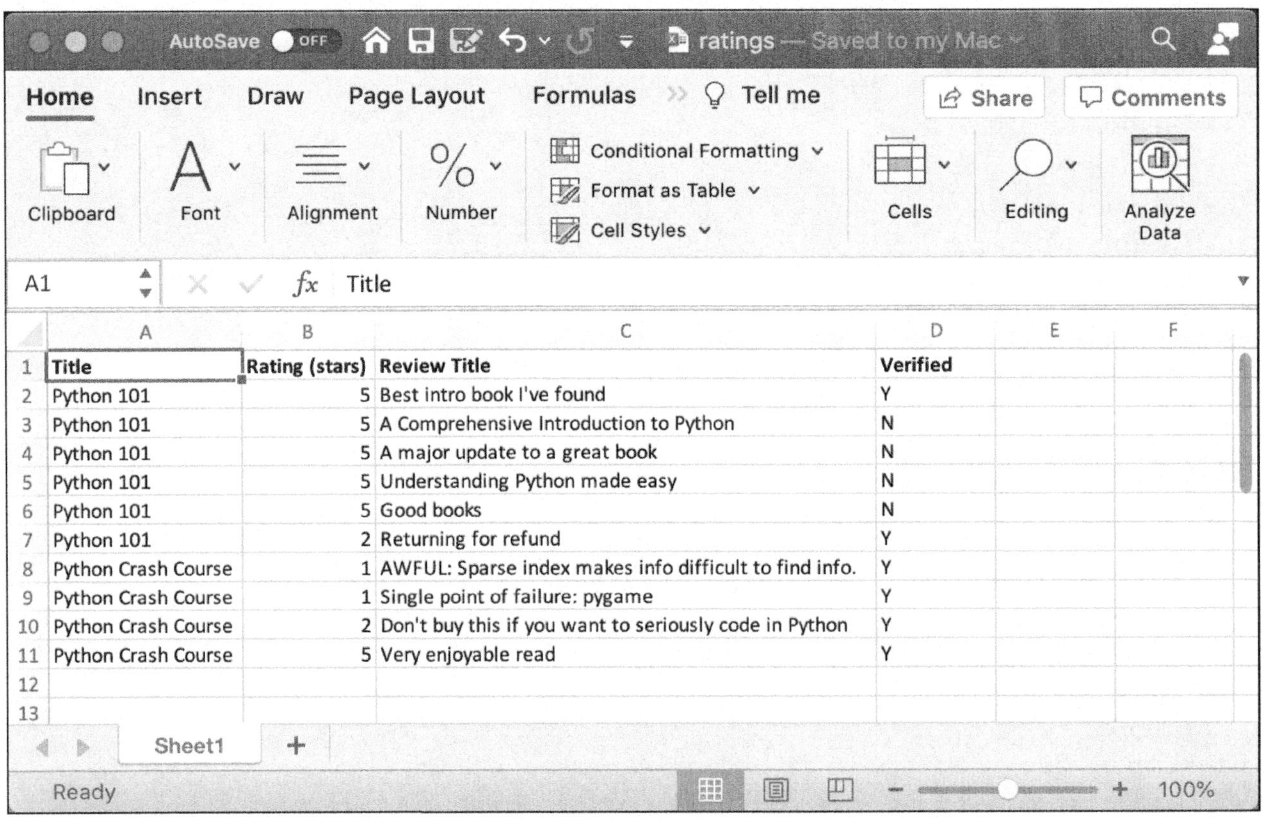

	A	B	C	D
1	Title	Rating (stars)	Review Title	Verified
2	Python 101	5	Best intro book I've found	Y
3	Python 101	5	A Comprehensive Introduction to Python	N
4	Python 101	5	A major update to a great book	N
5	Python 101	5	Understanding Python made easy	N
6	Python 101	5	Good books	N
7	Python 101	2	Returning for refund	Y
8	Python Crash Course	1	AWFUL: Sparse index makes info difficult to find info.	Y
9	Python Crash Course	1	Single point of failure: pygame	Y
10	Python Crash Course	2	Don't buy this if you want to seriously code in Python	Y
11	Python Crash Course	5	Very enjoyable read	Y

Fig. 5-1: Book Ratings

[10] https://github.com/driscollis/automating_excel_with_python

This data is loosely based on ratings of one of the author's books on Amazon and another popular Python book on Amazon. Feel free to add more data to the spreadsheet as you see fit.

Now that you have some data to work with, you are ready to write some code! Open up your Python editor and create a new file named `using_colorscale.py`. Then enter the following code:

```
# using_colorscale.py

from openpyxl import load_workbook
from openpyxl.formatting.rule import ColorScale, FormatObject, Rule
from openpyxl.styles import Color


def applying_colorscale(path, output_path):
    workbook = load_workbook(filename=path)
    sheet = workbook.active

    first = FormatObject(type='min')
    last = FormatObject(type="max")

    colors = [Color('AA0000'),    # red
              Color('00AA00')]    # green
    color_scale = ColorScale(cfvo=[first, last], color=colors)

    rule = Rule(type="colorScale", colorScale=color_scale)

    sheet.conditional_formatting.add("B1:B100", rule)
    workbook.save(output_path)


if __name__ == "__main__":
    applying_colorscale("ratings.xlsx",
                        output_path="colorscale.xlsx")
```

This code imports the classes you need: `ColorScale`, `FormatObject`, `Rule`, and `Color`. You create two instances of `FormatObject` to create a minimum and maximum format objects. Then you make a list that contains two `Color` objects. Finally, you instantiate `ColorScale` and pass in your format objects and colors

To use your color scale, you add it to a `Rule` object. You need to set the `type` of the `Rule` to a "colorScale". Note that you need to use a lowercase "c" here, whereas the class name uses an uppercase "C".

Lastly, you call your `sheet` object's `conditional_formatting.add()` method to apply your rule to the spreadsheet. The `add()` function is where you tell OpenPyXL which rows or columns you want to apply the rule on. In this case, you apply the rule to the cells in column **B**, starting at cell one and going through cell 100.

When you run this code, your spreadsheet will look like this:

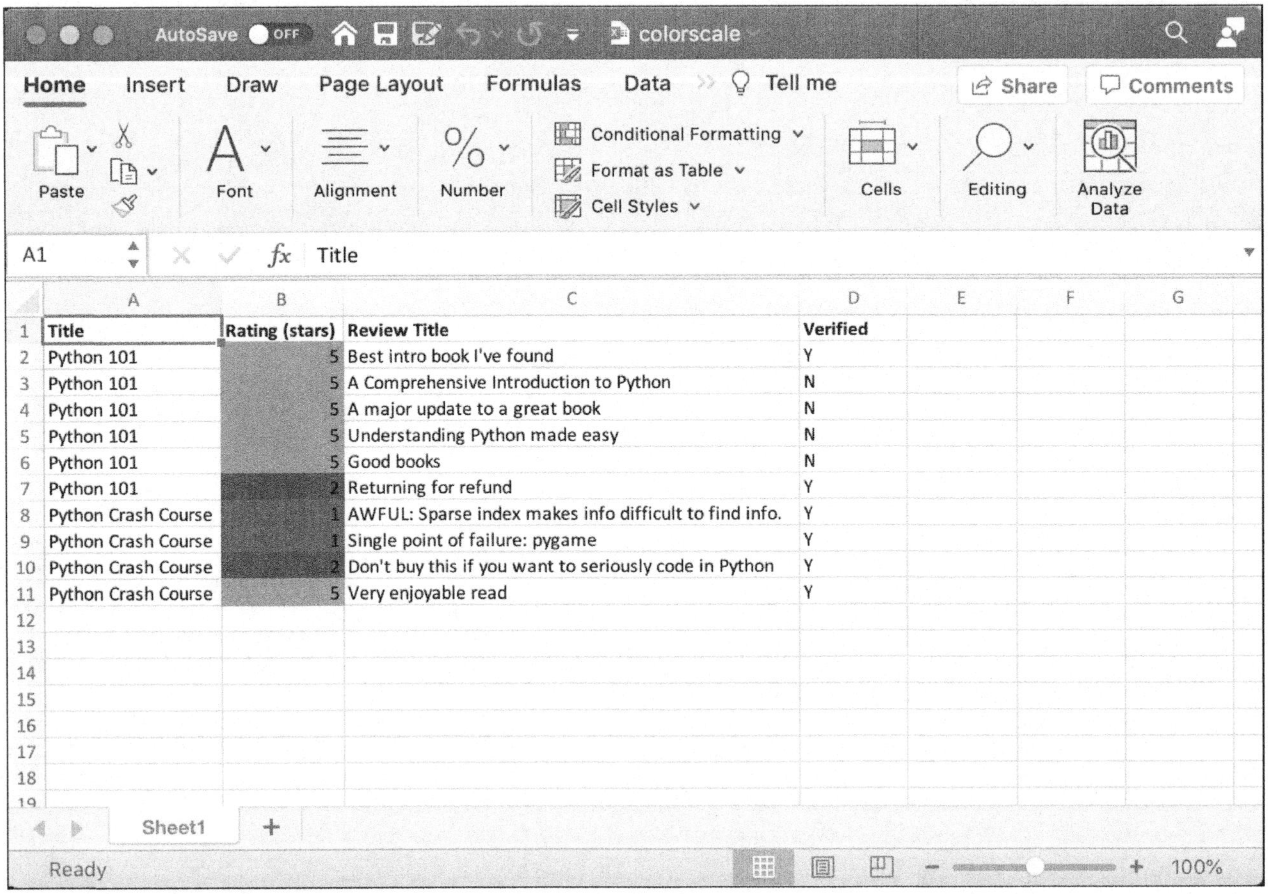

Fig. 5-2: Using a ColorScale

The lower the value in column **B**, the redder it becomes. You can see this in the screenshot above. You can add a third color to your list of colors to get more fine-grained control over how the colors change over a range of values. Give it a try and see what you can come up with.

You can simplify your code a bit by using a `ColorScaleRule` instead of all those other classes.

To see how that works, create a new file named `using_colorscalerule.py` and add this code:

```python
# using_colorscalerule.py

from openpyxl import load_workbook
from openpyxl.formatting.rule import ColorScaleRule


def applying_colorscalerule(path, output_path):
    workbook = load_workbook(filename=path)
    sheet = workbook.active

    red = "AA0000"
    yellow = "00FFFF00"
    green = "00AA00"

    color_scale_rule = ColorScaleRule(start_type="num",
                                      start_value=1,
                                      start_color=red,
                                      mid_type="num",
                                      mid_value=3,
                                      mid_color=yellow,
                                      end_type="num",
                                      end_value=5,
                                      end_color=green)

    sheet.conditional_formatting.add("B1:B100", color_scale_rule)
    workbook.save(output_path)


if __name__ == "__main__":
    applying_colorscalerule("ratings.xlsx",
                            output_path="colorscalerule.xlsx")
```

This example demonstrates adding three colors to your color scale. The `ColorScaleRule` class does not require you to add three colors. You can pass in only the start and end values instead, and it will happily create a spreadsheet that is the same as the previous code.

This code makes you set the `start_type` (a number in this case), the `start_value`, and the `start_-color`. You use the same start color that you used in the previous example. Then you add a mid-type, color, and value. Finally, you add an end-type, value, and color. The mid-color is a new color, yellow, while the end-color is still green.

You apply the `ColorScaleRule` the same way that you applied the previous rule.

When you run this code, you will create the following spreadsheet:

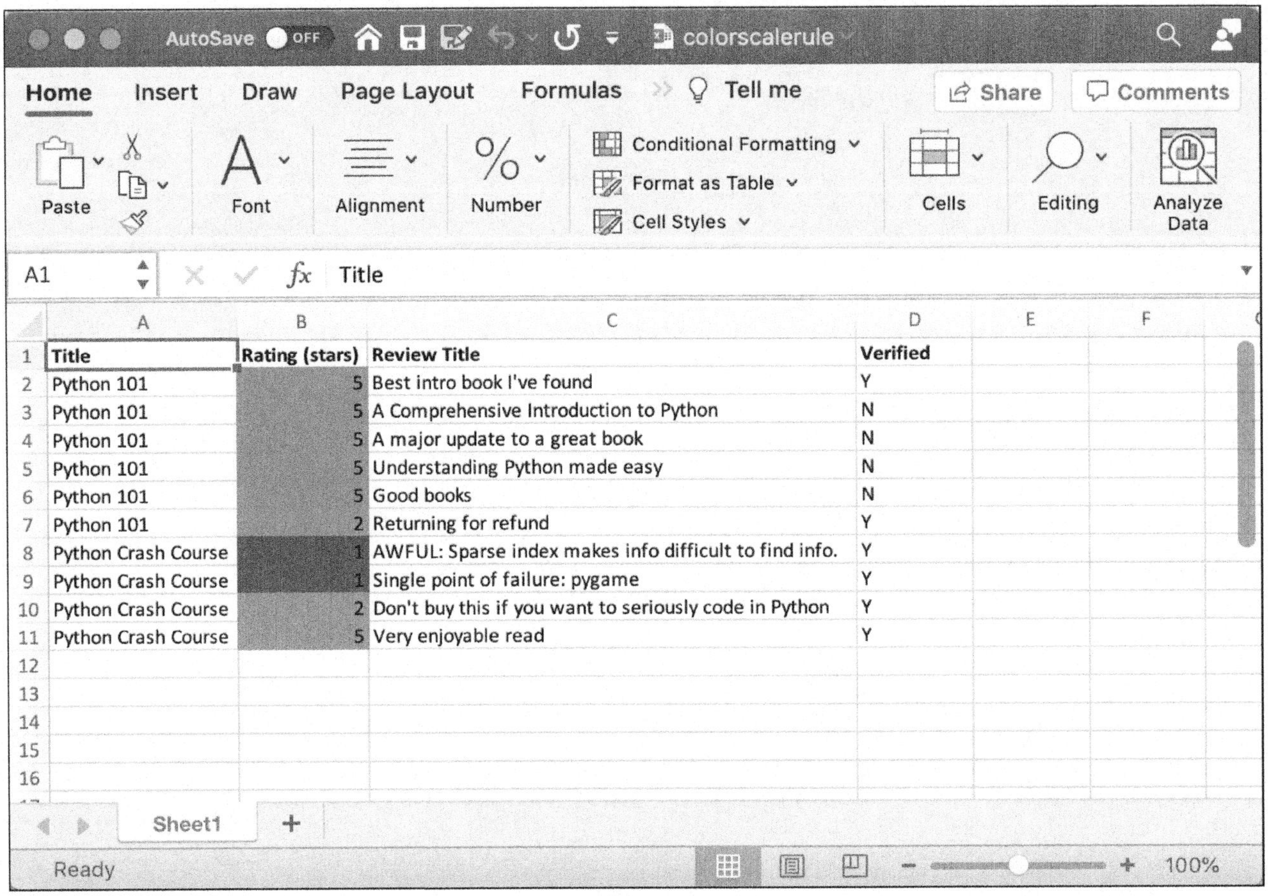

Fig. 5-3: Using a ColorScaleRule

Adding that extra color made a difference in the output. Compare this screenshot to the one from the previous example. Try changing the colors to something else or change the range of values in the data to see how your spreadsheet changes. You can have a lot of fun by experimenting with these values while getting your spreadsheet looking nice and professional.

Now you're ready to move on and learn about `IconSets`!

Adding `IconSets`

OpenPyXL has an interesting built-in format called an `IconSet`. The `IconSet` will replace the values in your spreadsheet with icons, which can be more eye-catching than simple numbers.

You can choose from the following sets of icons: '3Arrows', '3ArrowsGray', '3Flags', '3TrafficLights1', '3TrafficLights2', '3Signs', '3Symbols', '3Symbols2', '4Arrows', '4ArrowsGray', '4RedToBlack', '4Rating', '4TrafficLights', '5Arrows', '5ArrowsGray', '5Rating', '5Quarters'.

An `IconSet` does not support using the `Color` class you learned about when creating a `ColorScale`. Since you don't need to import `Color`, your code is a bit more compact.

To see how you can use an `IconSet`, create a new file and name it `using_iconset.py`. Then enter the following:

```
# using_iconset.py

from openpyxl import load_workbook
from openpyxl.formatting.rule import IconSet, FormatObject, Rule


def applying_iconset(path, output_path):
    workbook = load_workbook(filename=path)
    sheet = workbook.active

    first = FormatObject(type='num', val=0)
    mid = FormatObject(type="num", val=3)
    last = FormatObject(type="num", val=5)

    iconset = IconSet(iconSet='3TrafficLights1', cfvo=[first, mid, last],
                      showValue=None, percent=None, reverse=None)

    rule = Rule(type="iconSet", iconSet=iconset)

    sheet.conditional_formatting.add("B1:B100", rule)
    workbook.save(output_path)


if __name__ == "__main__":
    applying_iconset("ratings.xlsx",
                     output_path="iconset.xlsx")
```

Here you create three format objects: one for the first value, one for the middle value, and one for the last value. By setting these bounds, you are telling OpenPyXL what to use for the icons. Next, you create an `IconSet`, making sure to pass in your format objects as a list to `cfvo`. Then you pass the `IconSet` object to your `Rule`. Note that you set the `type` of the rule to "iconSet", which has the same odd capitalization as the "colorScale" did.

The last step is to apply the rule using the `conditional_formatting.add()` method. When you run this code, you will create a spreadsheet that looks like this:

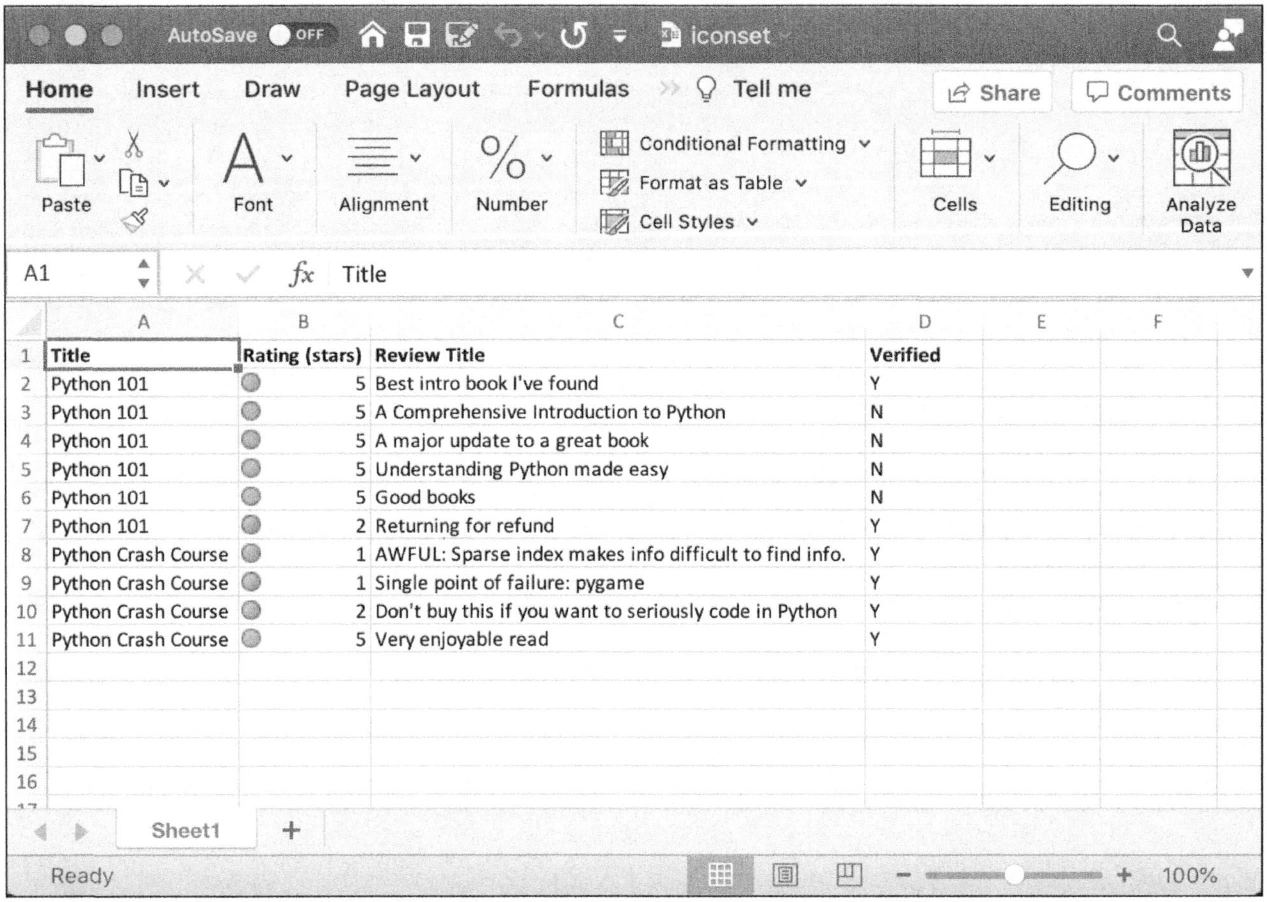

Fig. 5-4: Using an IconSet

In this example, you used the "3TrafficLights1" icon set and applied it to column B. Try swapping out that icon set for one of the others to see how it changes your spreadsheet.

Note: The IconSet's color may be slightly different on different operating systems. For example, this example was run on Mac but you ran it on Windows 10, the colors may be slightly muted.

OpenPyXL provides a convenience function called `IconSetRule` that simplifies creating an `IconSet` in much the same way as a `ColorScaleRule` simplifies creating a `ColorScale`.

To see how you would use an `IconSetRule`, create a new file and name it `using_iconsetrule.py`. Now enter this code in your new file:

```python
# using_iconsetrule.py

from openpyxl import load_workbook
from openpyxl.formatting.rule import IconSetRule


def applying_iconsetrule(path, output_path):
    workbook = load_workbook(filename=path)
    sheet = workbook.active

    icon_set_rule = IconSetRule("5Arrows", "num", [1, 2, 3, 4, 5])
    sheet.conditional_formatting.add("B1:B100", icon_set_rule)
    workbook.save(output_path)


if __name__ == "__main__":
    applying_iconsetrule("ratings.xlsx",
                         output_path="iconsetrule.xlsx")
```

This code is significantly shorter than the previous example. Here you only need to import `IconSetRule`. You tell it which icons you want to use ("5Arrows"), the format object type ("num"), and then the range of values. You apply this rule the same way you have used the previous rules.

When you run this code, your spreadsheet will look like this:

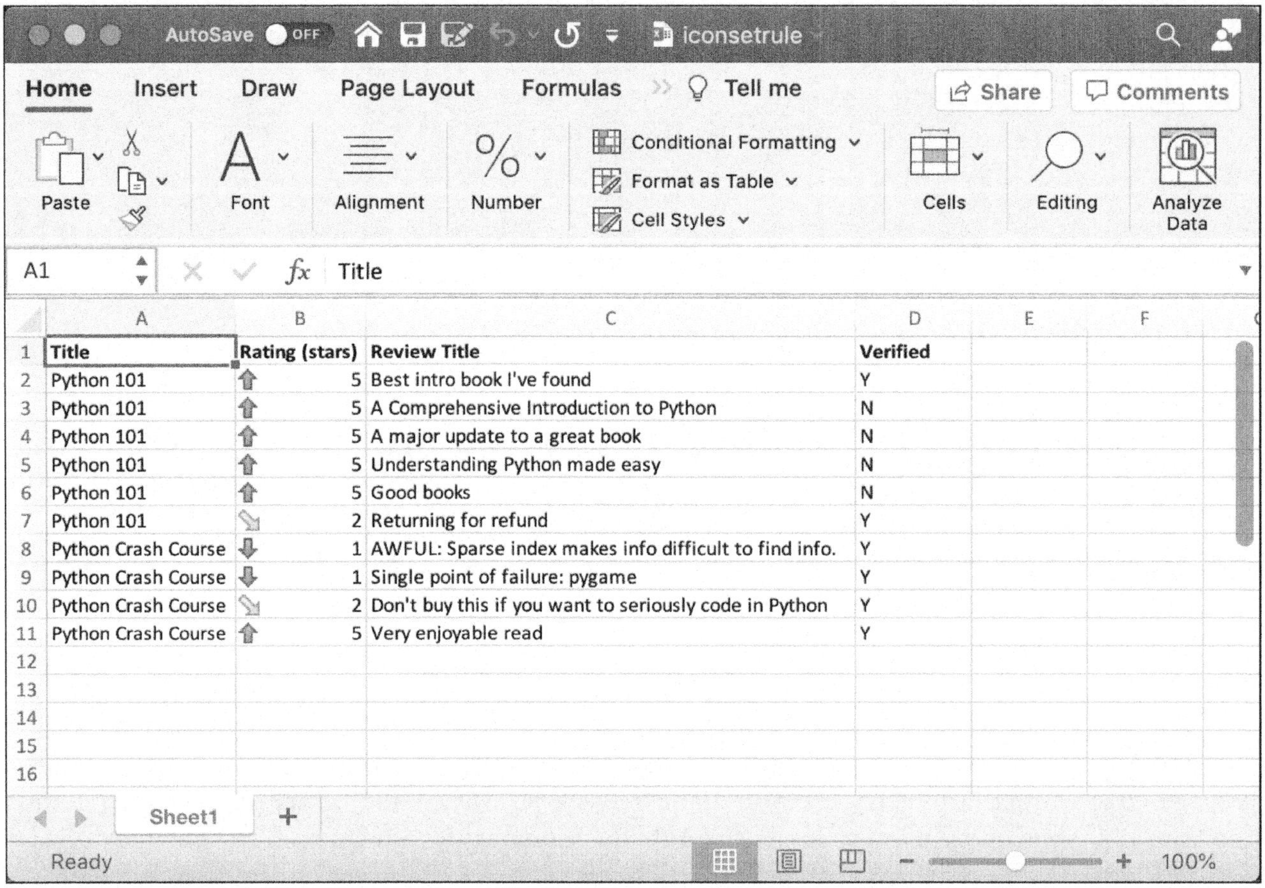

Fig. 5-5: Using an IconSetRule

Isn't that an excellent little enhancement for your spreadsheet? Give both versions of the `IconSet` a try and see which one you like better.

Note: If you run this code on Windows 10, the arrows will look different then the ones shown in this screenshot.

Now let's move on and learn about the `DataBar`!

Creating a `DataBar`

OpenPyXL supports adding a "progress bar" in your cells as well. The progress bar is called a `DataBar`. The `DataBar` is an excellent way to visualize data where you might be trying to reach a goal. For example, you might have a column of weekly sales numbers, and you want to show the progress, week-over-week, of your sales. OpenPyXL makes that straightforward.

Open up your Python editor and create a new file. Save your file with the name `using_databar.py`. Then add the following code:

```python
# using_databar.py

from openpyxl import load_workbook
from openpyxl.formatting.rule import DataBar, FormatObject, Rule


def applying_databar(path, output_path):
    workbook = load_workbook(filename=path)
    sheet = workbook.active

    first = FormatObject(type='num', val=1)
    last = FormatObject(type="num", val=5)
    green = "00AA00"
    data_bar = DataBar(cfvo=[first, last], color=green,
                       showValue=None, minLength=None, maxLength=None)

    rule = Rule(type='dataBar', dataBar=data_bar)
    sheet.conditional_formatting.add("B1:B100", rule)
    workbook.save(output_path)


if __name__ == "__main__":
    applying_databar("ratings.xlsx",
                     output_path="databar.xlsx")
```

In this example, you create two format objects and set their `type` to "num" and their `val` to the bounds you want your progress bar to use. For this case, your bounds are 1-5. Then you create a `DataBar` and pass in the format objects as a Python list to the `cfvo` parameter. Next, you set the color to green.

Finally, you add the `DataBar` object to your `Rule`. You need to set the rule's `type` to "dataBar" to make the rule work correctly.

When you run this code, your spreadsheet will look like this:

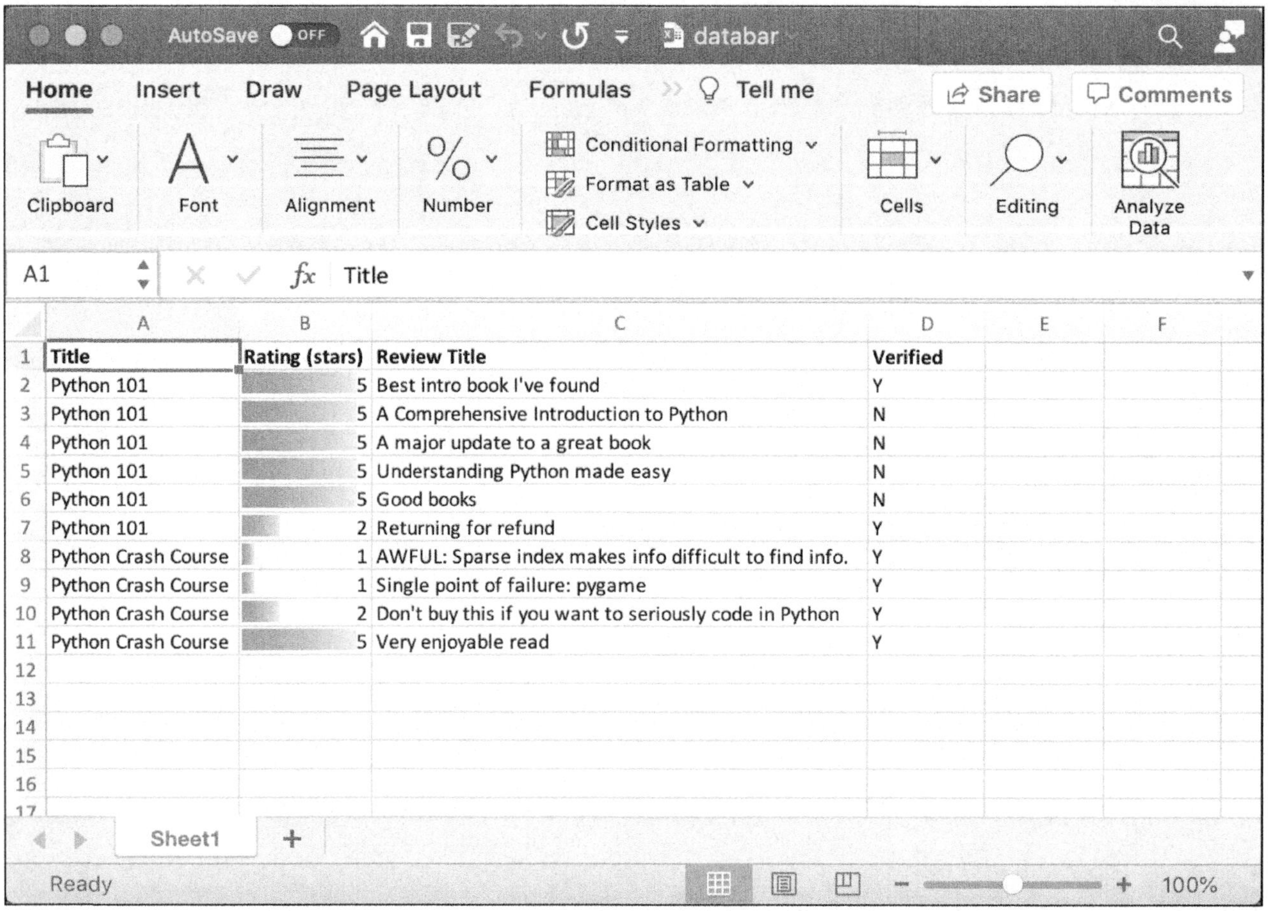

Fig. 5-6: Using a DataBar

The screenshot shows how you can create a column of progress bars quickly, with only a few lines of code. However, OpenPyXL makes it even easier by providing yet another convenience function: `DataBarRule`.

To see that class in action, create a new file named `using_databarrule.py`. Then add this code to your new file:

```
# using_databarrule.py

from openpyxl import load_workbook
from openpyxl.formatting.rule import DataBarRule


def applying_databar_rule(path, output_path):
    workbook = load_workbook(filename=path)
    sheet = workbook.active

    red = "AA0000"
```

```
    data_bar_rule = DataBarRule(start_type="num",
                                start_value=1,
                                end_type="num",
                                end_value="5",
                                color=red)

    sheet.conditional_formatting.add("B1:B100", data_bar_rule)
    workbook.save(output_path)


if __name__ == "__main__":
    applying_databar_rule("ratings.xlsx",
                          output_path="databarrule.xlsx")
```

This code reduces the number of imports that you need and the number of objects you need to create. Here you make only the `DataBarRule`. You give it a start type and end type, both of which are "num". Then you set the start and end values, which are `1` (one) and `5` (five), respectively. Finally, you set the color to red to easily differentiate the output of this code from your regular `DataBar` output.

When you run this code, your new spreadsheet will have nice, red progress bars in it:

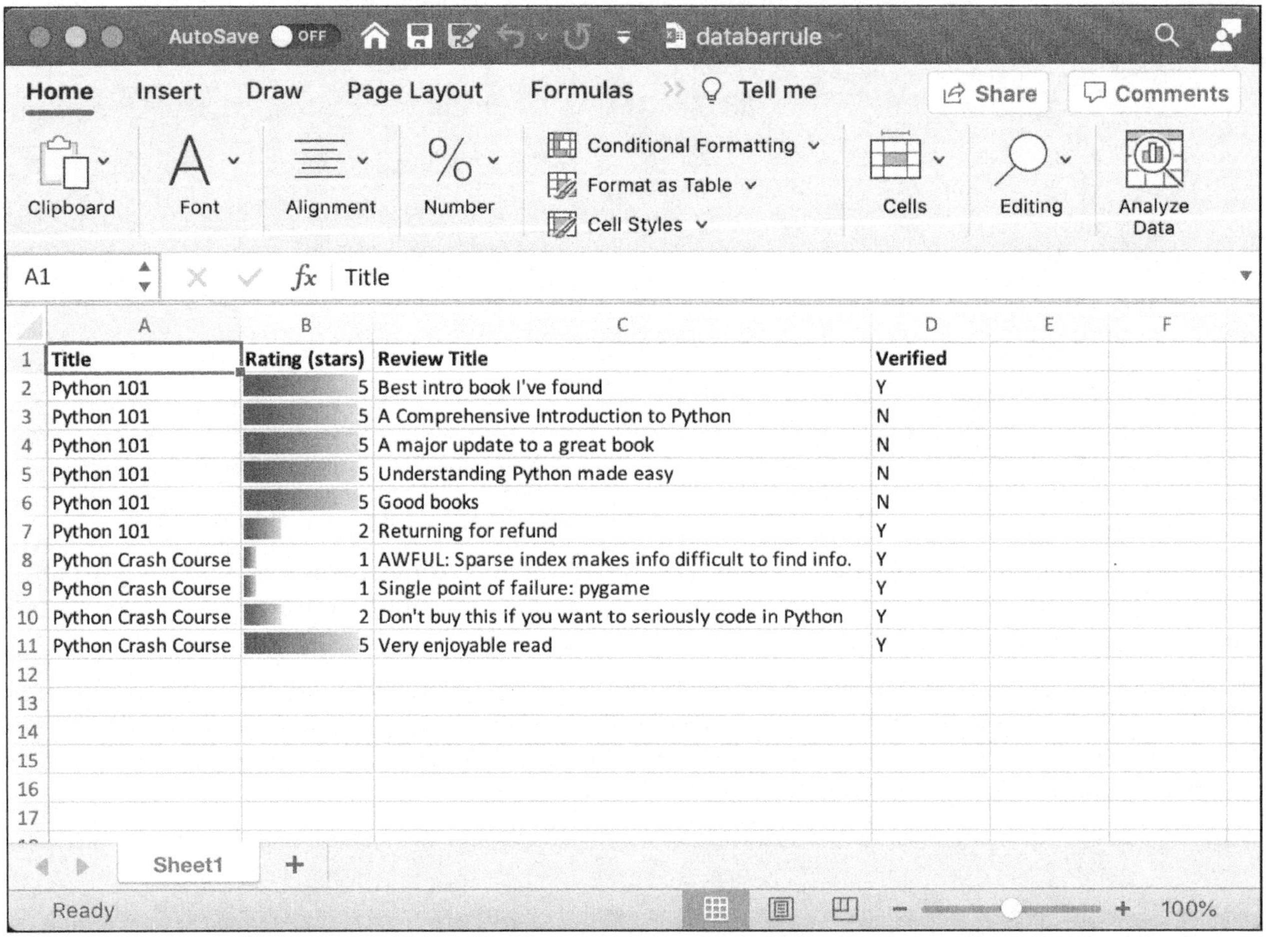

Fig. 5-7: Using a DataBarRule

Isn't that lovely? It would be great if you tried changing the color to one that you enjoy. Or you can add more data and then tweak the data bounds some more.

Now it's time to turn your attention to this chapter's final section: `DifferentialStyles`!

Using `DifferentialStyles`

A `DifferentialStyle` is a type of `NamedStyle`, which you learned about in **chapter 4**. You use a `DifferentialStyle` for packaging up multiple styles, like fonts, border, alignments, etc. When you combine a `DifferentialStyle` with a `Rule`, you can do some custom conditional formatting!

For this example, you will use a `DifferentialStyle` to change the background color of an entire row. Create a new file and name it `using_rules.py`, then add the following code:

```python
# using_rules.py

from openpyxl import load_workbook
from openpyxl.formatting.rule import Rule
from openpyxl.styles import PatternFill
from openpyxl.styles.differential import DifferentialStyle


def applying_rules(path, rule_formula, output_path):
    workbook = load_workbook(filename=path)
    sheet = workbook.active

    yellow = PatternFill(bgColor="00FFFF00")
    diff_style = DifferentialStyle(fill=yellow)
    rule = Rule(type="expression", dxf=diff_style)
    rule.formula = [rule_formula]

    sheet.conditional_formatting.add("A1:F100", rule)
    workbook.save(output_path)


if __name__ == "__main__":
    applying_rules("ratings.xlsx", rule_formula="$B1<3",
                   output_path="rules.xlsx")
```

This code creates a `PatternFill` object, which you use to create your background color. Then you instantiate your `DifferentialStyle` object and pass in the background color that you created.

Now you can create a `Rule`. For this to work, you set the rule's `type` to an "expression". To apply the style, you pass it to the `dxf` parameter. You also pass in a rule formula: the value must be less than 3 for the background color to change to yellow.

When you run this code, your spreadsheet will look like this:

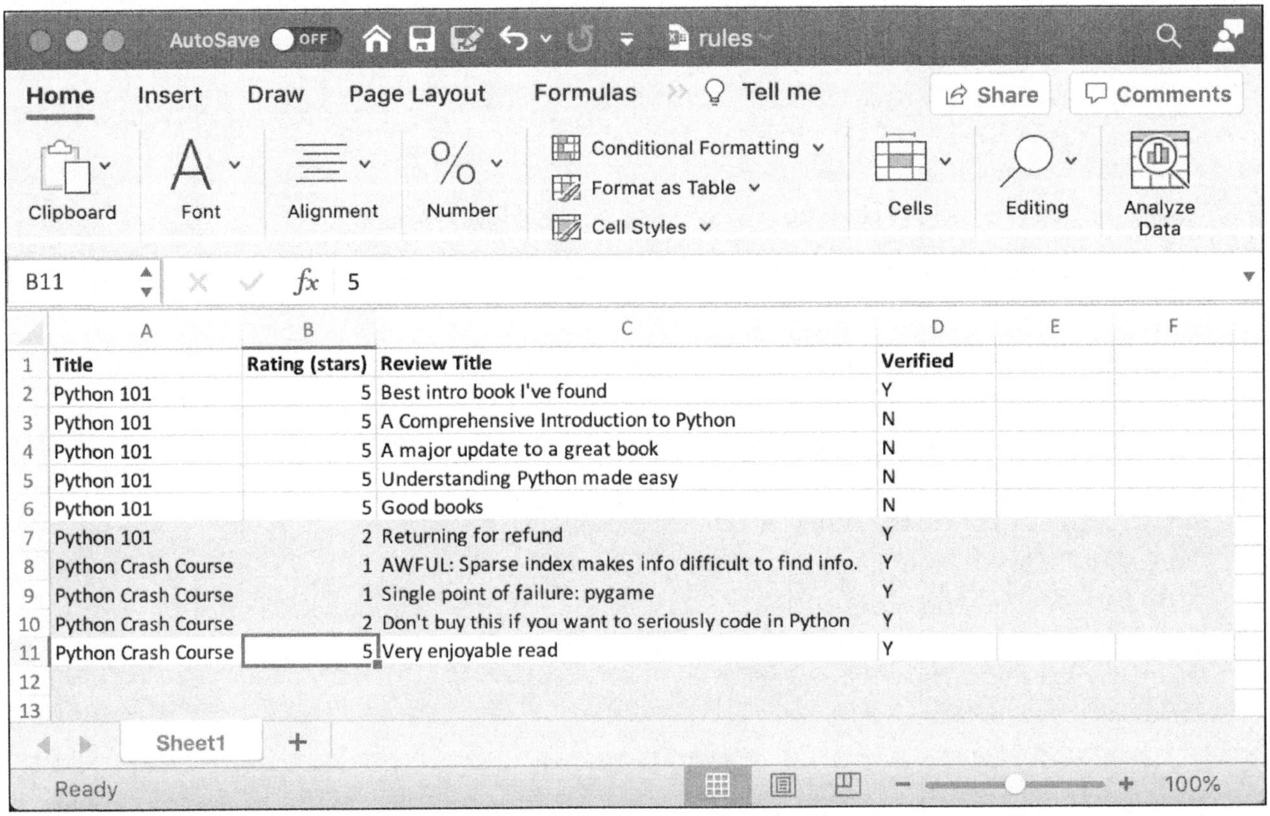

Fig. 5-8: Book Ratings with OpenPyXL DifferentialStyle Rules Applied

This looks pretty good, but you may have noticed that the empty rows are also yellow. This seems to occur because there are no values set, so Microsoft Excel interprets them as less than 3.

Wrapping Up

Conditional formatting gives you the ability to use formulas and boundaries to format your spreadsheets dynamically. After applying conditional formatting, you can change your data and see how the formatting will change automatically.

In this chapter, you learned about the following:

- Builtin formats
- Working with `ColorScales`
- Adding `IconSets`
- Creating a `DataBar`
- Using `DifferentialStyles`

You can take the code examples in this code and use these concepts together to do complex formatting of your spreadsheets. You need to spend some time experimenting with different rules and formatting objects, but once you understand the fundamentals, you will be creating unique spreadsheets quickly and confidently!

Chapter 6 - Creating Charts

OpenPyXL supports many different kinds of charts. These charts are an excellent way to convey information to the user and help them understand the data in the spreadsheet. The most common charts include the bar chart, pie chart, and line chart.

The focus of this chapter is to get you familiar with how to create a chart and edit its many different parts. When you create a chart, you will need to define the type of chart you want to use, such as `BarChart` or `LineChart`. You will also need to provide the data that the chart uses, which is called a `Reference`.

In this chapter, you will learn how to:

- Add Titles to a chart
- Change axis orientation
- Modify chart layout
- Change the chart size
- Use Styles
- Create Chartsheets

Let's get started by creating your first chart!

Making Your First Chart

OpenPyXL supports many different types of charts. You will be focusing primarily on the `BarChart` in this chapter and learn about other chart types in the following chapter.

The charts don't have any required arguments to pass to them. You can initialize them by doing the following:

```
from openpyxl.chart import BarChart

bar_chart = BarChart()
```

Once you have a chart instance, you can add it to your worksheet. To learn how to do that, create a new Python file and name it `first_chart.py`.

Then enter the following code:

```
# first_chart.py

from openpyxl import Workbook
from openpyxl.chart import BarChart, Reference


def main(filename):
    workbook = Workbook()
    sheet = workbook.active

    # Add data to spreadsheet
    data_rows = [
        ["Book", "Kindle", "Paperback"],
        [1, 9.99, 15.99],
        [2, 9.99, 25.99],
        [3, 9.99, 25.99],
        [4, 4.99, 29.99],
        [5, 14.99, 39.99],
    ]

    for row in data_rows:
        sheet.append(row)

    # Create the bar chart
    bar_chart = BarChart()

    data = Reference(worksheet=sheet,
                     min_row=1,
                     max_row=10,
                     min_col=2,
                     max_col=3)
    bar_chart.add_data(data, titles_from_data=True)
    sheet.add_chart(bar_chart, "E2")

    workbook.save(filename)


if __name__ == "__main__":
    main("bar_chart.xlsx")
```

Here you create a `Worksheet` the same way that you have in the past. Then you make some data and add it to the worksheet using `append()`. Next, you create the `BarChart` and a `Reference` object. The `Reference` class tells OpenPyXL what data to use to create the chart.

In this case, you tell it to use rows one through ten and columns two through three. That allows you to skip the first column, which is the book number. You then add the `Reference` to the chart by passing it to the chart's `add_data()` method. You set `titles_from_data` to `True`, which tells the chart to use the column labels for the chart's legend.

If you do not set `titles_from_data` to `True`, then the legend will say "Series 1", "Series 2", etcetera.

Finally, you attach the chart to the worksheet using `add_chart()`, which takes the chart object and a cell name. The cell name is the position where the chart will appear in the worksheet.

When you run this code, your spreadsheet will look like this:

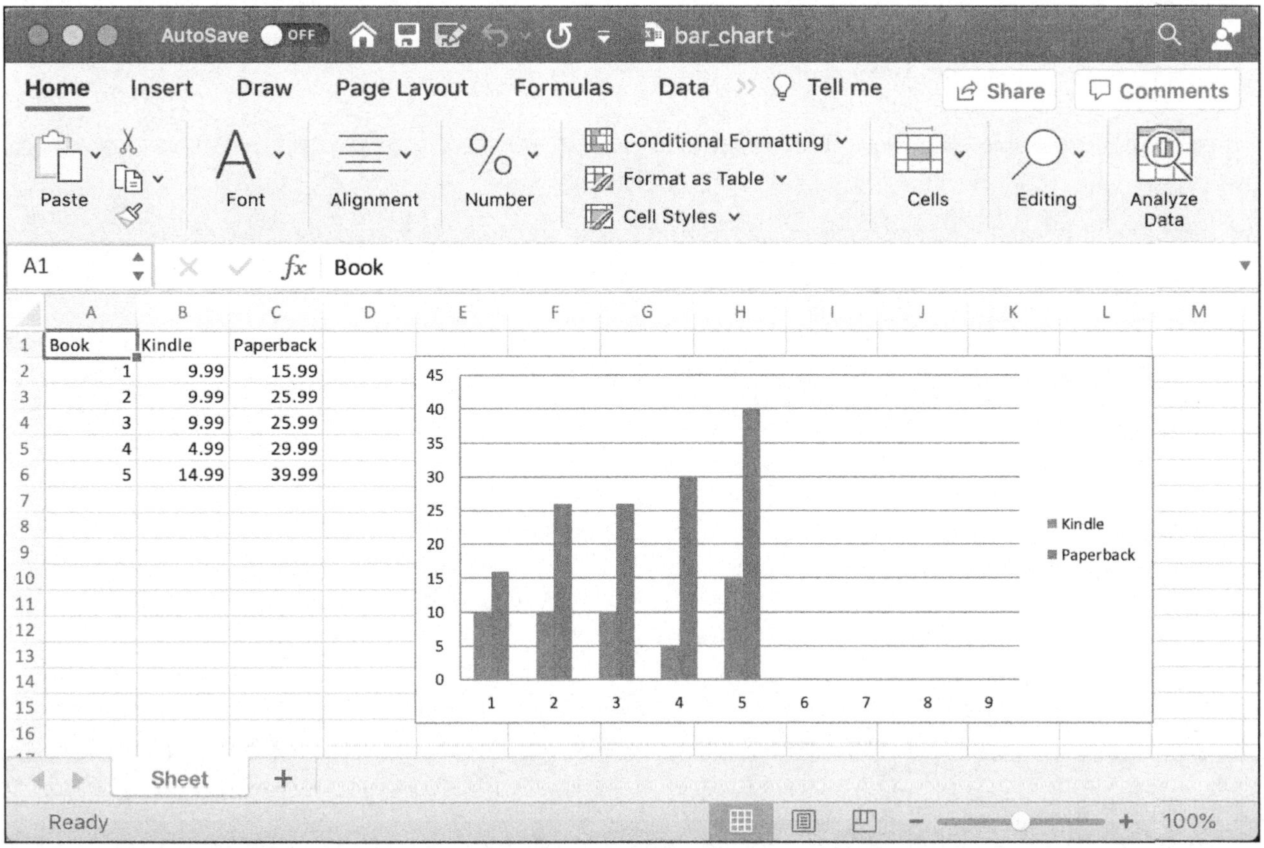

Fig. 6-1: Creating a BarChart

Isn't that a nice-looking little chart? But wait! It's missing something. It needs a chart title, and some axis titles would be good to have too.

You will learn how to add all of those items in the next section!

Adding Titles to the Chart

Charts can be confusing if they aren't clearly labeled. Fortunately, OpenPyXL gives you the ability to add a descriptive title to your chart. You will also learn how to add titles to the x and y axes.

To see how this works, create a new file and name it `first_chart_titles.py`. Once you create your file, you will need to add this code to it:

```
# first_chart_titles.py

from openpyxl import Workbook
from openpyxl.chart import BarChart, Reference


def main(filename):
    workbook = Workbook()
    sheet = workbook.active

    # Add data to spreadsheet
    data_rows = [
        ["Book", "Kindle", "Paperback"],
        ["Python 101", 9.99, 15.99],
        ["Python 201", 9.99, 25.99],
        ["ReportLab", 9.99, 25.99],
        ["wxPython", 4.99, 29.99],
        ["Jupyter", 14.99, 39.99],
    ]

    for row in data_rows:
        sheet.append(row)

    # Create the bar chart
    bar_chart = BarChart()
    bar_chart.title = "Book Prices by Type"
    bar_chart.x_axis.title = "Book Types"
    bar_chart.y_axis.title = "Prices"

    data = Reference(worksheet=sheet,
                     min_row=1,
                     max_row=10,
                     min_col=2,
                     max_col=3)
    bar_chart.add_data(data, titles_from_data=True)
    sheet.add_chart(bar_chart, "E2")

    workbook.save(filename)
```

```
if __name__ == "__main__":
    main("bar_chart_titles.xlsx")
```

This code is a copy of the code from the last section. You need to focus on the following new lines of code:

```
bar_chart.title = "Book Prices by Type"
bar_chart.x_axis.title = "Book Types"
bar_chart.y_axis.title = "Prices"
```

The bar chart instance has many methods that you can use to modify the chart in different ways. In this case, you want to add a title to the chart. Since this data is about the prices of various book types, you give it a "Book Prices by Type" title.

Next, you want to add some labels or titles to each axis. The x-axis represents the various book types (i.e. eBook and paperback). To add a title to the x-axis, you need to set `x_axis.title` to a string.

Finally, you add a title to the y-axis. The y-axis in this chart represents the price of the book. So you set `y_axis.title` to "Prices".

Now that you understand what the new lines of code are doing, you should run this program.

When you do, you will see that your chart updates to look like this:

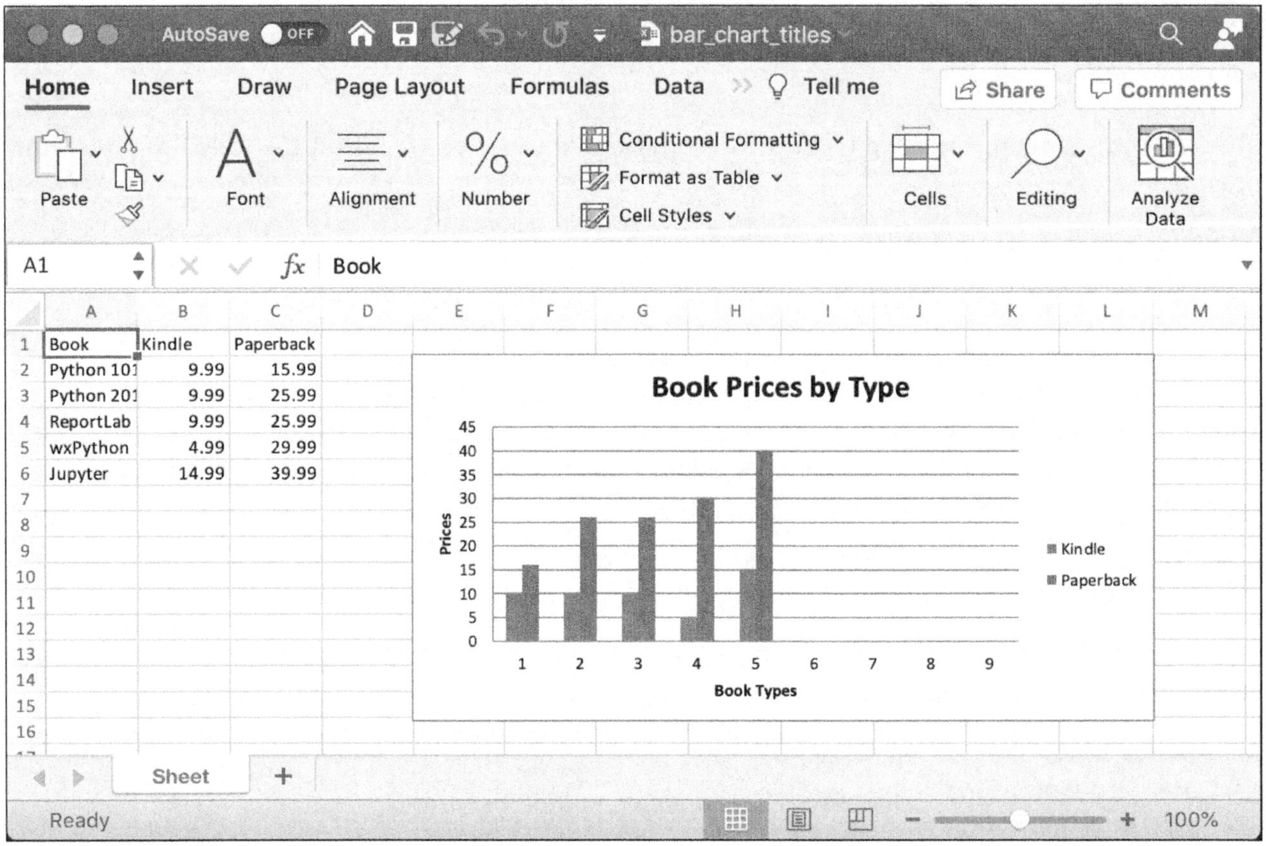

Fig. 6-2: Creating a BarChart with Titles

Your chart has some friendly, new titles. Try changing the titles to something different, or play around with the data to make your chart more unique!

Now you are ready to move on and learn about how to change your chart's axis orientation!

Changing Axis Orientation

OpenPyXL allows you to set the axis orientation for the chart. The default orientation is where the x-axis and the y-axis increases from minimum to maximum. You can change one or both axis settings to cause the chart to draw itself differently.

Open up your Python editor and create a new file. Save the file with the name `axis_orientations.py`.

Then enter the following code:

```python
# axis_orientations.py

from openpyxl import Workbook
from openpyxl.chart import BarChart, Reference
from openpyxl.chart.layout import Layout, ManualLayout


def create_chart(title, sheet, x_orientation=None, y_orientation=None):
    chart = BarChart()
    chart.title = title
    chart.x_axis.title = "Book Types"
    chart.y_axis.title = "Prices"

    data = Reference(worksheet=sheet,
                     min_row=1,
                     max_row=10,
                     min_col=2,
                     max_col=3)
    chart.add_data(data, titles_from_data=True)

    if x_orientation:
        chart.x_axis.scaling.orientation = x_orientation
    if y_orientation:
        chart.y_axis.scaling.orientation = y_orientation

    return chart


def main(filename):
    workbook = Workbook()
    sheet = workbook.active

    # Add data to spreadsheet
    data_rows = [
        ["Book", "Kindle", "Paperback"],
        [1, 9.99, 15.99],
        [2, 9.99, 25.99],
        [3, 9.99, 25.99],
        [4, 4.99, 29.99],
        [5, 14.99, 39.99],
    ]

    for row in data_rows:
```

```
        sheet.append(row)

    # Create the bar charts
    sheet.add_chart(create_chart("Defaults", sheet), "D1")
    sheet.add_chart(create_chart("Flip X", sheet,
                                 x_orientation="maxMin",
                                 y_orientation="minMax"), "J1")
    sheet.add_chart(create_chart("Flip Y", sheet,
                                 x_orientation="minMax",
                                 y_orientation="maxMin"), "D15")
    sheet.add_chart(create_chart("Flip Both", sheet,
                                 x_orientation="maxMin",
                                 y_orientation="maxMin"), "J15")

    workbook.save(filename)


if __name__ == "__main__":
    main("axis_orientations.xlsx")
```

Since this code is a bit longer than the previous examples were, you will go over each function individually.

The first half of the code contains your imports and the `create_chart()` function:

```
# axis_orientations.py

from openpyxl import Workbook
from openpyxl.chart import BarChart, Reference
from openpyxl.chart.layout import Layout, ManualLayout


def create_chart(title, sheet, x_orientation=None, y_orientation=None):
    chart = BarChart()
    chart.title = title
    chart.x_axis.title = "Book Types"
    chart.y_axis.title = "Prices"

    data = Reference(worksheet=sheet,
                     min_row=1,
                     max_row=10,
                     min_col=2,
                     max_col=3)
```

```
    chart.add_data(data, titles_from_data=True)

    if x_orientation:
        chart.x_axis.scaling.orientation = x_orientation
    if y_orientation:
        chart.y_axis.scaling.orientation = y_orientation

    return chart
```

You use `create_chart()` to create multiple charts that you then insert into the worksheet. The `create_chart()` function takes in the following arguments:

- title - The title of the chart
- sheet - The worksheet that contains the data for the chart
- x_orientation - What orientation the x-axis should be in
- y_orientation - What orientation the y-axis should be in

Most of the code in `create_chart()` will look familiar. The new change here is setting the `scaling.orientation` on the x and y axes. When you change the `scaling.orientation`, the chart draws itself differently.

At the end of the function, you return the `chart`.

Now you're ready to learn about the `main()` function:

```
def main(filename):
    workbook = Workbook()
    sheet = workbook.active

    # Add data to spreadsheet
    data_rows = [
        ["Book", "Kindle", "Paperback"],
        [1, 9.99, 15.99],
        [2, 9.99, 25.99],
        [3, 9.99, 25.99],
        [4, 4.99, 29.99],
        [5, 14.99, 39.99],
    ]

    for row in data_rows:
        sheet.append(row)

    # Create the bar charts
```

```
    sheet.add_chart(create_chart("Defaults", sheet), "D1")
    sheet.add_chart(create_chart("Flip X", sheet,
                                 x_orientation="maxMin",
                                 y_orientation="minMax"), "J1")
    sheet.add_chart(create_chart("Flip Y", sheet,
                                 x_orientation="minMax",
                                 y_orientation="maxMin"), "D15")
    sheet.add_chart(create_chart("Flip Both", sheet,
                                 x_orientation="maxMin",
                                 y_orientation="maxMin"), "J15")

    workbook.save(filename)


if __name__ == "__main__":
    main("axis_orientations.xlsx")
```

Here you create the actual `Workbook` and grab the active worksheet. Then you add the data that you will use for your charts. Finally, you make four charts with different scaling orientations.

To set the x and y axis orientation, you need to set one or both of them to either "maxMin" or "minMax".

When you run the code, you will end up with four charts in your spreadsheet. Here are the charts:

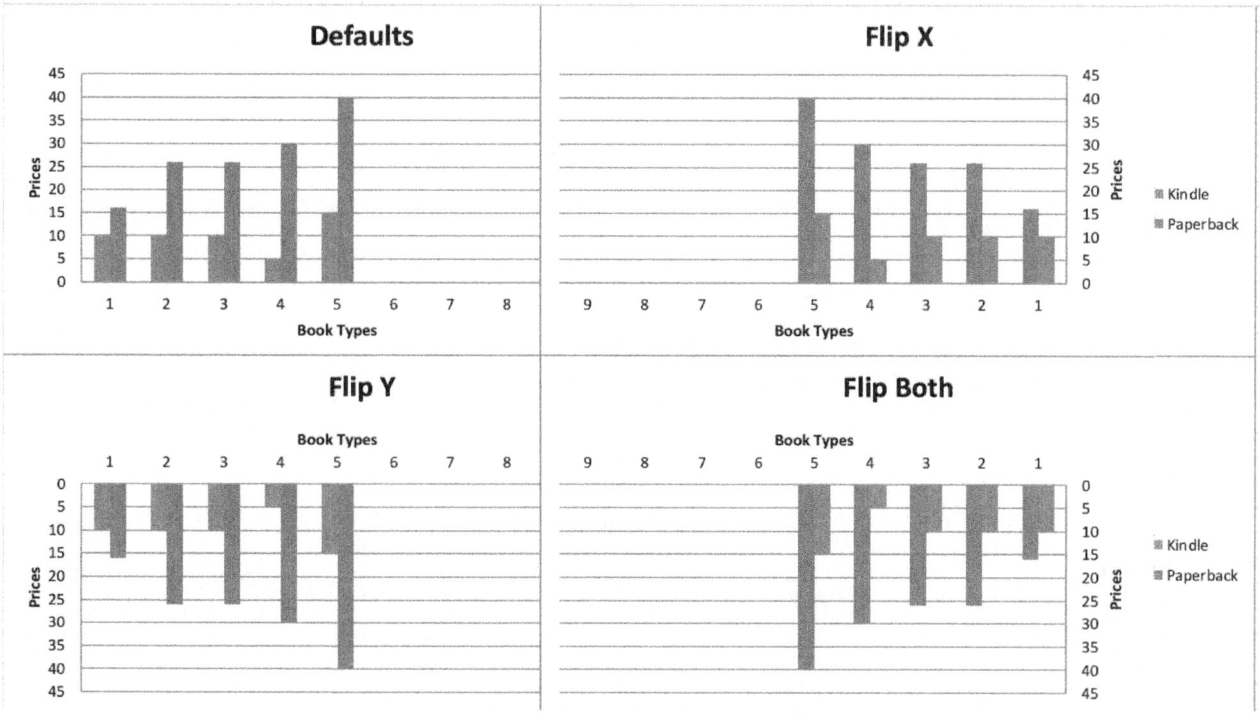

Fig. 6-3: Changing Axis Orientation

This screenshot demonstrates what happens when different combinations of "maxMin" and "minMax" for and x and y scaling orientation values. You should experiment with this code and try editing it in different ways to learn how this works on your own.

Now you are ready to learn about modifying a chart's layout!

Modifying Chart Layout

When you add a chart to a spreadsheet, that chart is within a drawing container object. You can control your chart's position and size within that container. You do this by creating a `Layout` object.

The recommended way of modifying the position and size of a chart is to use a `ManualLayout` object. The arguments that control the position and size of the chart are as follows:

- `x` - The horizontal position from the left
- `y` - The vertical position from the top
- `h` - The height of the chart relative to its container
- `w` - The width of the box

You can also use the `ManualLayout` to control the position and size of the chart's legend. You control the position of the chart's legend by setting its position to one of the following:

- `r` - right (default)

- `l` - left
- `t` - top
- `b` - bottom
- `tr` - top right

Now that you have a basic understanding of how to position the chart and the legend, you can write some code. Create a new file and name it `manual_chart_layout.py`. Then add the following code to your file:

```
# manual_chart_layout.py

from openpyxl import Workbook
from openpyxl.chart import BarChart, Reference
from openpyxl.chart.layout import Layout, ManualLayout


def main(filename):
    workbook = Workbook()
    sheet = workbook.active

    # Add data to spreadsheet
    data_rows = [
        ["Book", "Kindle", "Paperback"],
        [1, 9.99, 15.99],
        [2, 9.99, 25.99],
        [3, 9.99, 25.99],
        [4, 4.99, 29.99],
        [5, 14.99, 39.99],
    ]

    for row in data_rows:
        sheet.append(row)

    # Create the bar chart
    chart = BarChart()
    chart.title = "Manual chart layout"
    chart.legend.position = "tr"
    chart.layout = Layout(
        manualLayout=ManualLayout(
            x=0.25, y=0.25,
            h=0.5, w=0.5,
        )
    )
```

```
    data = Reference(worksheet=sheet,
                     min_row=1,
                     max_row=10,
                     min_col=2,
                     max_col=3)
    chart.add_data(data, titles_from_data=True)
    sheet.add_chart(chart, "E2")

    workbook.save(filename)


if __name__ == "__main__":
    main("manual_chart_layout.xlsx")
```

In this example, you want to focus on the section of code that comes right after you create your `BarChart`.

Here is the specific lines of code you should study:

```
# Create the bar chart
chart = BarChart()
chart.title = "Manual chart layout"
chart.legend.position = "tr"
chart.layout = Layout(
    manualLayout=ManualLayout(
        x=0.25, y=0.25,
        h=0.5, w=0.5,
    )
)
```

Here you set the `legend.position` to "tr" or top-right. Then you the set chart's `layout` attribute to a `Layout()` class, which contains a `ManualLayout` instance inside of it.

When you run this code, your spreadsheet will look like this:

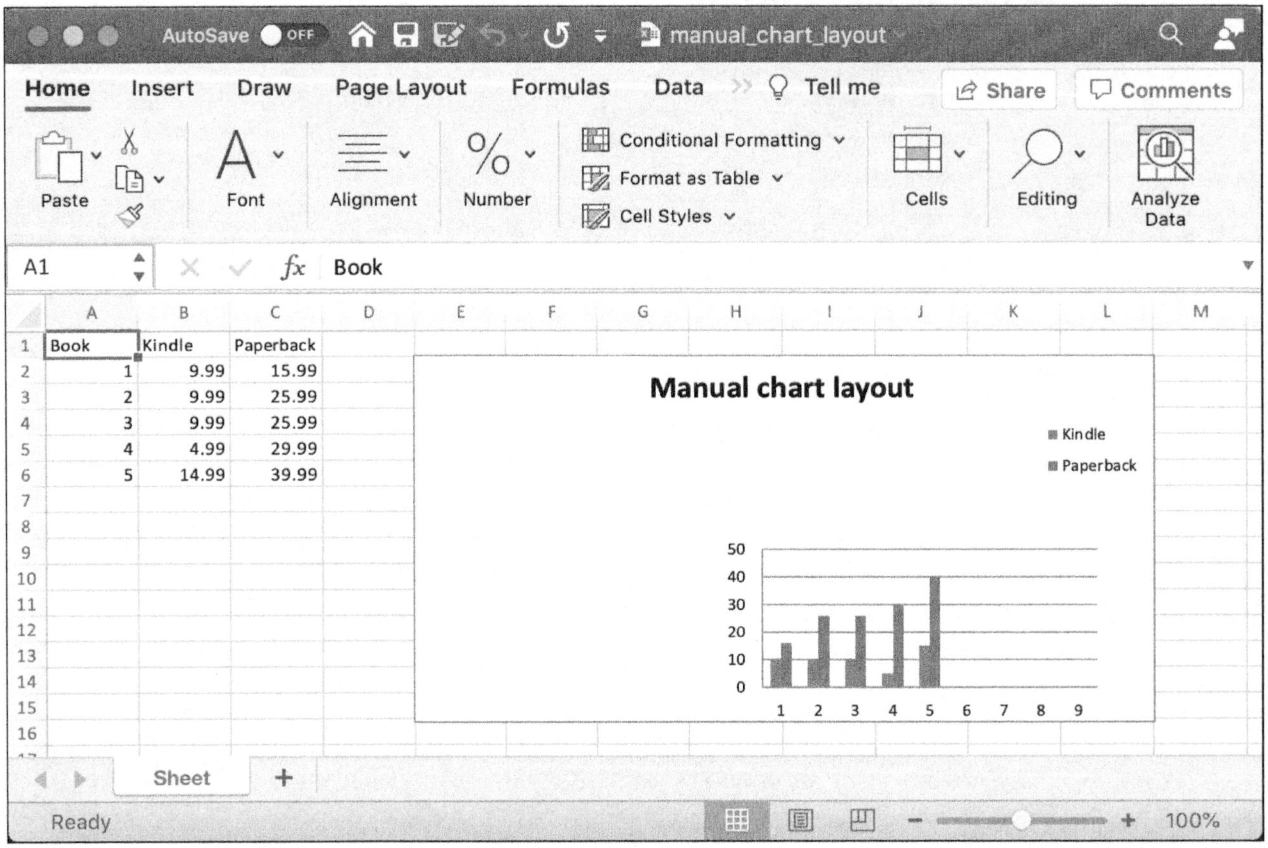

Fig. 6-4: Manual Chart Layout

You can see that the legend is no longer to the right of the chart like it has been in all the previous examples. Instead, the legend is in the top-right corner with the chart kind of underneath the legend!

If you have the time, you should play around with `ManualLayout` to see what you can do with it. You can change the way your chart looks with only some minor changes to its layout.

Now you are ready to learn about changing the size of your chart!

Changing the Chart Size

You learned that you could adjust the size and position of the chart within the drawing container. But what if you want to change the size of the drawing container itself? If you do that, the entire chart will be larger or smaller!

To change the container's size, you need to adjust the `height` and `width` of the chart object.

Create a new file and name it `chart_size.py`. Then enter the following code:

```python
# chart_size.py

from openpyxl import Workbook
from openpyxl.chart import BarChart, Reference


def main(filename):
    workbook = Workbook()
    sheet = workbook.active

    # Add data to spreadsheet
    data_rows = [
        ["Book", "Kindle", "Paperback"],
        [1, 9.99, 15.99],
        [2, 9.99, 25.99],
        [3, 9.99, 25.99],
        [4, 4.99, 29.99],
        [5, 14.99, 39.99],
    ]

    for row in data_rows:
        sheet.append(row)

    # Create the bar chart
    bar_chart = BarChart()
    bar_chart.height = 20
    bar_chart.width = 30

    data = Reference(worksheet=sheet,
                     min_row=1,
                     max_row=10,
                     min_col=2,
                     max_col=3)
    bar_chart.add_data(data, titles_from_data=True)
    sheet.add_chart(bar_chart, "E2")

    workbook.save(filename)


if __name__ == "__main__":
    main("bar_chart_size.xlsx")
```

Here you set the `height` of the chart to **20** and the `width` to **30**. That doesn't sound like much, but when you run this code, you can see that the chart is quite a bit larger:

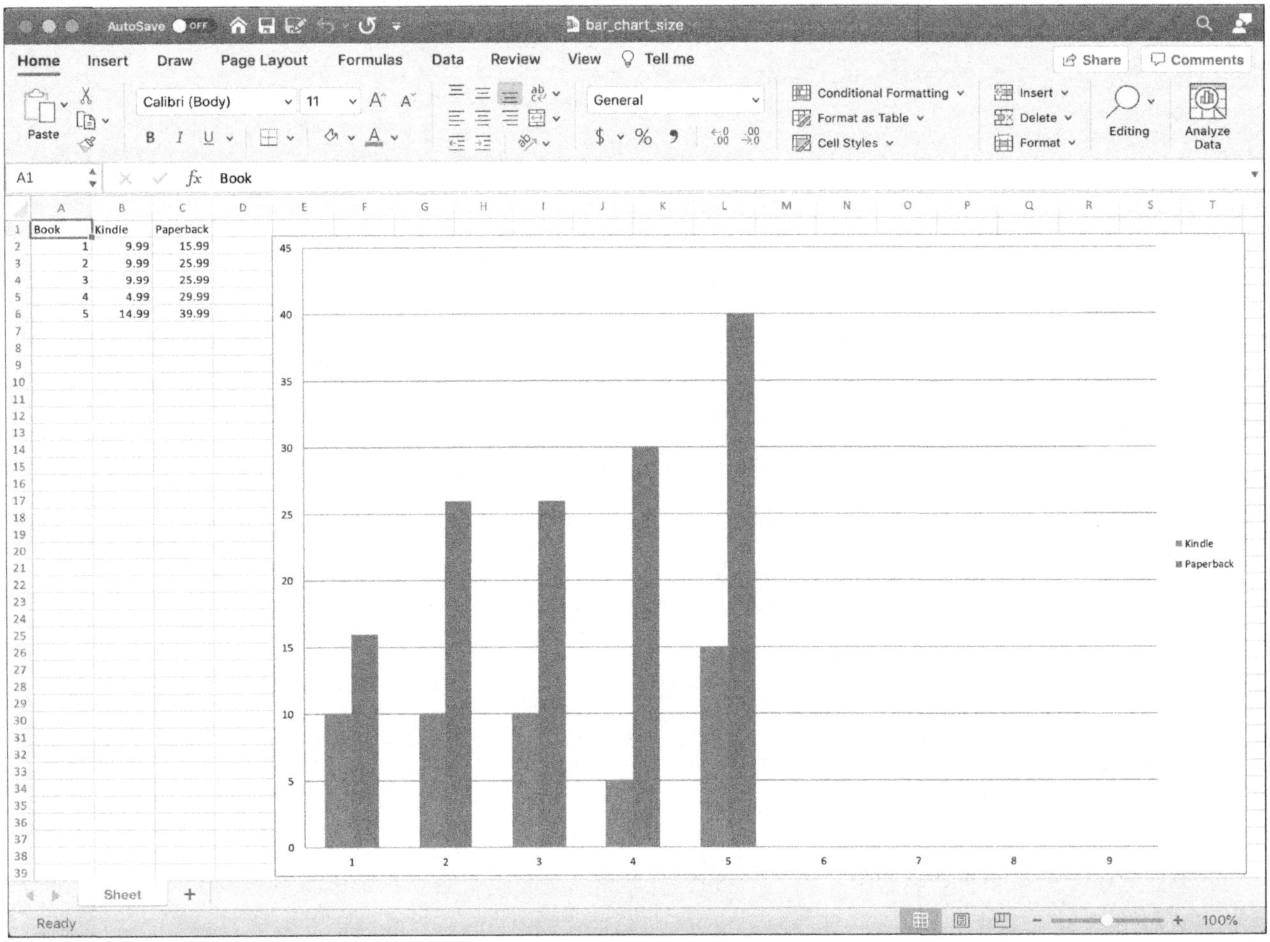

Fig. 6-5: Changing the Chart Size

You now have a couple of different tools that you can use to adjust the size of your charts. Give them a try and see what works best for you!

The next topic to learn about is how to change the style of your chart.

Using Styles

The chart object has forty-eight different styles. The style is a color scheme for your chart. To apply a style, you set the `style` attribute of the chart object to an integer from 1 to 48.

You can see how this works by creating a new Python script. After making your new file, name it `chart_styles.py` and enter the following code:

```python
# chart_styles.py

from openpyxl import Workbook
from openpyxl.chart import BarChart, Reference


def main(filename, style=None):
    workbook = Workbook()
    sheet = workbook.active

    # Add data to spreadsheet
    data_rows = [
        ["Book", "Kindle", "Paperback"],
        [1, 9.99, 15.99],
        [2, 9.99, 25.99],
        [3, 9.99, 25.99],
        [4, 4.99, 29.99],
        [5, 14.99, 39.99],
    ]

    for row in data_rows:
        sheet.append(row)

    # Create the bar chart
    bar_chart = BarChart()

    data = Reference(worksheet=sheet,
                     min_row=1,
                     max_row=10,
                     min_col=2,
                     max_col=3)
    bar_chart.add_data(data, titles_from_data=True)
    sheet.add_chart(bar_chart, "E2")

    if style is not None:
        bar_chart.style = style

    workbook.save(filename)


if __name__ == "__main__":
    for style in range(1, 4):
        main(f"chart_style{style}.xlsx", style)
```

Here you use Python's `range()` function to create three spreadsheets using the styles 1 - 3. The first style applies a gray color scheme to your chart:

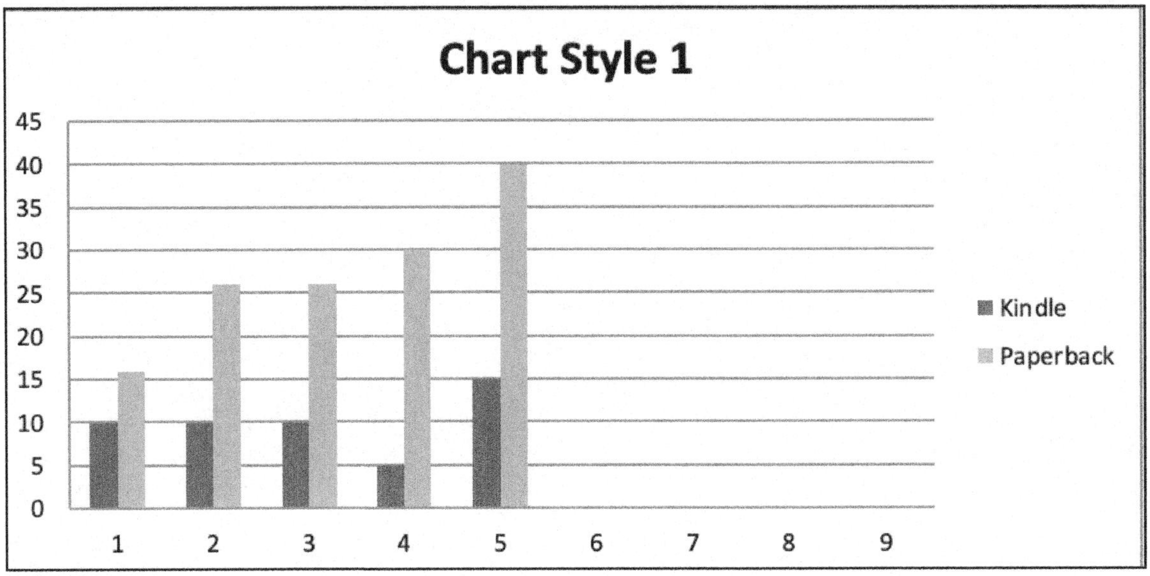

Fig. 6-6: Chart Style 1

When you use style two, your color scheme looks like the default color scheme:

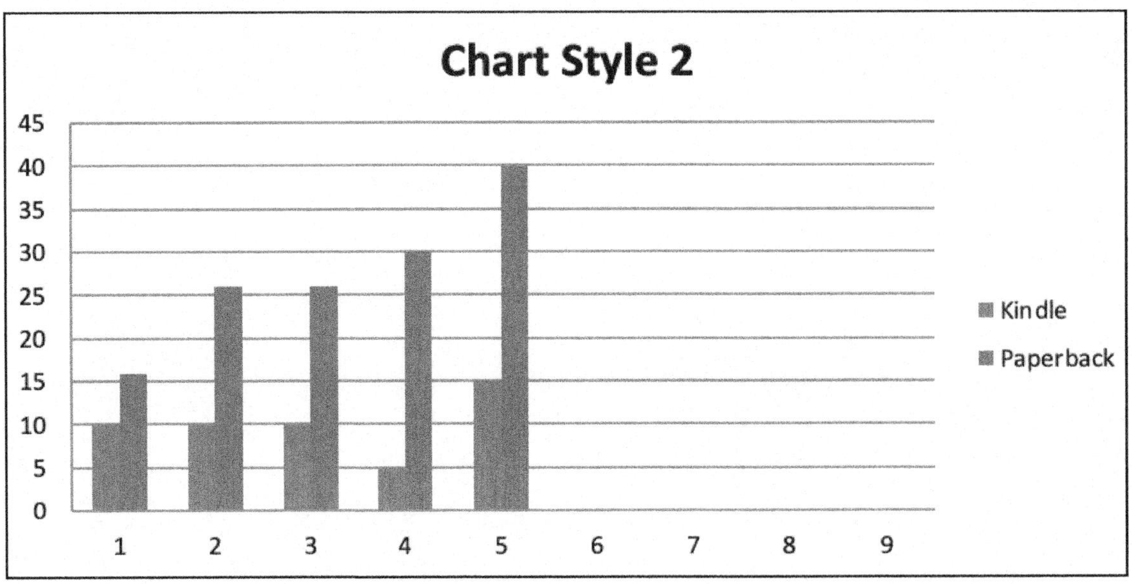

Fig. 6-7: Chart Style 2

The third color scheme uses shades of blue:

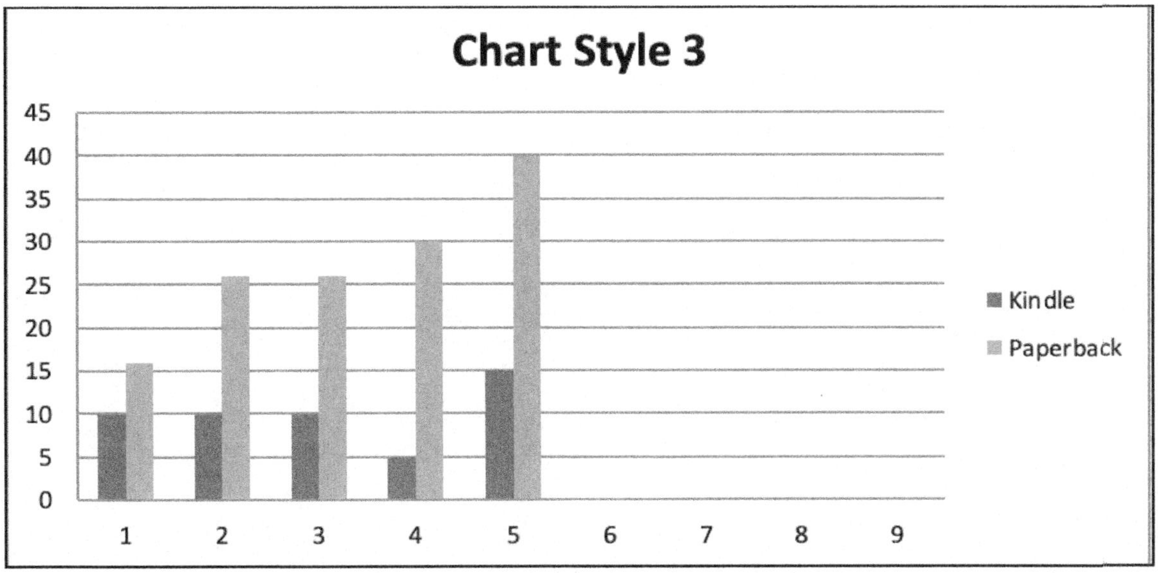

Fig. 6-8: Chart Style 3

You can update the code example above to create all forty-eight styles to see a sample of each of them. You should be able to find at least one color scheme that fits your needs.

The last subject that you will learn about are chartsheets!

Creating Chartsheets

A chartsheet is a special worksheet that only contains a chart. There is no data whatsoever on a chartsheet. OpenPyXL supports creating a chartsheet using the data from a different worksheet in your spreadsheet.

Note: Chartsheets may not work properly or at all in other spreadsheet programs, such as older versions of LibreOffice.

To make this example more interesting, you will be creating a `PieChart` and putting it into a chartsheet.

Create a new file and name it `chartsheet_demo.py`. Then enter the following code:

```
# chartsheet_demo.py

from openpyxl import Workbook
from openpyxl.chart import PieChart, Reference


def main(filename):
    wb = Workbook()
    ws = wb.active
    chart_sheet = wb.create_chartsheet()

    rows = [
        ["Python", 50],
        ["C++", 35],
        ["Java", 10],
        ["R", 5]
    ]

    for row in rows:
        ws.append(row)

    chart = PieChart()
    labels = Reference(ws, min_col=1, min_row=1, max_row=4)
    data = Reference(ws, min_col=2, min_row=1, max_row=5)
    chart.add_data(data, titles_from_data=True)
    chart.set_categories(labels)
    chart.title = "Programming Languages"

    chart_sheet.add_chart(chart)

    wb.save(filename)

if __name__ == "__main__":
    main("chartsheet.xlsx")
```

Here you import a `PieChart` instead of a `BarChart`. Then in your `main()` function, you call `create_-chartsheet()` to create the special chartsheet. The next few lines of code put some data into the first worksheet.

The next step is to create your `PieChart`:

```
chart = PieChart()
labels = Reference(ws, min_col=1, min_row=1, max_row=4)
data = Reference(ws, min_col=2, min_row=1, max_row=5)
chart.add_data(data, titles_from_data=True)
chart.set_categories(labels)
chart.title = "Programming Languages"

chart_sheet.add_chart(chart)
```

In the code above, you create two references. The first reference contains the legend's labels. The second reference is the data used to generate the chart. You use `set_categories()` to apply the labels to the legend, and you use `add_data()` to add the data to the chart.

When you run this code, you will create a Workbook that contains two worksheets. The first worksheet contains the data, and the second worksheet is the chartsheet.

Here is a screenshot of the chartsheet:

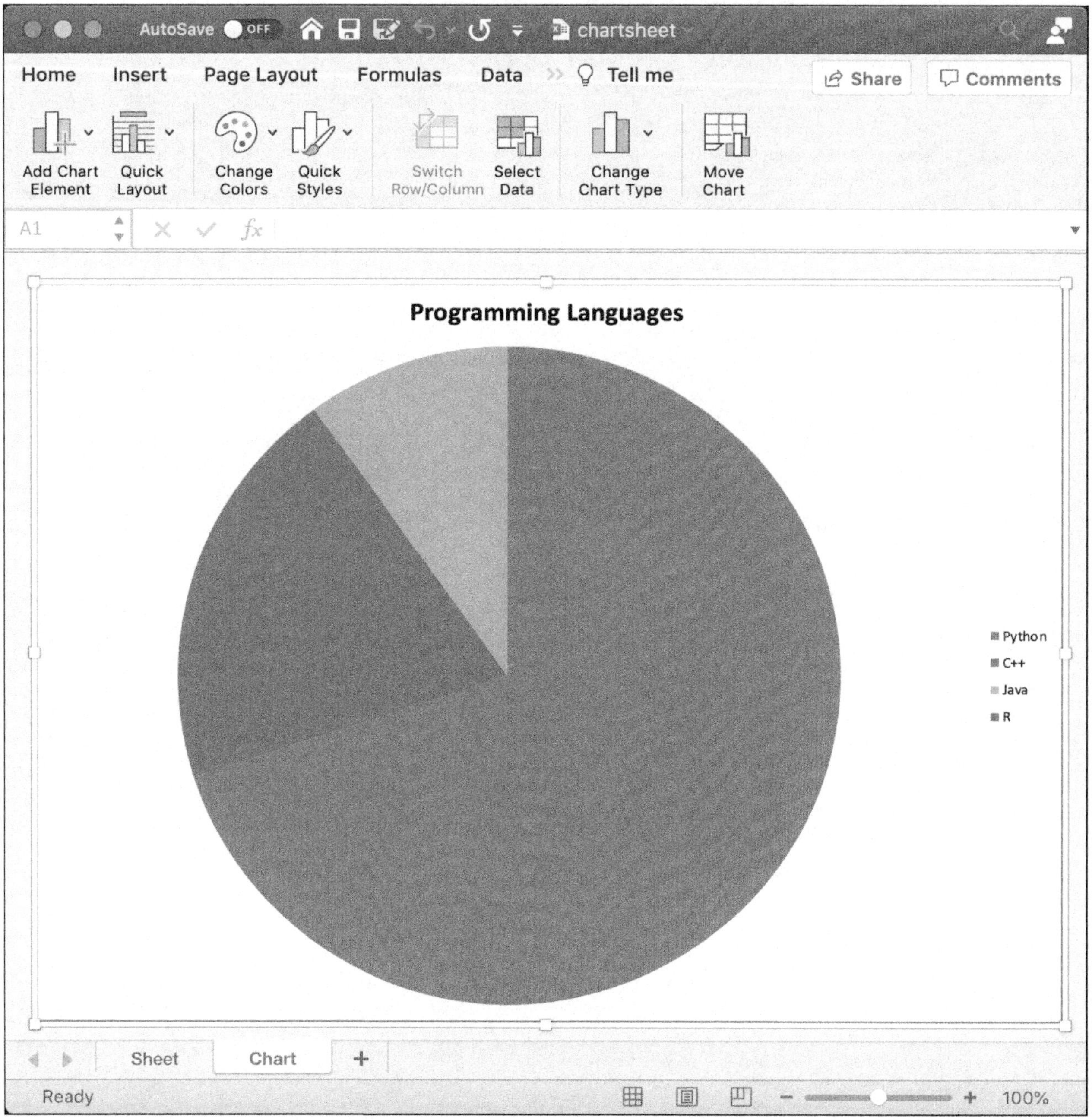

Fig. 6-9: A Chartsheet

Since the chartsheet only shows the chart, the chart is much bigger than if it was in a regular worksheet. Try editing this code to change it to a `BarChart` or another chart type. You can also modify some of the other settings to see how they affect the chart's appearance.

Wrapping Up

You can visualize your spreadsheet's data using charts. A chart can be easier to understand than raw numbers. Everyone is different, so it's good to be able to communicate the data in different ways.

In this chapter, you learned about the following topics:

- Adding Titles to the chart
- Changing axis orientation
- Modifying chart layout
- Changing the chart size
- Using Styles
- Creating Chartsheets

You can take any of the working examples in these chapters and modify them to help you cement what you have learned. You can take the tools you learned in this chapter and apply most of them to any of the supported chart types.

In the next chapter, you will learn about the many other chart types you can create in OpenPyXL.

Chapter 7 - Chart Types

There are many different kinds of charts that you can create using OpenPyXL. These different chart types give you many different ways to visualize and display your data to the user. You can help users better understand their data by putting it into a chart.

In this chapter, you will learn how to create the following chart types:

- Area Charts
- Bar Charts
- Bubble Charts
- Line Charts
- Scatter Charts
- Pie Charts
- Doughnut Charts
- Radar Charts
- Surface Charts

You won't learn every idiosyncrasy with every chart, but how to create most of the supported chart types. By doing so, you will learn to visualize your data in many different ways. Once you have learned about all the different types, you can experiment with them and see which ones work best for your audience.

WARNING: Some of the chart examples in this chapter do not work in non-Excel spreadsheets such as LibreOffice. Also, some examples may vary slightly in color or icon shape between Microsoft Excel versions or platforms (i.e. Mac vs Windows)

The first chart type you will learn about is the area chart!

Area Charts

OpenPyXL supports two different types of area charts. You can create a two-dimensional or a three-dimensional chart using OpenPyXL. The creation process of both charts is the same except that you use a different import.

An area chart is a special version of a line chart. Instead of simply connecting dots with a line, the chart will also fill in the region with a solid color underneath the line.

You will get started by learning how to create a two-dimensional area chart!

2D Area Charts

You can use an area chart to show the rise and fall of multiple data series effectively. They are also useful for demonstrating total amounts over a time period.

To see how you can create an area chart with OpenPyXL, create a new file and name it `area_chart.py`. Then enter the following code:

```
# area_chart.py

from openpyxl import Workbook
from openpyxl.chart import AreaChart, Reference


def create_excel_data(sheet):
    data_rows = [
        ["Book", "Kindle", "Paperback"],
        ["Python 101", 15, 5],
        ["Python 201", 5, 1],
        ["ReportLab", 10, 0],
        ["wxPython", 2, 2],
        ["Jupyter", 25, 15],
    ]

    for row in data_rows:
        sheet.append(row)


def create_chart(sheet):
    chart = AreaChart()
    chart.style = 23
    chart.title = "Book Prices by Type"
    chart.x_axis.title = "Book Types"
    chart.y_axis.title = "Prices"

    data = Reference(worksheet=sheet,
                     min_row=1,
                     max_row=10,
                     min_col=2,
                     max_col=3)
    chart.add_data(data, titles_from_data=True)
    sheet.add_chart(chart, "E2")
```

```
def main():
    workbook = Workbook()
    sheet = workbook.active
    create_excel_data(sheet)
    create_chart(sheet)
    workbook.save("area_chart_3d.xlsx")


if __name__ == "__main__":
    main()
```

This code should look familiar to you if you read the last chapter. The first function, `create_excel_data()`, creates a few rows of data using dummy book price information. Then you have `create_chart()`, where you instantiate `AreaChart()` and set the style and a couple of titles. You use `main()` to create the `Workbook` and call the other two functions.

When you run this code, your spreadsheet will look like this:

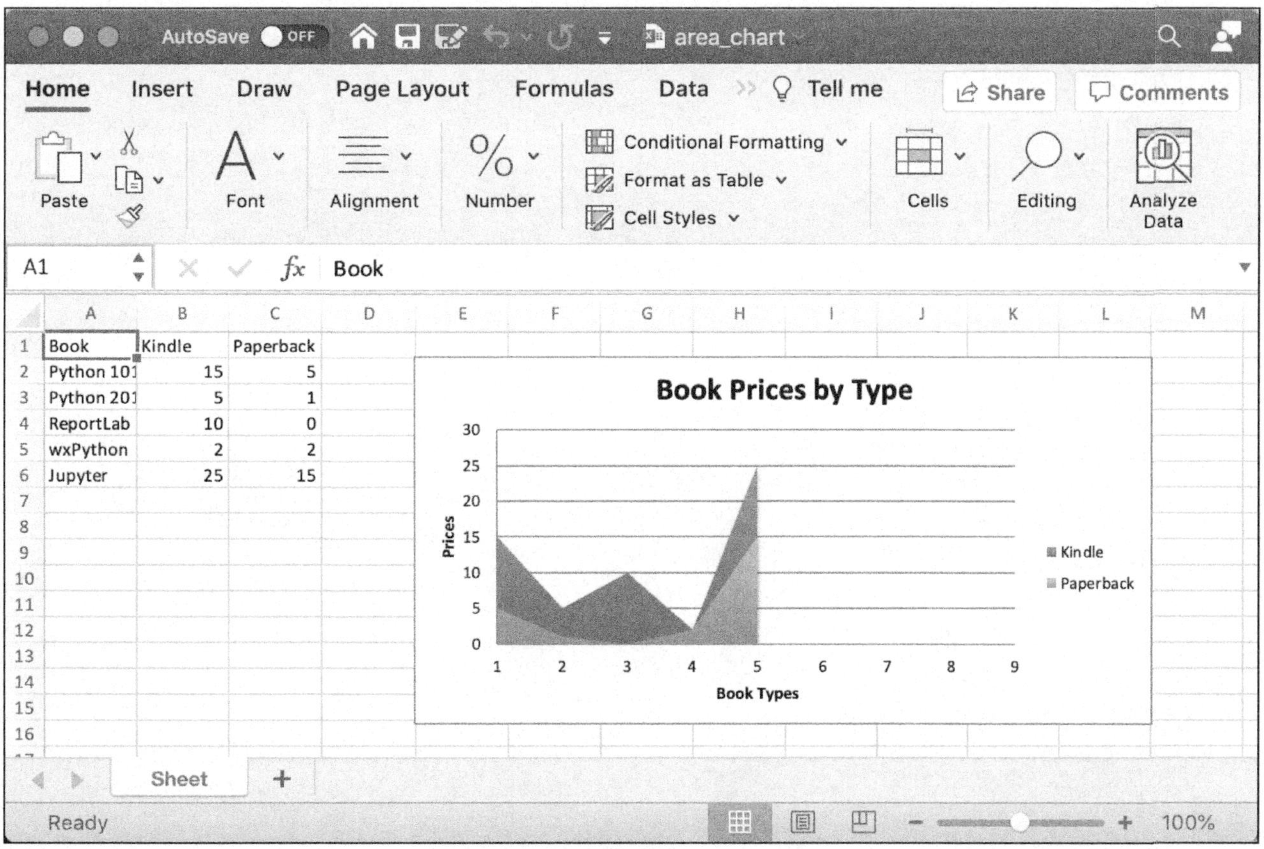

Fig. 7-1: Creating an Area Chart

Doesn't that look nice? You can experiment with different `style` values or change the `Reference` object to limit what data OpenPyXL uses to generate the chart.

Now you are ready to see what happens when you use a 3D area chart instead!

3D Area Charts

The 3D area chart conveys the same information as a 2D area chart. The difference is in the presentation. The chart appears to show the data in three dimensions instead of two. How well it accomplishes that feat is up for debate.

You can decide for yourself by creating a new file and naming it `area_chart_3d.py`. Then add this code to your new file:

```
# area_chart_3d.py

from openpyxl import Workbook
from openpyxl.chart import AreaChart3D, Reference

def main(filename):
    wb = Workbook()
    sheet = wb.active

    rows = [
        ["Book", "Kindle", "Paperback"],
        [2, 30, 40],
        [3, 25, 40],
        [4 ,30, 50],
        [5 ,10, 30],
        [6,  5, 25],
        [7 ,10, 50],
    ]

    for row in rows:
        sheet.append(row)

    chart = AreaChart3D()
    chart.title = "Area Chart 3D"
    chart.x_axis.title = "Books"
    chart.y_axis.title = "Copies Sold"
    chart.legend = None

    cats = Reference(sheet, min_col=1, min_row=1, max_row=7)
    data = Reference(sheet, min_col=2, min_row=1, max_col=3, max_row=7)
    chart.add_data(data, titles_from_data=True)
```

```
    chart.set_categories(cats)

    sheet.add_chart(chart, "E2")

    wb.save(filename)

if __name__ == "__main__":
    main("area_chart_3d.xlsx")
```

The main difference between this code and the code in the previous example is that you use `AreaChart3D` instead of `AreaChart`. The other change is that you set the chart title differently and you add some categories.

Go ahead and run the code. Your code will create the following spreadsheet:

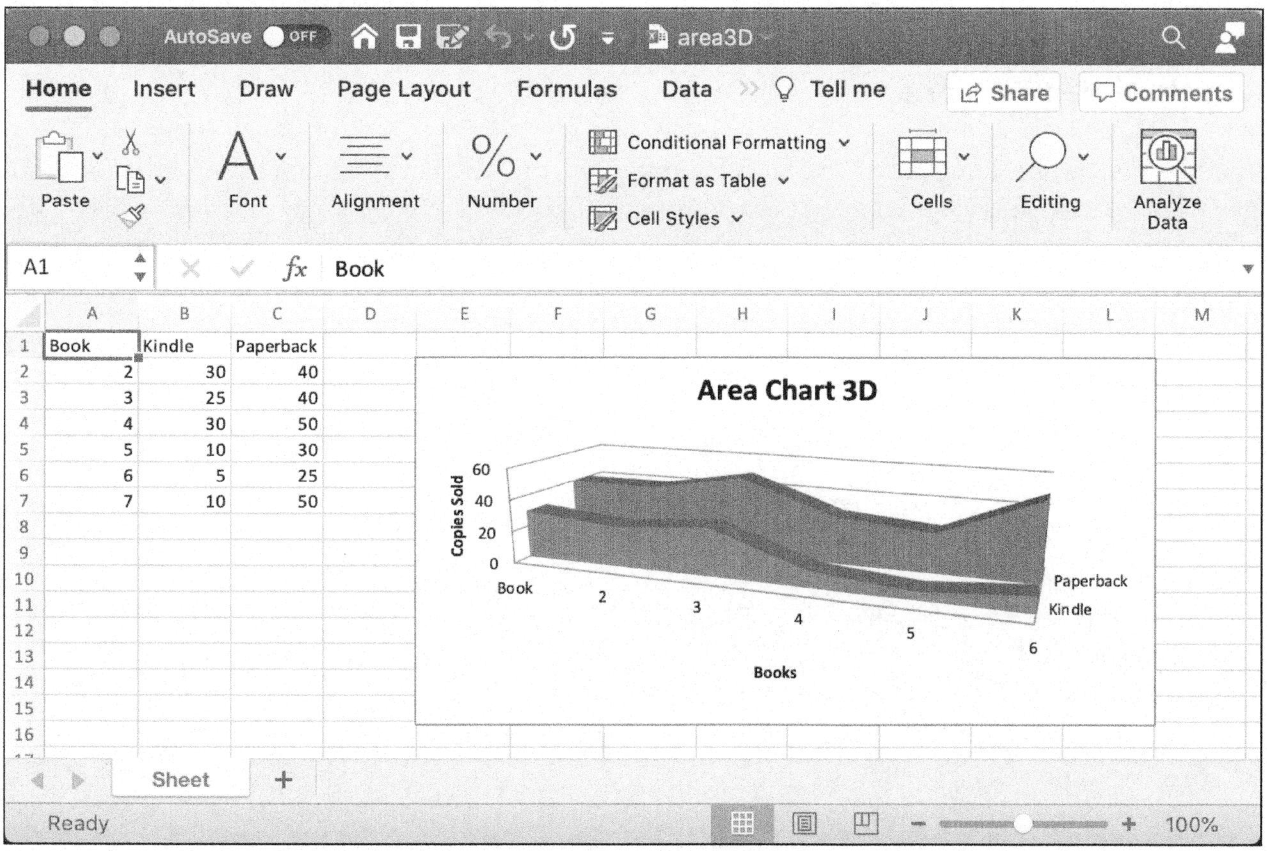

Fig. 7-2: Creating a 3D Area Chart

Now your data is shown in 3D! You can use this type of chart to add a little pizzazz to a presentation.

The next chart that you will learn about is the bar chart!

Bar Charts

Bar charts are one of the most common types of charts. A bar chart makes it easy to show the difference in sales figures or populations. You can visually compare these values and see their differences clearly in a bar chart.

OpenPyXL supports three different types of bar charts:

- Vertical
- Horizontal
- Stacked

The vertical version is probably the type of bar chart you will see most, and it is the one you will learn about first.

Vertical Bar Charts

The humble vertical bar chart is the most common type of bar chart. You have seen how to create one of these in the previous chapter. For completeness, you will create one in this section too.

Open up your Python editor and create a new file. You can name it `bar_chart.py`. Then enter the following code:

```
# bar_chart.py

from openpyxl import Workbook
from openpyxl.chart import BarChart, Reference


def create_excel_data(sheet):
    data_rows = [
        ('Number', 'Batch 1', 'Batch 2'),
        (2, 10, 30),
        (3, 40, 60),
        (4, 50, 70),
        (5, 20, 10),
        (6, 10, 40),
        (7, 50, 30),
    ]

    for row in data_rows:
        sheet.append(row)
```

```
def create_bar_chart(sheet):
    bar_chart = BarChart()

    data = Reference(worksheet=sheet,
                     min_row=1,
                     max_row=10,
                     min_col=2,
                     max_col=3)
    bar_chart.add_data(data, titles_from_data=True)
    sheet.add_chart(bar_chart, "E2")


def main():
    workbook = Workbook()
    sheet = workbook.active
    create_excel_data(sheet)
    create_bar_chart(sheet)
    workbook.save("bar_chart.xlsx")


if __name__ == "__main__":
    main()
```

In this example, you re-use the `main()` function from earlier in the chapter. The `create_excel_data()` is similar to the earlier ones, although the data is slightly different.

Then in `create_bar_chart()`, you create the `BarChart` using its defaults. When you run this code, your spreadsheet will look like this:

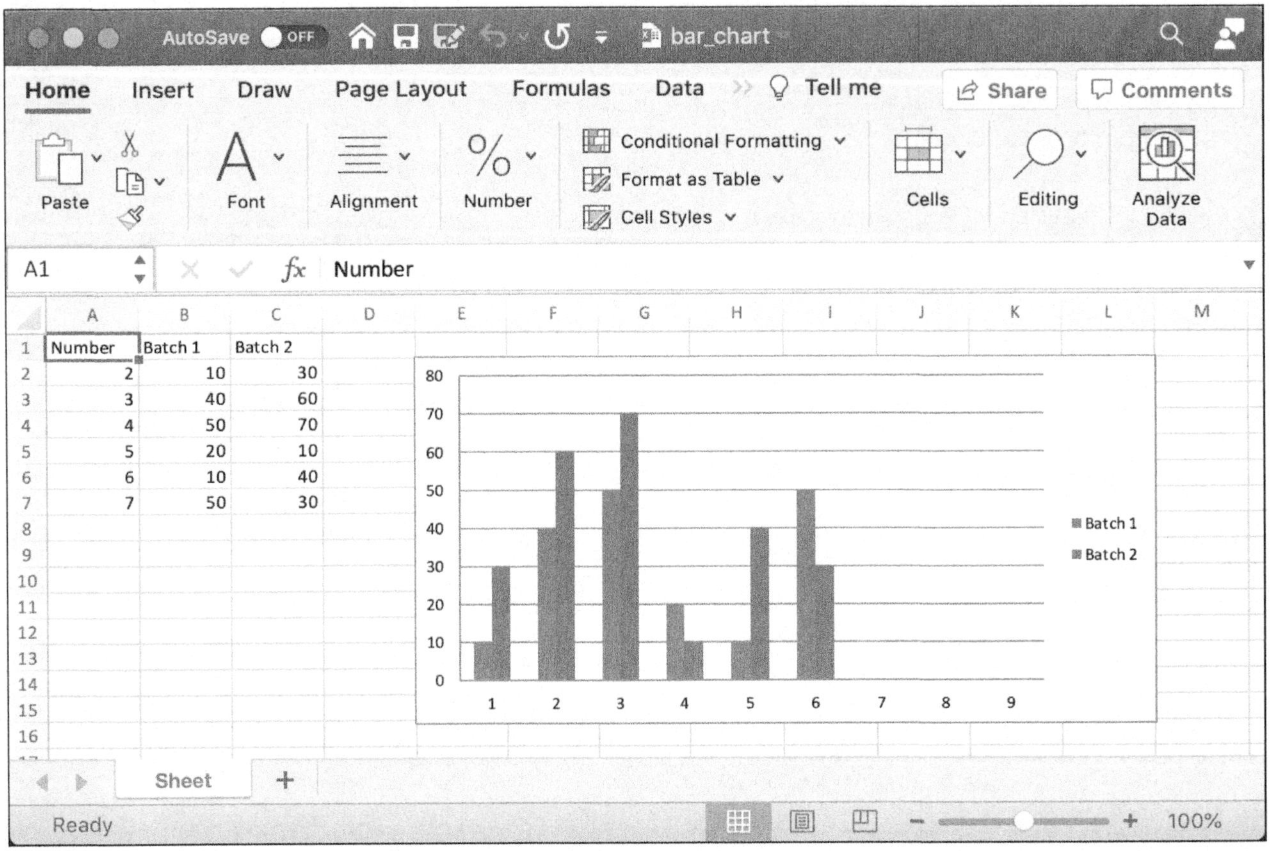

Fig. 7-3: Creating a Vertical Bar Chart

The screenshot above shows your standard vertically oriented bar chart. If you like, you can change its style by setting the `style` attribute to a different value, which you learned about in chapter 6.

Now you are ready to see how to transform this chart into a horizontally-oriented bar chart!

Horizontal Bar Charts

A horizontal bar chart is where the bars grow from left to right instead of from bottom to top. You will still use the `BarChart` class that you used in the previous example.

However, to get it to grow horizontally instead of vertically, you must set the bar chart's `type` attribute to "bar".

You can see how this works by creating a new file named `bar_chart_horizontal.py` and entering the following code:

```python
# bar_chart_horizontal.py

from openpyxl import Workbook
from openpyxl.chart import BarChart, Reference


def create_excel_data(sheet):
    data_rows = [
        ('Number', 'Batch 1', 'Batch 2'),
        (2, 10, 30),
        (3, 40, 60),
        (4, 50, 70),
        (5, 20, 10),
        (6, 10, 40),
        (7, 50, 30),
    ]

    for row in data_rows:
        sheet.append(row)


def create_bar_chart(sheet):
    bar_chart = BarChart()
    bar_chart.type = "bar"
    bar_chart.style = 31

    data = Reference(worksheet=sheet,
                     min_row=1,
                     max_row=10,
                     min_col=2,
                     max_col=3)
    bar_chart.add_data(data, titles_from_data=True)
    sheet.add_chart(bar_chart, "E2")


def main():
    workbook = Workbook()
    sheet = workbook.active
    create_excel_data(sheet)
    create_bar_chart(sheet)
    workbook.save("bar_chart_horizontal.xlsx")
```

```
if __name__ == "__main__":
    main()
```

This code looks almost exactly the same as the previous example. The part you want to focus on here is as follows:

```
def create_bar_chart(sheet):
    bar_chart = BarChart()
    bar_chart.type = "bar"
    bar_chart.style = 31
```

Here you set the `bar_chart.type` to "bar". When you run this code, you will see that the bar chart it creates is now horizontally oriented:

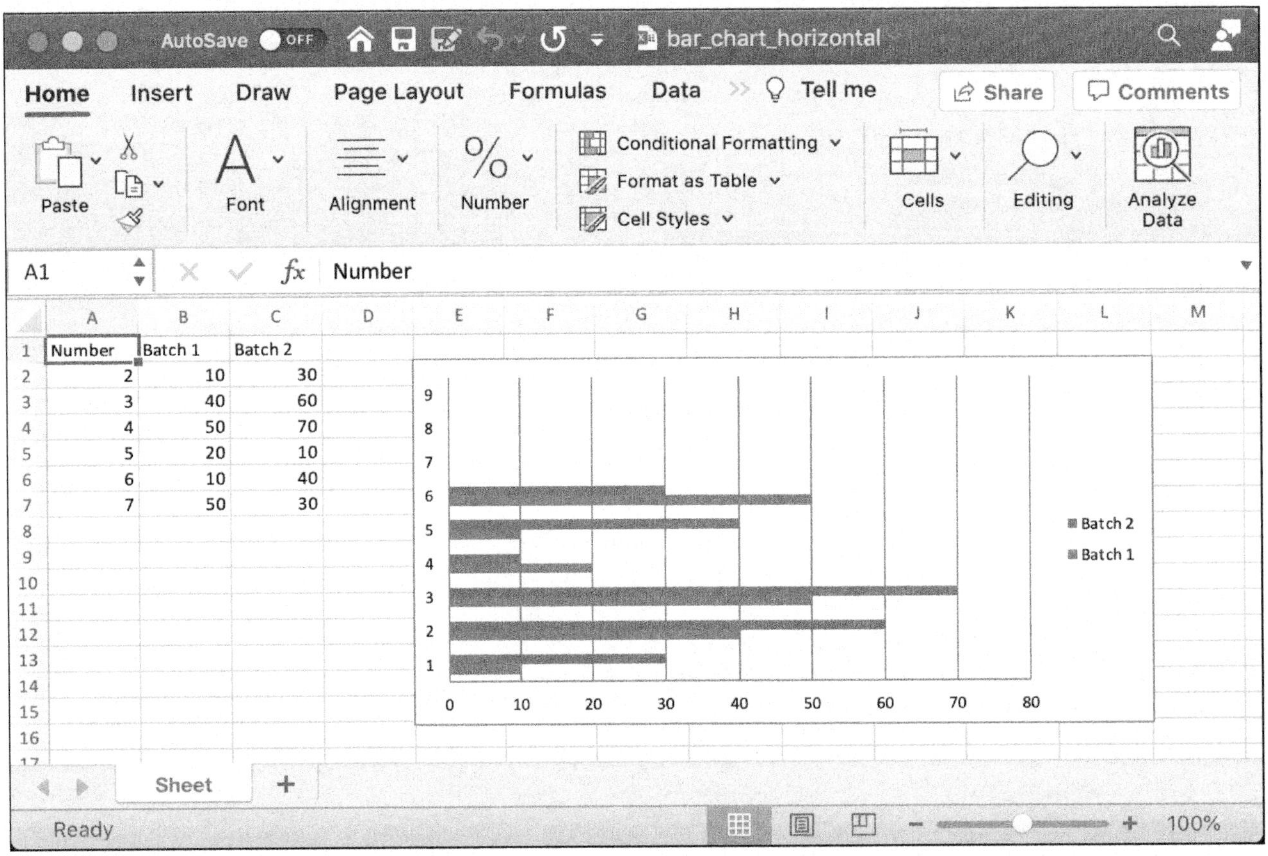

Fig. 7-4: Creating a Horizontal Bar Chart

That looks a little different than the vertical bar chart. Both of these versions of bar charts are easy to interpret. Give them each a try so you can see which one works best for your data.

Now you are ready to learn about stacked bar charts.

Stacked Bar Charts

A stacked bar chart shows how a larger category is divided into smaller ones and the relationship between each part and the total. OpenPyXL supports two different types of stacked bar charts:

- A regular stacked bar chart
- A percent stacked bar chart

To create a regular stacked bar chart with OpenPyXL, you must set the `grouping` attribute to "stacked". Create a new file and name it `bar_chart_stacked.py`. Then enter the following:

```
# bar_chart_stacked.py

from openpyxl import Workbook
from openpyxl.chart import BarChart, Reference


def create_excel_data(sheet):
    data_rows = [
        ('Number', 'Batch 1', 'Batch 2'),
        (2, 10, 30),
        (3, 40, 60),
        (4, 50, 70),
        (5, 20, 10),
        (6, 10, 40),
        (7, 50, 30),
    ]

    for row in data_rows:
        sheet.append(row)


def create_bar_chart(sheet):
    bar_chart = BarChart()
    bar_chart.type = "col"
    bar_chart.style = 12
    bar_chart.grouping = "stacked"
    bar_chart.overlap = 100
    bar_chart.title = 'Stacked Chart'

    data = Reference(worksheet=sheet,
                     min_row=1,
```

```
                         max_row=7,
                         min_col=2,
                         max_col=3)
    bar_chart.add_data(data, titles_from_data=True)
    sheet.add_chart(bar_chart, "E2")


def main():
    workbook = Workbook()
    sheet = workbook.active
    create_excel_data(sheet)
    create_bar_chart(sheet)
    workbook.save("bar_chart_stacked.xlsx")


if __name__ == "__main__":
    main()
```

This code is also similar to the other bar chart examples. You can focus in on `creare_bar_chart()` to see what's different:

```
def create_bar_chart(sheet):
    bar_chart = BarChart()
    bar_chart.type = "col"
    bar_chart.style = 12
    bar_chart.grouping = "stacked"
    bar_chart.overlap = 100
    bar_chart.title = 'Stacked Chart'
```

Here you set the bar chart `type` to **"col"** and the `grouping` to **"stacked"**. You also set the `overlap` value to 100.

When you run this code, you will get the following chart:

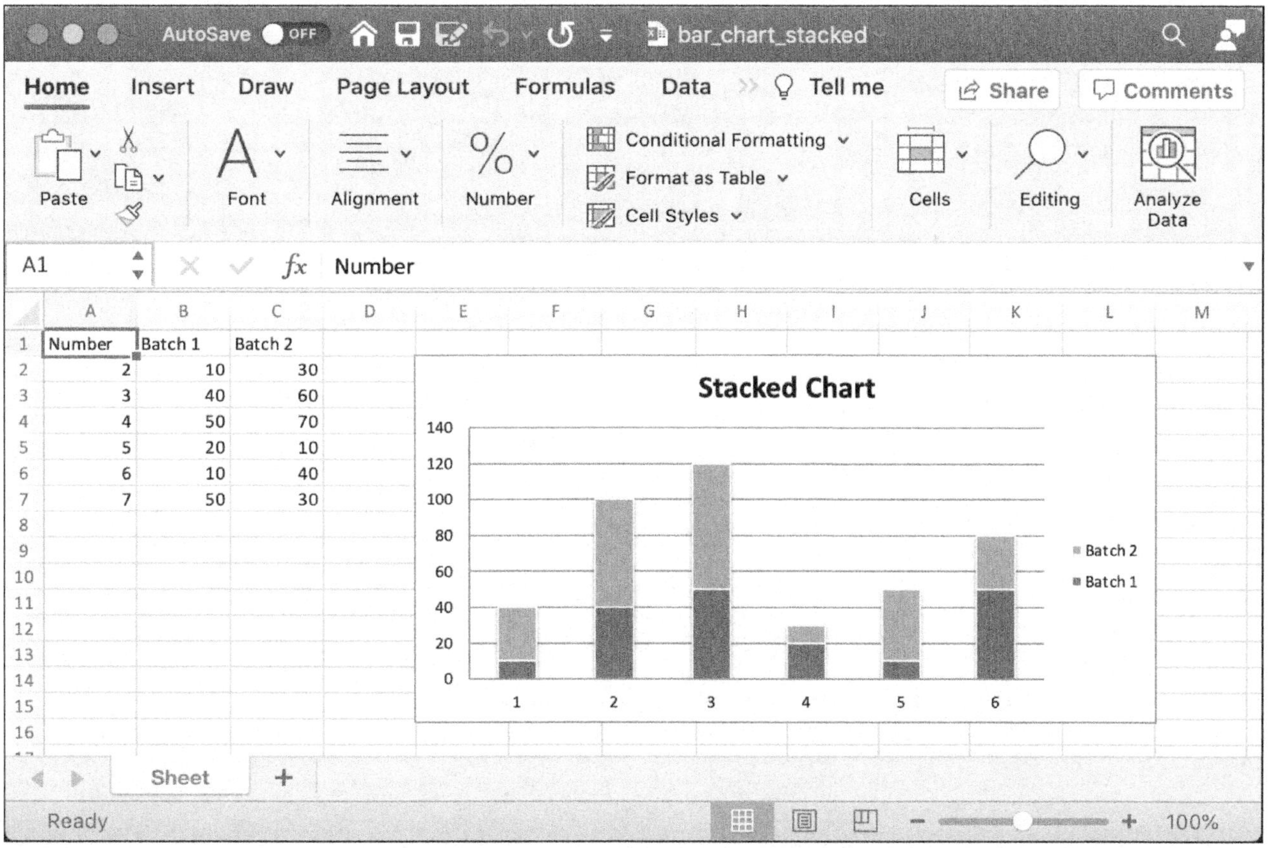

Fig. 7-5: Creating a Stacked Bar Chart

If you want to see how a percent stacked bar chart differs from a regular one, you will need to make some minor edits.

All you will need to do is change the following code to make a **Percent Stacked Bar Chart**:

```
def create_bar_chart(sheet):
    bar_chart = BarChart()
    bar_chart.type = "bar"
    bar_chart.style = 13
    bar_chart.grouping = "percentStacked"
    bar_chart.overlap = 100
    bar_chart.title = 'Percent Stacked Chart'

    data = Reference(worksheet=sheet,
                     min_row=1,
                     max_row=10,
                     min_col=2,
                     max_col=3)
    bar_chart.add_data(data, titles_from_data=True)
    sheet.add_chart(bar_chart, "E2")
```

Re-run the code, and your spreadsheet will update to look like this:

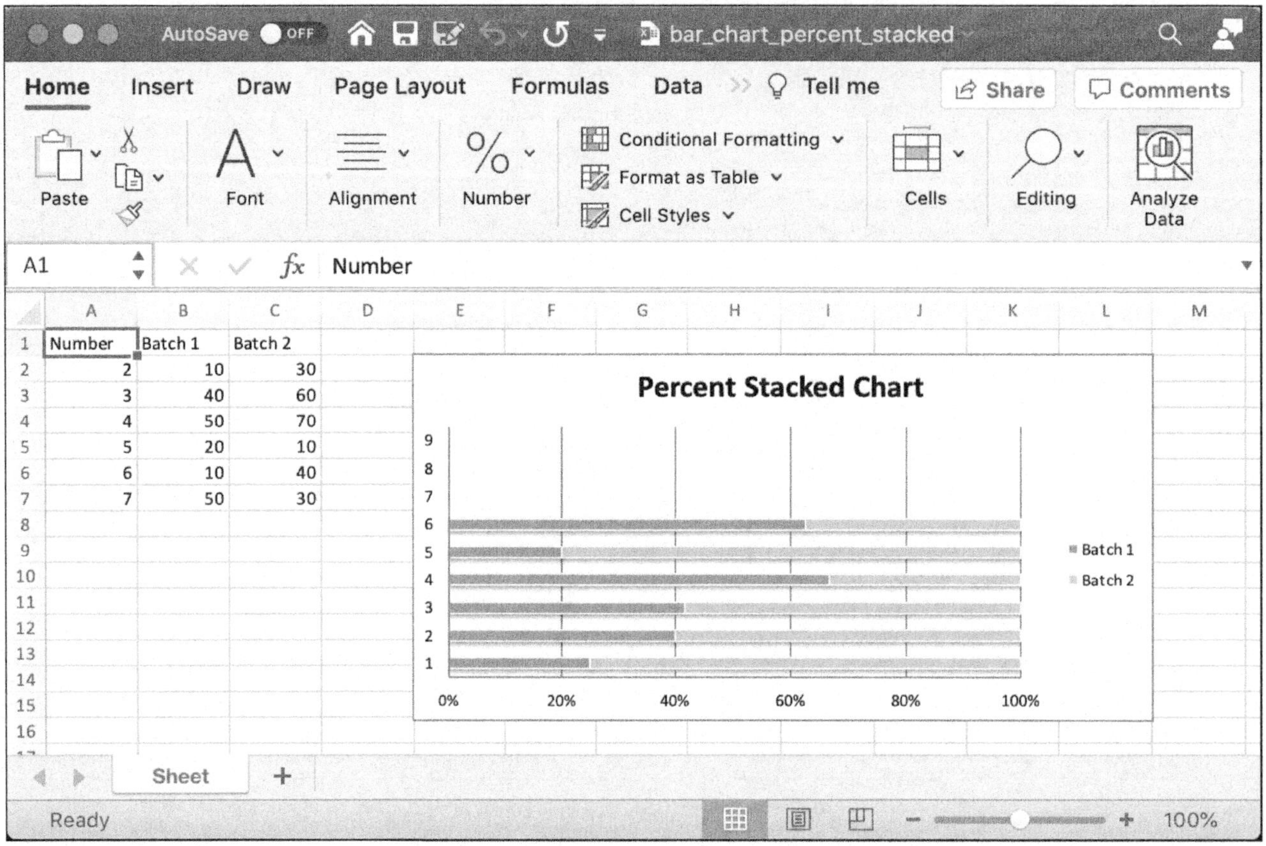

Fig. 7-6: Creating a Percent Stacked Bar Chart

Now you know how to create stacked bar charts! Feel free to edit the data or try them out with your own data sets.

The last bar chart you will learn about is the 3D bar chart!

3D Bar Charts

The 3D bar chart is kind of fun. You can use the 3D bar chart to make your data stand out. While this bar chart version doesn't add anything new to your visualization, it is a nice effect.

Create a new file named `bar_chart_3d.py` and enter this code:

```python
# bar_chart_3d.py

from openpyxl import Workbook
from openpyxl.chart import BarChart3D, Reference


def create_excel_data(sheet):
    data_rows = [
        ["", "Kindle", "Paperback"],
        ["Python 101", 9.99, 25.99],
        ["Python 201: Intermediate Python", 9.99, 25.99],
        ["wxPython Cookbook", 9.99, 25.99],
        ["ReportLab: PDF Processing with Python", 4.99, 29.99],
        ["Jupyter Notebook 101", 4.99, 29.99],
        ["Creating GUI Applications with wxPython", 24.99, 29.99],
        ["Python Interviews", 24.99, 65.00],
        ["Pillow: Image Processing with Python", 24.99, 69.00],
        ["Automating Excel with Python", 24.99, 69.00],
    ]

    for row in data_rows:
        sheet.append(row)


def create_bar_chart(sheet):
    bar_chart = BarChart3D()
    bar_chart.title = "Book Prices by Type"
    bar_chart.height = 20
    bar_chart.width = 30

    data = Reference(worksheet=sheet,
                     min_row=2,
                     max_row=10,
                     min_col=2,
                     max_col=3)
    titles = Reference(sheet, min_col=1, min_row=2, max_row=10)
    bar_chart.add_data(data, titles_from_data=True)
    bar_chart.set_categories(titles)
    sheet.add_chart(bar_chart, "E2")


def main():
    workbook = Workbook()
```

```
    sheet = workbook.active
    create_excel_data(sheet)
    create_bar_chart(sheet)
    workbook.save("bar_chart_3d.xlsx")


if __name__ == "__main__":
    main()
```

To make things a little more interesting, the data added to this chart is slightly different from before (see `create_excel_data()`). The other change is to import `BarChart3D` and use that instead of `BarChart`.

You set the `height` and `width` of the 3D bar chart to make it easier to view. When you run this code, you will get the following spreadsheet:

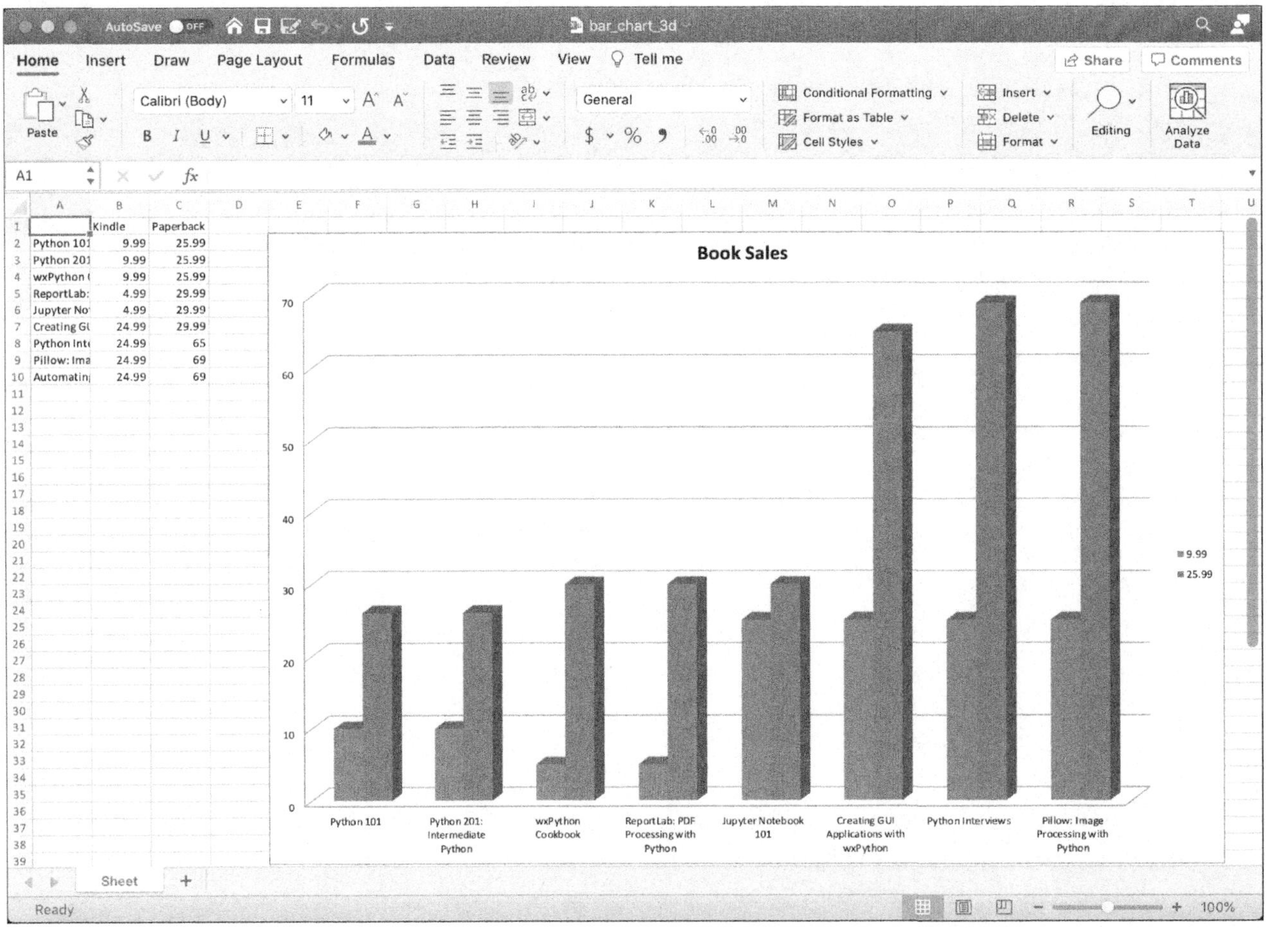

Fig. 7-7: Creating a 3D Bar Chart

Isn't that a nice-looking chart? You should try changing the data around or pick a different style to use.

The next chart type to discover is the bubble chart!

Bubble Charts

A bubble chart is a way to visualize your data using multiple circles (bubbles) in a two-dimensional plot. They are a variation of the scatter plot, but instead of dots, you use bubbles.

The bubble chart requires at least three sets of values or columns of data:

- One column is used for the size of the bubbles
- The other two columns show the horizontal and vertical position of the points

The OpenPyXL documentation[11] for the Bubble Chart has a good example. You will use a variant of that code.

To get started, create a new file named `bubble_chart.py` and add the following code:

```
# bubble_chart.py

from openpyxl import Workbook
from openpyxl.chart import Series, Reference, BubbleChart


def main():
    workbook = Workbook()
    sheet = workbook.active

    rows = [
        ("Number of Products", "Sales in USD", "Market share"),
        (14, 12200, 15),
        (20, 60000, 33),
        (18, 24400, 10),
        (22, 32000, 42),
        (),
        (12, 8200, 18),
        (15, 50000, 30),
        (19, 22400, 15),
        (25, 25000, 50),
    ]

    for row in rows:
```

[11]https://openpyxl.readthedocs.io/en/stable/charts/bubble.html

```
        sheet.append(row)

    chart = BubbleChart()
    chart.style = 18

    # add the first series of data
    xvalues = Reference(sheet, min_col=1, min_row=2, max_row=5)
    yvalues = Reference(sheet, min_col=2, min_row=2, max_row=5)
    size = Reference(sheet, min_col=3, min_row=2, max_row=5)
    series = Series(values=yvalues, xvalues=xvalues, zvalues=size, title="2013")
    chart.series.append(series)

    # add the second series of data
    xvalues = Reference(sheet, min_col=1, min_row=7, max_row=10)
    yvalues = Reference(sheet, min_col=2, min_row=7, max_row=10)
    size = Reference(sheet, min_col=3, min_row=7, max_row=10)
    series = Series(values=yvalues, xvalues=xvalues, zvalues=size, title="2014")
    chart.series.append(series)

    # place the chart starting in cell E1
    sheet.add_chart(chart, "E1")
    workbook.save("bubble.xlsx")

if __name__ == "__main__":
    main()
```

OpenPyXL uses multiple `Reference` objects and a `Series` object to generate the bubble chart. A data series is a row or column of numbers that you use to plot the chart. You can see in the example above that you create two `Series` objects containing three `Reference` objects.

Once you finish creating a `Series`, you add it to the chart using `series.append()`. When you run this code, your new spreadsheet will have a bubble chart:

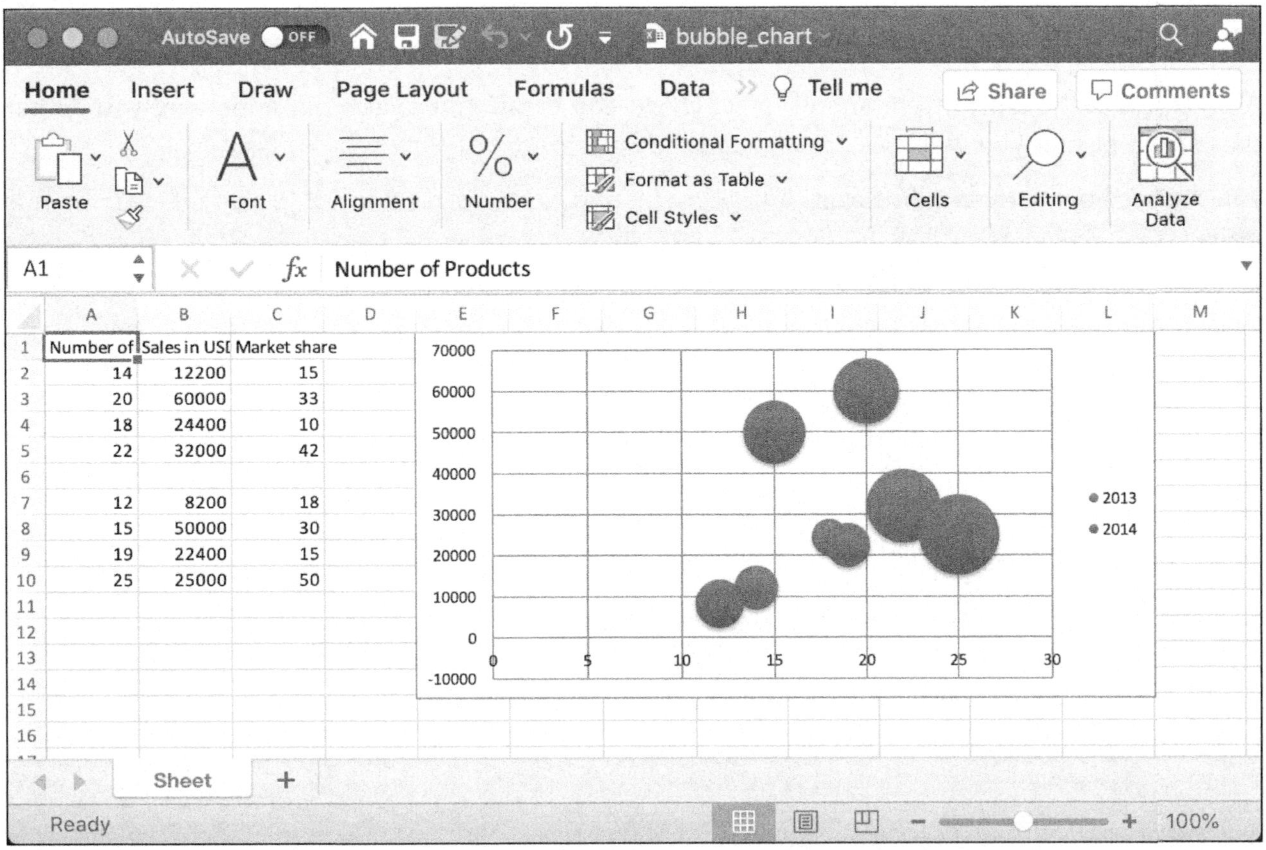

Fig. 7-8: Creating a Bubble Chart

Bubble charts are a fun way to display your data visually. You don't see bubble charts used very often, so keep them handy when you need to add a little extra pop to your presentation or report.

Now it is time to learn about line charts!

Line Charts

OpenPyXL supports several different types of line charts:

* Two-dimensional line charts
* Three-dimensional line charts

There are also a couple of variations of the two-dimensional line charts.

In this section, you will focus on a regular two-dimensional and a regular three-dimensional line chart. You can learn more about line charts in OpenPyXL's documentation[12].

[12] https://openpyxl.readthedocs.io/en/stable/charts/line.html

2D Line Charts

A 2D line chart is a pretty common type of chart. You create line charts the same way you do bar charts, except that you will use `LineChart` instead of `BarChart`.

You can see how to make a line chart by creating a new file named `line_chart.py` and entering this code:

```
# line_chart.py

from openpyxl import Workbook
from openpyxl.chart import LineChart, Reference


def create_excel_data(sheet):
    data_rows = [
        ["Book", "Kindle", "Paperback"],
        [1, 9.99, 25.99],
        [2, 9.99, 25.99],
        [3, 9.99, 25.99],
        [4, 4.99, 29.99],
        [5, 4.99, 29.99],
        [6, 24.99, 29.99],
        [7, 24.99, 65.00],
        [8, 24.99, 69.00],
        [9, 24.99, 69.00],
    ]

    for row in data_rows:
        sheet.append(row)


def create_line_chart(sheet):
    chart = LineChart()
    chart.title = "Line Chart"
    chart.style = 15
    chart.y_axis.title = 'Sales'
    chart.x_axis.title = 'Books'

    data = Reference(sheet, min_col=2, min_row=2, max_col=3, max_row=9)
    chart.add_data(data)

    sheet.add_chart(chart, "E2")
```

```
def main():
    workbook = Workbook()
    sheet = workbook.active
    create_excel_data(sheet)
    create_line_chart(sheet)
    workbook.save("line_chart.xlsx")


if __name__ == "__main__":
    main()
```

There isn't anything truly new in this code. The only difference here is that you are creating a `LineChart` object.

Go ahead and run this code, and you will have created your first line chart:

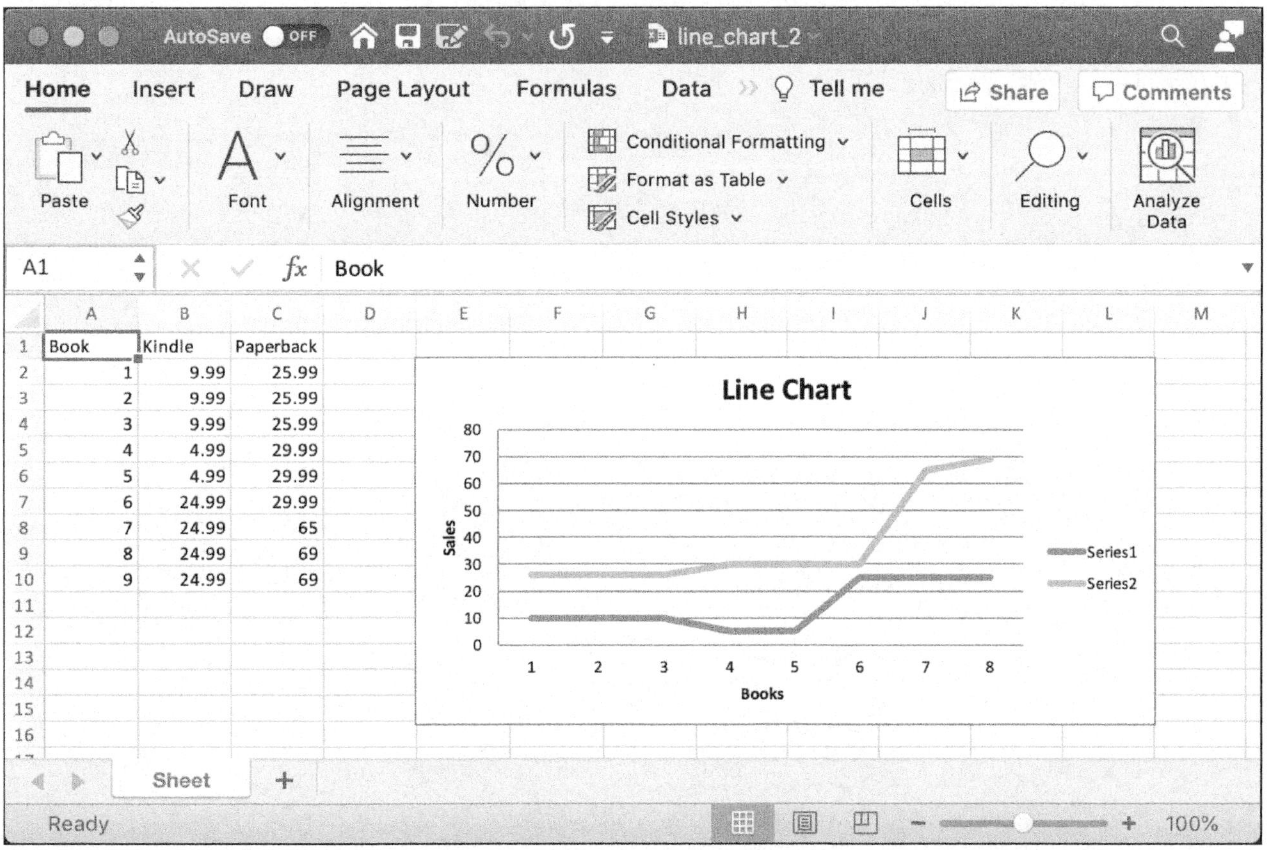

Fig. 7-10: Creating a Line Chart

That looks pretty good! Now you're ready to make your line chart three-dimensional!

3D Line Charts

The 3D line chart is another type of line chart, only drawn such that it looks three-dimensional. The only difference is that you need to use `LineChart3D` to create one.

Open your Python editor back up and create a new file named `line_chart_3d.py`. Then enter this code:

```
# line_chart_3d.py

from openpyxl import Workbook
from openpyxl.chart import LineChart3D, Reference


def create_excel_data(sheet):
    data_rows = [
        ["Book", "Kindle", "Paperback"],
        [1, 9.99, 25.99],
        [2, 9.99, 25.99],
        [3, 9.99, 25.99],
        [4, 4.99, 29.99],
        [5, 4.99, 29.99],
        [6, 24.99, 29.99],
        [7, 24.99, 65.00],
        [8, 24.99, 69.00],
        [9, 24.99, 69.00],
    ]

    for row in data_rows:
        sheet.append(row)


def create_line_chart(sheet):
    chart = LineChart3D()
    chart.title = "Line Chart"
    chart.style = 15
    chart.y_axis.title = 'Sales'
    chart.x_axis.title = 'Books'

    data = Reference(sheet, min_col=2, min_row=2, max_col=3, max_row=9)
    chart.add_data(data)

    sheet.add_chart(chart, "E2")
```

```python
def main():
    workbook = Workbook()
    sheet = workbook.active
    create_excel_data(sheet)
    create_line_chart(sheet)
    workbook.save("line_chart_3d.xlsx")


if __name__ == "__main__":
    main()
```

This code is the same as the previous example except for the new import. Go ahead and run this example to see what a 3D line chart looks like:

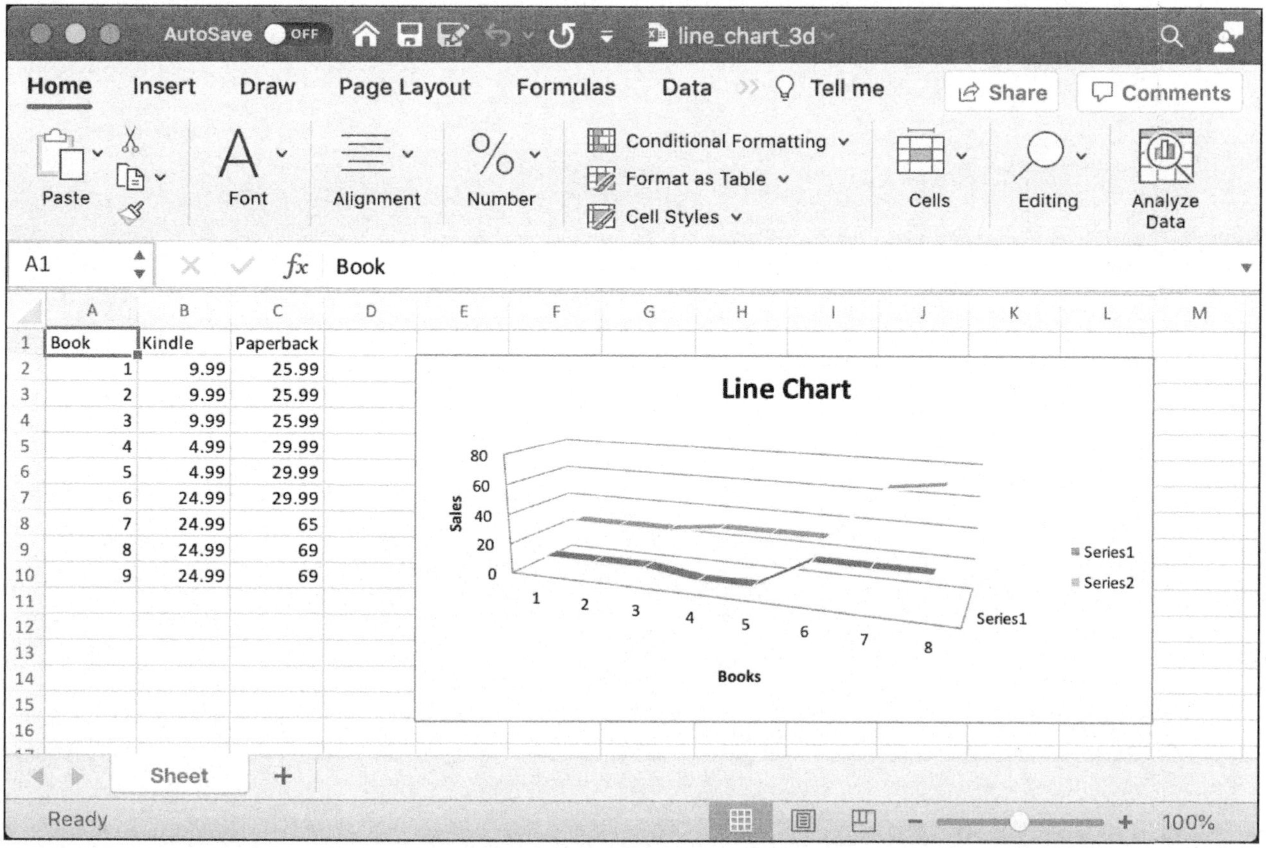

Fig. 7-11: Creating a 3D Line Chart

Now you know how to create two different kinds of line charts. The next chart type to learn about is the scatter chart!

Scatter Charts

The scatter chart is a type of plot that uses Cartesian coordinates to display values for two variables for a set of data. Your data is a collection of points.

The two variables define the horizontal and vertical positions of each point on the chart.

OpenPyXL draws a line between the points by default in its scatter charts, so they look like a line chart. You can see this happen by creating a new Python file named `scatter_chart.py` and entering this code:

```
# scatter_chart.py

from openpyxl import Workbook
from openpyxl.chart import ScatterChart, Reference, Series


def main(filename):
    workbook = Workbook()
    sheet = workbook.active

    rows = [
        ["Book", "Kindle", "Paperback"],
        [1, 9.99, 25.99],
        [2, 9.99, 25.99],
        [3, 9.99, 25.99],
        [4, 4.99, 29.99],
        [5, 4.99, 29.99],
        [6, 24.99, 29.99],
        [7, 24.99, 65.00],
        [8, 24.99, 69.00],
        [9, 24.99, 69.00],
    ]

    for row in rows:
        sheet.append(row)

    chart = ScatterChart()
    chart.title = "Scatter Chart"
    chart.style = 13
    chart.x_axis.title = 'Size'
    chart.y_axis.title = 'Percentage'
```

```
    xvalues = Reference(sheet, min_col=1, min_row=2, max_row=7)
    for i in range(2, 4):
        values = Reference(sheet, min_col=i, min_row=1, max_row=7)
        series = Series(values, xvalues, title_from_data=True)
        chart.series.append(series)

    sheet.add_chart(chart, "E2")

    workbook.save(filename)


if __name__ == "__main__":
    main("scatter_chart.xlsx")
```

This code creates the values to plot by creating a `Reference` that you name `xvalues`. You then loop over a small `range` to create a couple of `Series` objects that will plot out your chart using the `xvalues` you created.

When you run this code, your spreadsheet will look like this:

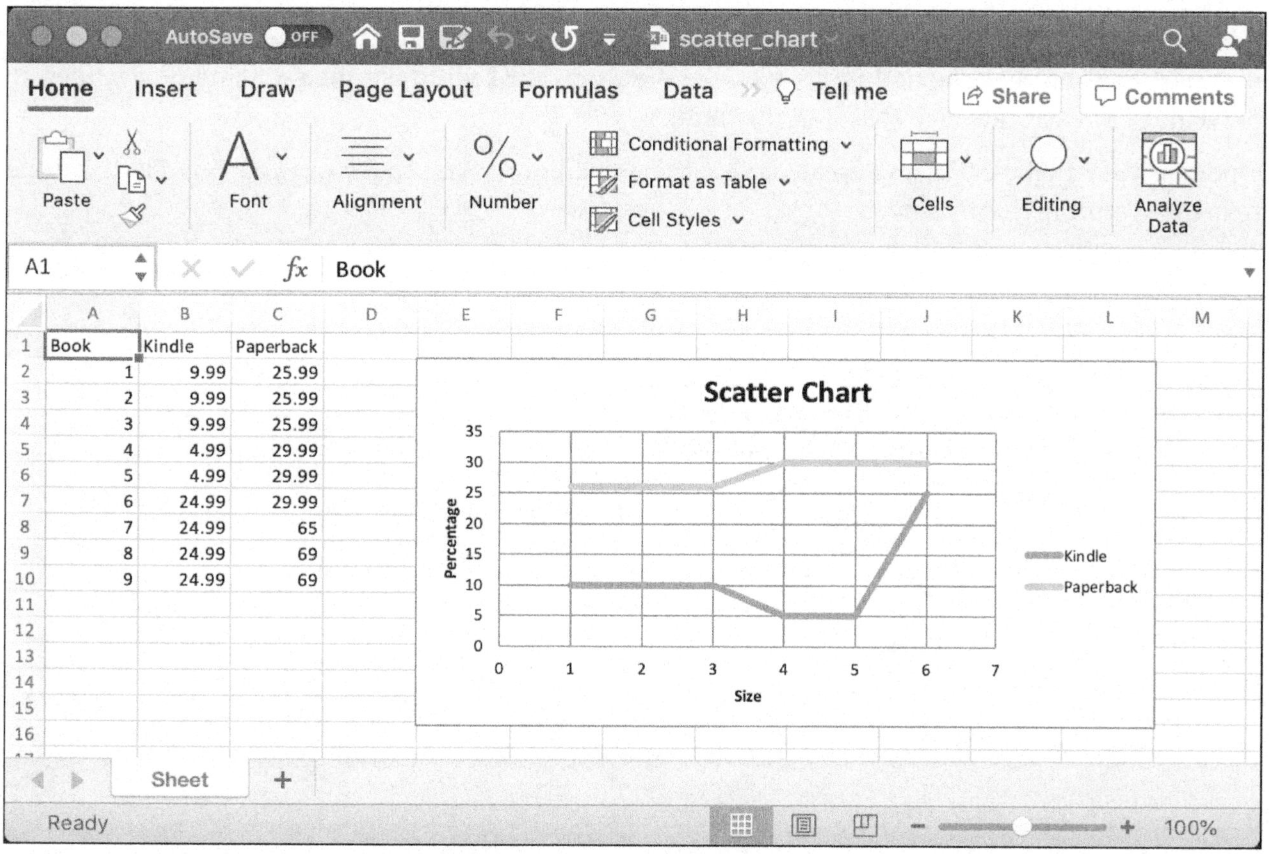

Fig. 7-12: Creating a Scatter Chart

Feel free to try a different data set with your scatter chart.

The next chart type to learn about are pie charts!

Pie Charts

A pie chart is a type of graph that is a circle divided into sections that represent a proportion of the whole. OpenPyXL supports three different types of pie charts:

- The regular pie chart
- Project pie charts
- 3D pie charts

Pie charts are a great way to show percentages in a population. You will learn how to create a pie chart now!

Regular Pie Charts

You can create a pie chart with OpenPyXL using the `PieChart` class. The data that you add to a pie chart does not have to add up to 100. The `PieChart` class will take the data and determine the percentage of each category based on the total.

Open up your Python IDE and create a new file named `pie_chart.py`. Now you can add this code to create your pie chart:

```
# pie_chart.py

from openpyxl import Workbook
from openpyxl.chart import PieChart, Reference
from openpyxl.chart.series import DataPoint


def main(filename):
    workbook = Workbook()
    sheet = workbook.active

    data = [
        ['Pizza', 'Sold'],
        ['Pepperoni', 50],
        ['Sausage', 30],
        ['Cheese', 10],
        ['Supreme', 40],
```

```
    ]

    for row in data:
        sheet.append(row)

    chart = PieChart()
    chart.title = "Pizza Pie Chart"
    labels = Reference(sheet, min_col=1, min_row=2, max_row=5)
    data = Reference(sheet, min_col=2, min_row=1, max_row=5)
    chart.add_data(data, titles_from_data=True)
    chart.set_categories(labels)

    # Cut the first slice of pizza from the pie
    slice = DataPoint(idx=0, explosion=20)
    chart.series[0].data_points = [slice]

    sheet.add_chart(chart, "E2")

    workbook.save(filename)


if __name__ == "__main__":
    main("pie_chart.xlsx")
```

You don't need to use a `Series` object with a pie chart. You only need a couple of `Reference` objects. However, if you want to pop out a slice of the pie chart, you need to use a `DataPoint` object.

To use the `DataPoint` object, you need to create some code like this:

```
slice = DataPoint(idx=0, explosion=20)
chart.series[0].data_points = [slice]
```

When you run the full code above, you will get a spreadsheet with a pie chart that looks like this:

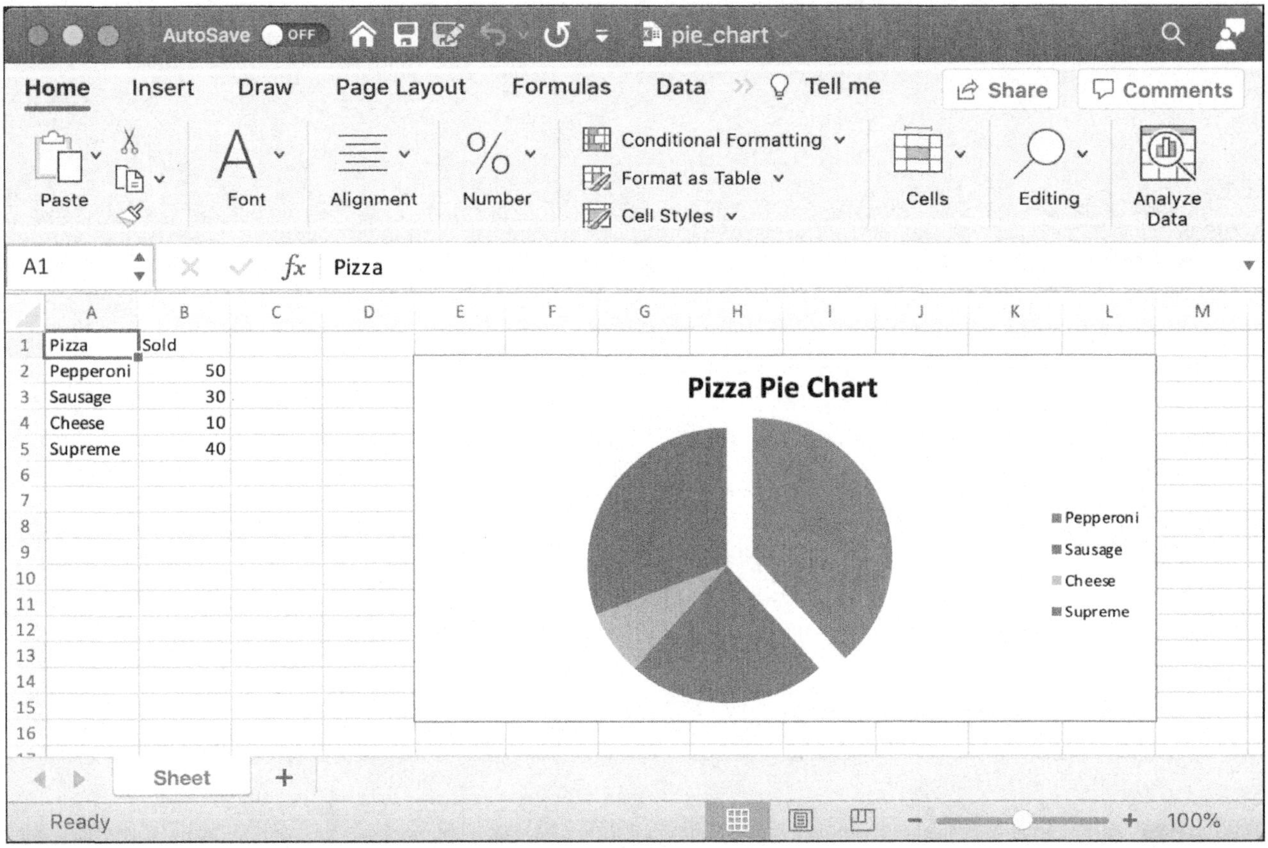

Fig. 7-13: Creating a Pie Chart

That's a neat-looking chart! You should experiment with the `DataPoint` object and see how you change it to make the pie chart draw differently.

Now that you have created a normal pie chart, it's time to learn about the projected pie chart variety!

Projected Pie Charts

Projected pie charts are a little different than a regular pie chart. According to the documentation, a projected pie chart will "extract some slices from a pie chart and project them into a second pie or bar chart".

You will take the projected pie chart example[13] from the OpenPyXL documentation and modify it slightly for your code. Create a new file named `projected_pie_chart.py` and add the following:

[13]https://openpyxl.readthedocs.io/en/stable/charts/pie.html#projected-pie-charts

```python
# projected_pie_chart.py

from copy import deepcopy

from openpyxl import Workbook
from openpyxl.chart import ProjectedPieChart, Reference


def main(filename):
    workbook = Workbook()
    sheet = workbook.active

    data = [
        ['Page', 'Views'],
        ['Search', 95],
        ['Products', 4],
        ['Offers', 0.5],
        ['Sales', 0.5],
    ]

    for row in data:
        sheet.append(row)

    projected_pie = ProjectedPieChart()
    projected_pie.type = "pie"
    projected_pie.splitType = "val" # split by value
    labels = Reference(sheet, min_col=1, min_row=2, max_row=5)
    data = Reference(sheet, min_col=2, min_row=1, max_row=5)
    projected_pie.add_data(data, titles_from_data=True)
    projected_pie.set_categories(labels)
    sheet.add_chart(projected_pie, "E2")

    projected_bar = deepcopy(projected_pie)
    projected_bar.type = "bar"
    projected_bar.splitType = 'pos' # split by position
    sheet.add_chart(projected_bar, "E19")

    workbook.save(filename)


if __name__ == "__main__":
    main("project_pie_chart.xlsx")
```

This code will create two projected pie charts. The first projected pie chart will project a pie chart, while the second will project a bar chart. You can specify the project by setting the `type` attribute to "pie" or "bar". You can also set the `splitType` to be split by value ("val") or split by position ("pos").

When you run this example, your spreadsheet will look like the following screenshot:

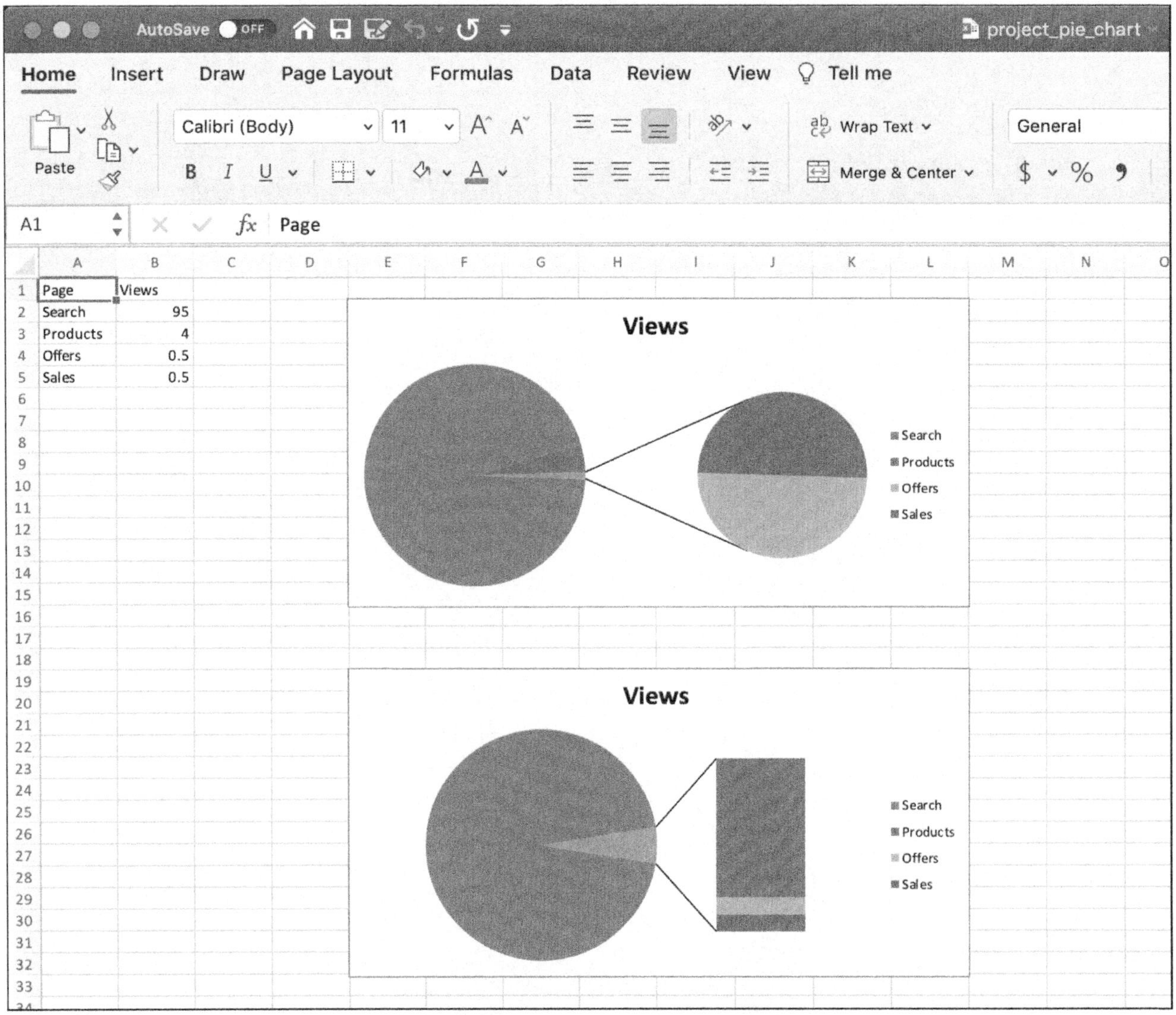

Fig. 7-14: Creating a Projected Pie Chart

The projected pie chart is unique from the other charts in that it is kind of a chart within a chart. You should try editing the code and experimenting with the values that you pass to the project pie chart. It's the best way to familiarize yourself with how it functions.

The last pie chart type to learn is the 3D pie chart.

3D Pie Charts

You can create a pie chart with a 3D effect applied by using `PieChart3D`.

To get started, create a new file named `pie_chart_3d.py` and add this code to your file:

```
# pie_chart_3d.py

from copy import deepcopy

from openpyxl import Workbook
from openpyxl.chart import PieChart3D, Reference


def main(filename):
    workbook = Workbook()
    sheet = workbook.active

    data = [
        ['Pizza', 'Sold'],
        ['Pepperoni', 50],
        ['Sausage', 30],
        ['Cheese', 10],
        ['Supreme', 40],
    ]

    for row in data:
        sheet.append(row)

    pie = PieChart3D()
    labels = Reference(sheet, min_col=1, min_row=2, max_row=5)
    data = Reference(sheet, min_col=2, min_row=1, max_row=5)
    pie.add_data(data, titles_from_data=True)
    pie.set_categories(labels)
    pie.title = "Pizza Pies sold by type"
    sheet.add_chart(pie, "E2")

    workbook.save(filename)


if __name__ == "__main__":
    main("pie_chart_3d.xlsx")
```

This code is the same as the first pie chart code you saw in this section, except you are using

`PieChart3D` here. When you execute this code, you will end up with this spreadsheet:

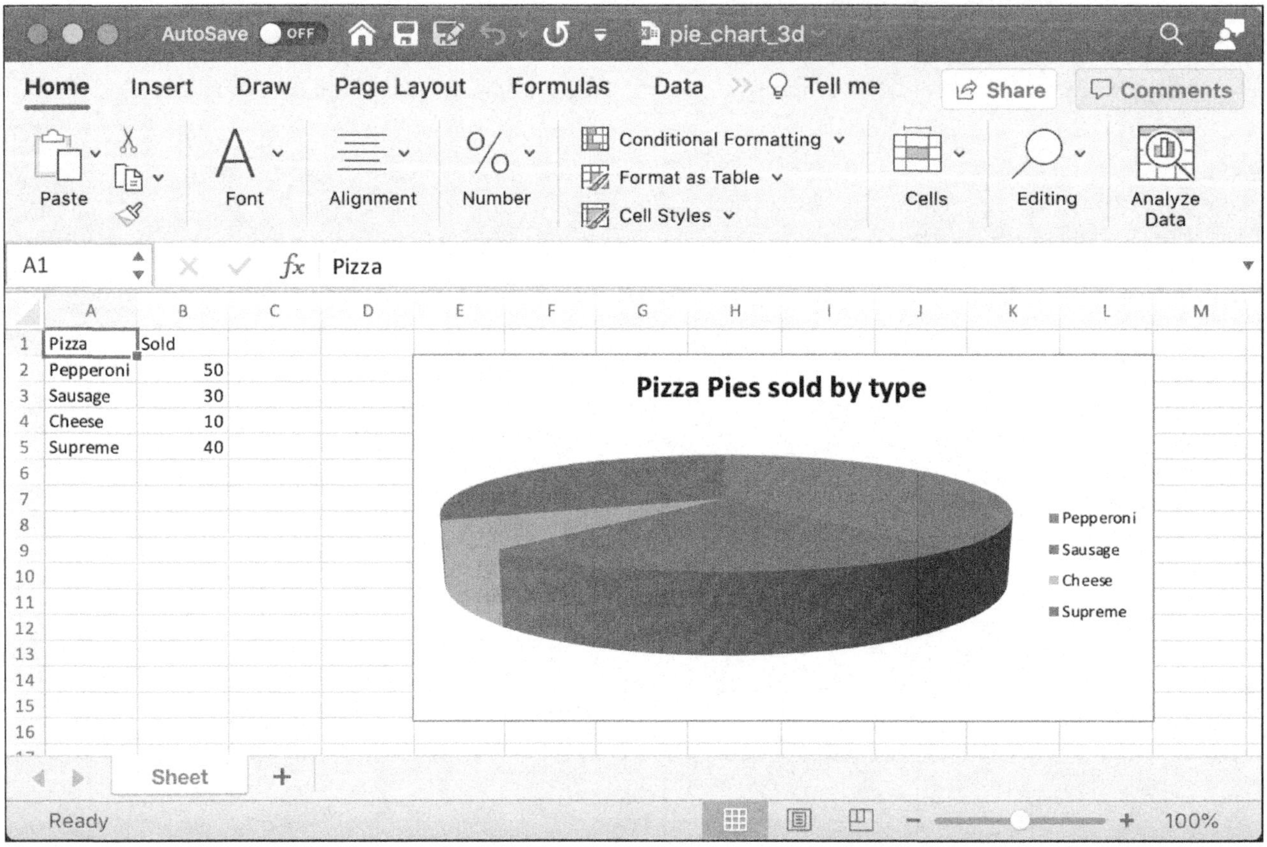

Fig. 7-15: Creating a 3D Pie Chart

The spreadsheet above shows you what the pie chart looks like with a 3D effect applied to it.

You are now ready to learn about doughnut charts!

Doughnut Charts

A doughnut chart is closely related to pie charts. The pie chart is a circle, while the doughnut chart is a ring or series of concentric rings.

For this example, you will take the code from OpenPyXL's documentation[14] and modify it a bit to use some of the sample data that you have used in some of your previous examples.

To get started, create a new file named `doughnut_chart.py`, then enter this code:

[14]https://openpyxl.readthedocs.io/en/stable/charts/doughnut.html

```python
# doughnut_chart.py

from copy import deepcopy

from openpyxl import Workbook
from openpyxl.chart import DoughnutChart, Reference, Series
from openpyxl.chart.series import DataPoint


def main(filename):
    workbook = Workbook()
    sheet = workbook.active

    data = [
        ['Books', 2019, 2020],
        ['Python 101', 40, 50],
        ['Python 201', 2, 10],
        ['ReportLab', 20, 30],
        ['Jupyter', 30, 40],
    ]

    for row in data:
        sheet.append(row)

    chart = DoughnutChart()
    labels = Reference(sheet, min_col=1, min_row=2, max_row=5)
    data = Reference(sheet, min_col=2, min_row=1, max_row=5)
    chart.add_data(data, titles_from_data=True)
    chart.set_categories(labels)
    chart.title = "Books sold by title"
    chart.style = 26

    # Cut the first slice out of the doughnut
    slices = [DataPoint(idx=i) for i in range(4)]
    plain, jam, lime, chocolate = slices
    chart.series[0].data_points = slices
    plain.graphicalProperties.solidFill = "FAE1D0"
    jam.graphicalProperties.solidFill = "BB2244"
    lime.graphicalProperties.solidFill = "22DD22"
    chocolate.graphicalProperties.solidFill = "61210B"
    chocolate.explosion = 10

    sheet.add_chart(chart, "E1")
```

```
    chart2 = deepcopy(chart)
    chart2.title = None
    data = Reference(sheet, min_col=3, min_row=1, max_row=5)
    series2 = Series(data, title_from_data=True)
    series2.data_points = slices
    chart2.series.append(series2)

    sheet.add_chart(chart2, "E17")

    workbook.save(filename)


if __name__ == "__main__":
    main("doughnut_chart.xlsx")
```

This code will create two doughnut charts. They both pull from the same dataset, but they load it differently using different rows and columns. In the first doughnut chart, you split out the slices to apply custom colors to each slice. You also set the `explosion` value of the `chocolate` ring to **10**. That will separate the chocolate portion of the doughnut from the rest of the doughnut.

The second doughnut chart doesn't have any customization applied to it. You don't set the `explosion` either. By using the defaults, you get to see what a normal doughnut chart looks like:

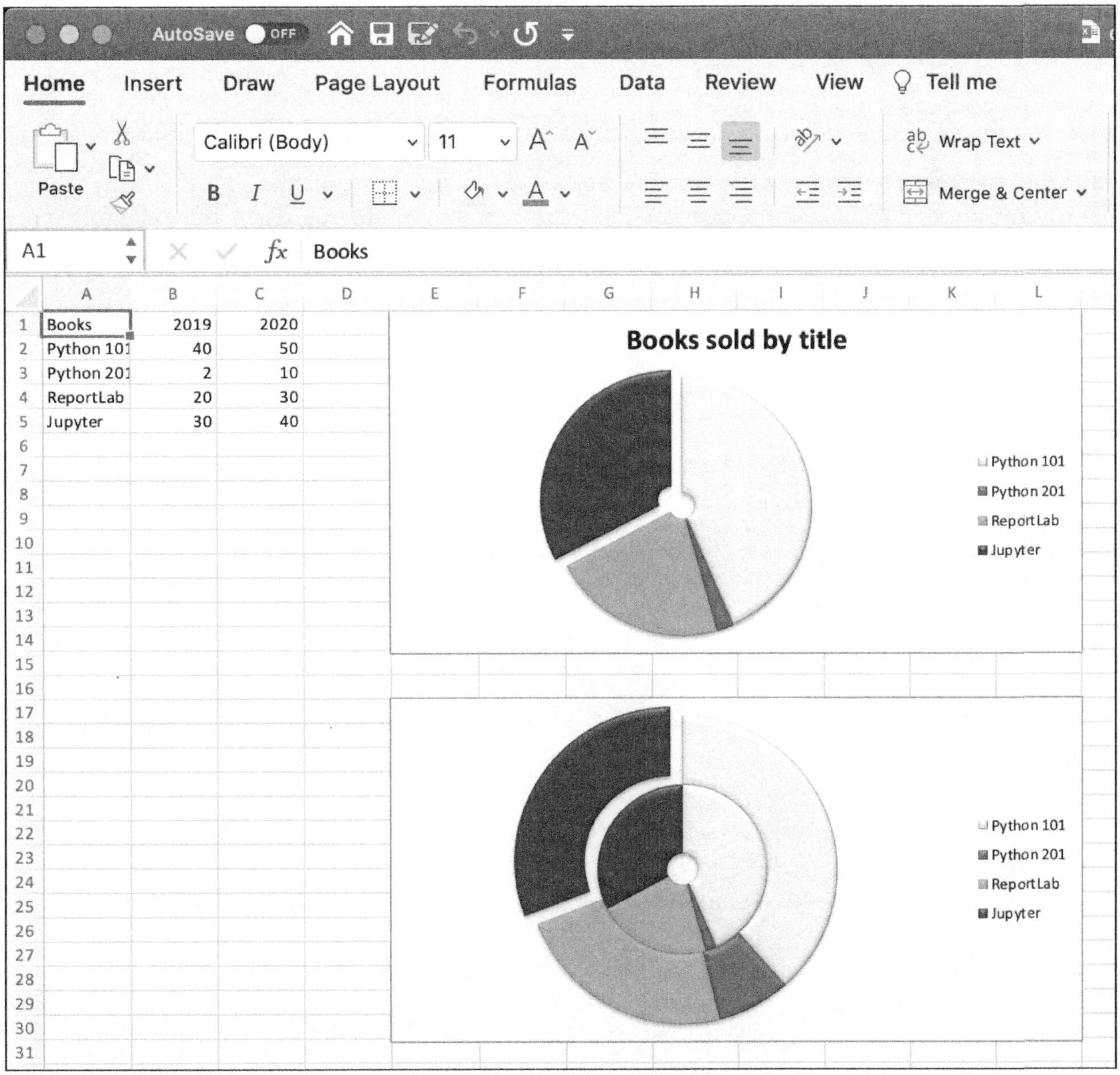

Fig. 7-16: Creating a Doughnut Chart

The doughnut chart is a fun way to make a pie chart look different. If you need an alternative way to showing your data, you may want to consider using the doughnut instead of the pie chart.

Radar charts are the next chart type that you will discover.

Radar Charts

Radar charts compare the aggregate values of multiple data series. OpenPyXL describes them as a "projection of an area chart on a circular x-axis". OpenPyXL supports two versions of the radar chart:

- Standard - where the area is marked with a line
- Filled - where the whole area is filled

There is a third type called "marker", but it has no effect. You can add markers via the `Series` object.

You will be taking the radar chart example from the OpenPyXL documentation[15] and modifying it slightly for your code. Open up a new file and name it `radar_chart.py`. Then enter the following code:

```
# radar_chart.py

from openpyxl import Workbook
from openpyxl.chart import RadarChart, Reference


def main(filename):
    workbook = Workbook()
    sheet = workbook.active

    data = [
        ['Month', "Bulbs", "Seeds", "Flowers", "Trees & shrubs"],
        ['Jan', 0, 2500, 500, 0,],
        ['Feb', 0, 5500, 750, 1500],
        ['Mar', 0, 9000, 1500, 2500],
        ['Apr', 0, 6500, 2000, 4000],
        ['May', 0, 3500, 5500, 3500],
        ['Jun', 0, 0, 7500, 1500],
        ['Jul', 0, 0, 8500, 800],
        ['Aug', 1500, 0, 7000, 550],
        ['Sep', 5000, 0, 3500, 2500],
        ['Oct', 8500, 0, 2500, 6000],
        ['Nov', 3500, 0, 500, 5500],
        ['Dec', 500, 0, 100, 3000 ],
    ]


    for row in data:
        sheet.append(row)

    chart = RadarChart()
    chart.type = "filled"
    labels = Reference(sheet, min_col=1, min_row=2, max_row=13)
```

[15] https://openpyxl.readthedocs.io/en/stable/charts/radar.html

```
    data = Reference(sheet, min_col=2, max_col=5, min_row=1, max_row=13)
    chart.add_data(data, titles_from_data=True)
    chart.set_categories(labels)
    chart.style = 26
    chart.title = "Garden Centre Sales"
    chart.y_axis.delete = True

    sheet.add_chart(chart, "G2")

    workbook.save(filename)


if __name__ == "__main__":
    main("radar_chart.xlsx")
```

When you create your radar chart, you choose to use the "filled" version. Then you create a couple of references, one to contain the `labels` and one for the `data`. Then you set up the chart.

Run your code, and the spreadsheet that it creates will look like this:

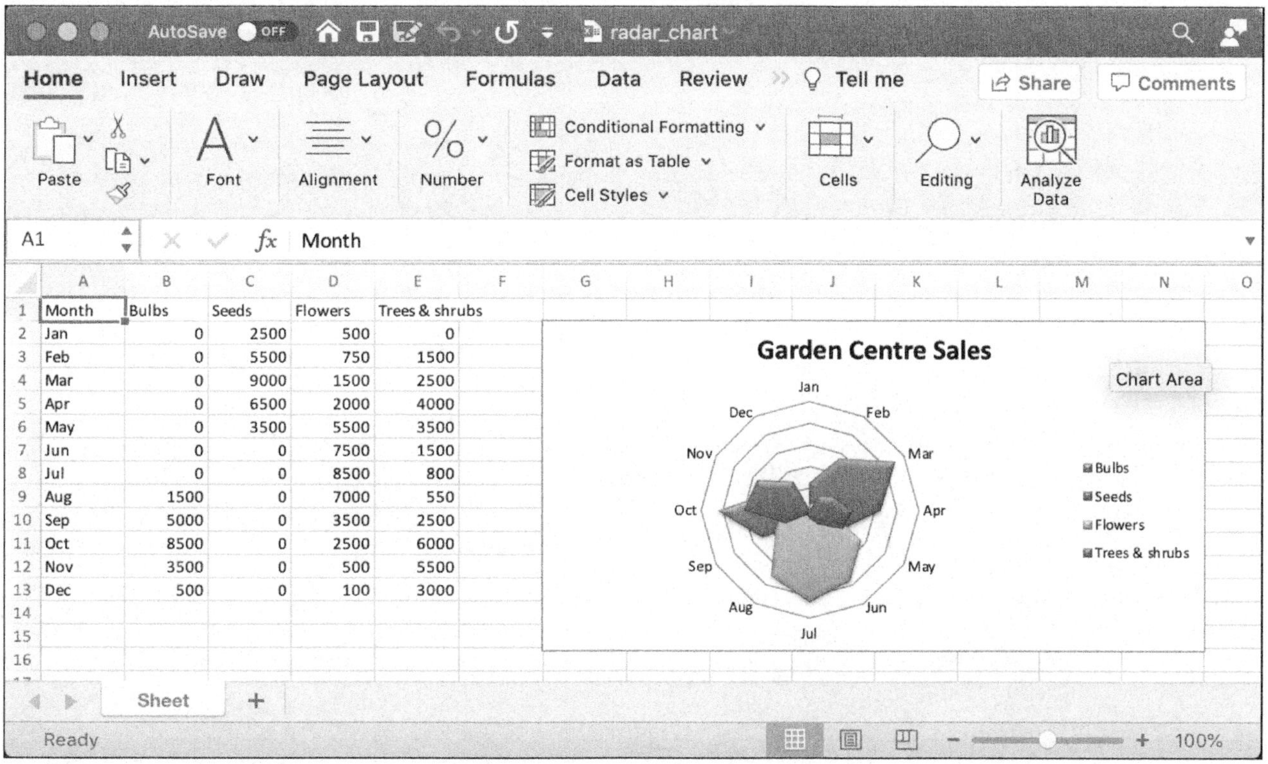

Fig. 7-17: Creating a Radar Chart

The radar chart is very unique-looking. Use it wisely.

The last chart to learn about is the surface chart!

Surface Charts

Your data must be arranged as columns and rows in a spreadsheet to allow you to plot them in a surface chart. According to the documentation[16], a "surface chart is useful when you want to find optimum combinations between two sets of data".

By default, OpenPyXL draws its surface charts in 3D. You can create 2D surface charts by setting the rotation and perspective in the chart, if you so desire.

The example in the documentation does an excellent job of showing you how to create four different surface charts. You will take that example and modify it slightly.

Create a new Python file named `surface_chart.py` that contains this code:

```
# surface_chart.py

from copy import deepcopy

from openpyxl import Workbook
from openpyxl.chart import SurfaceChart, SurfaceChart3D
from openpyxl.chart import Reference


def main(filename):
    workbook = Workbook()
    sheet = workbook.active

    data = [
        [None, 10, 20, 30, 40, 50,],
        [0.1, 15, 65, 105, 65, 15,],
        [0.2, 35, 105, 170, 105, 35,],
        [0.3, 55, 135, 215, 135, 55,],
        [0.4, 75, 155, 240, 155, 75,],
        [0.5, 80, 190, 245, 190, 80,],
        [0.6, 75, 155, 240, 155, 75,],
        [0.7, 55, 135, 215, 135, 55,],
        [0.8, 35, 105, 170, 105, 35,],
        [0.9, 15, 65, 105, 65, 15],
    ]

    for row in data:
        sheet.append(row)
```

[16]https://openpyxl.readthedocs.io/en/stable/charts/surface.html

```
    chart1 = SurfaceChart()
    ref = Reference(sheet, min_col=2, max_col=6, min_row=1, max_row=10)
    labels = Reference(sheet, min_col=1, min_row=2, max_row=10)
    chart1.add_data(ref, titles_from_data=True)
    chart1.set_categories(labels)
    chart1.title = "Contour"

    sheet.add_chart(chart1, "A12")

    # wireframe
    chart2 = deepcopy(chart1)
    chart2.wireframe = True
    chart2.title = "2D Wireframe"

    sheet.add_chart(chart2, "G12")

    # 3D Surface
    chart3 = SurfaceChart3D()
    chart3.add_data(ref, titles_from_data=True)
    chart3.set_categories(labels)
    chart3.title = "Surface"

    sheet.add_chart(chart3, "A29")

    chart4 = deepcopy(chart3)
    chart4.wireframe = True
    chart4.title = "3D Wireframe"

    sheet.add_chart(chart4, "G29")

    workbook.save(filename)

if __name__ == "__main__":
    main("surface_chart.xlsx")
```

This code will create the following surface chart types:

- A regular surface chart (top-left)
- A wireframe surface chart (top right)
- A 3D surface chart (bottom left)
- A 3D wireframe surface chart (bottom right)

You can set the `wireframe` attribute to `True` for the `SurfaceChart` and the `SurfaceChart3D` objects to enable wireframe drawing.

When you run this code, you will get the following spreadsheet:

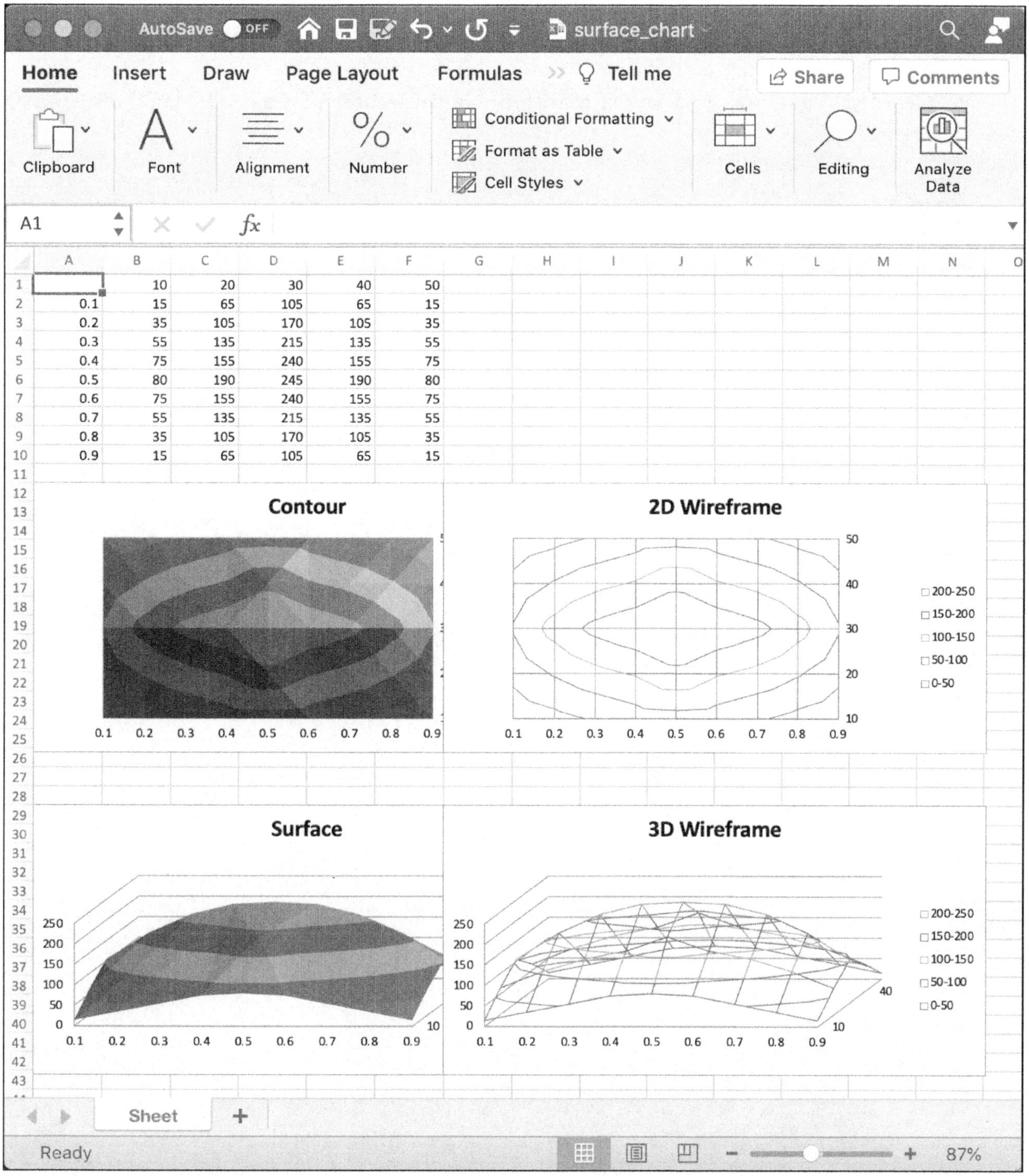

Fig. 7-18: Creating Surface Charts

Aren't those charts fun? They are very different than the other charts in this chapter.

Wrapping Up

You have learned about a wide variety of chart types in this chapter. Specifically, you have learned how to create:

- Area Charts
- Bar Charts
- Bubble Charts
- Line Charts
- Scatter Charts
- Pie Charts
- Doughnut Charts
- Radar Charts
- Surface Charts

You can use these charts to visualize a large number of different data types. From sales figures to populations and beyond, you will be able to plot your data in one or more of these fun charts. Your spreadsheets will look much more interesting when they contain charts.

Give these charts a try. Experiment with them using the knowledge you gained in the previous chapter. Soon you will have your amazing custom charts!

Chapter 8 - Converting CSV to Excel

There are many common file types that you will need to work with as a software developer. One such format is the CSV file. CSV stands for "Comma-Separated Values" and is a text file format that uses a comma as a delimiter to separate values from one another. Each row is its own record and each value is its own field. Most CSV files have records that are all the same length.

Microsoft Excel opens CSV files with no problem. You can open one yourself with Excel and then save it yourself in an Excel format. The purpose of this chapter is to teach you the following concepts:

- Converting a CSV file to Excel
- Converting an Excel spreadsheet to CSV

You will be using Python to do the conversion from one file type to the other.

Converting a CSV file to Excel

You will soon see that converting a CSV file to an Excel spreadsheet doesn't take very much code. However, you do need to have a CSV file to get started. With that in mind, open up your favorite text editor (Notepad, SublimeText, or something else) and add the following:

```
book_title,author,publisher,pub_date,isbn
Python 101,Mike Driscoll, Mike Driscoll,2020,123456789
wxPython Recipes,Mike Driscoll,Apress,2018,978-1-4842-3237-8
Python Interviews,Mike Driscoll,Packt Publishing,2018,9781788399081
```

Save this file as **books.txt**. You can also download the CSV file from this book's GitHub code repository[17].

Now that you have the CSV file, you need to create a new Python file too. Open up your Python IDE and create a new file named `csv_to_excel.py`. Then enter the following code:

[17]https://github.com/driscollis/automating_excel_with_python

```
# csv_to_excel.py

import csv
import openpyxl


def csv_to_excel(csv_file, excel_file):
    csv_data = []
    with open(csv_file) as file_obj:
        reader = csv.reader(file_obj)
        for row in reader:
            csv_data.append(row)

    workbook = openpyxl.Workbook()
    sheet = workbook.active
    for row in csv_data:
        sheet.append(row)
    workbook.save(excel_file)


if __name__ == "__main__":
    csv_to_excel("books.csv", "converted_books.xlsx")
```

Your code uses Python's `csv` module in addition to OpenPyXL. You create a function, `csv_to_excel()`, that accepts two arguments:

- `csv_file` - The path to the input CSV file
- `excel_file` - The path to the Excel file that you want to create

You want to extract each row of data from the CSV. To extract the data, you create a `csv.reader()` object and then iterate over one row at a time. For each iteration, you append the row to `csv_data`. A `row` is a list of strings.

The next step of the process is to create the Excel spreadsheet. To add data to your `Workbook`, you iterate over each row in `csv_data` and `append()` them to your Worksheet. Finally, you save the Excel spreadsheet.

When you run this code, you will have an Excel spreadsheet that looks like this:

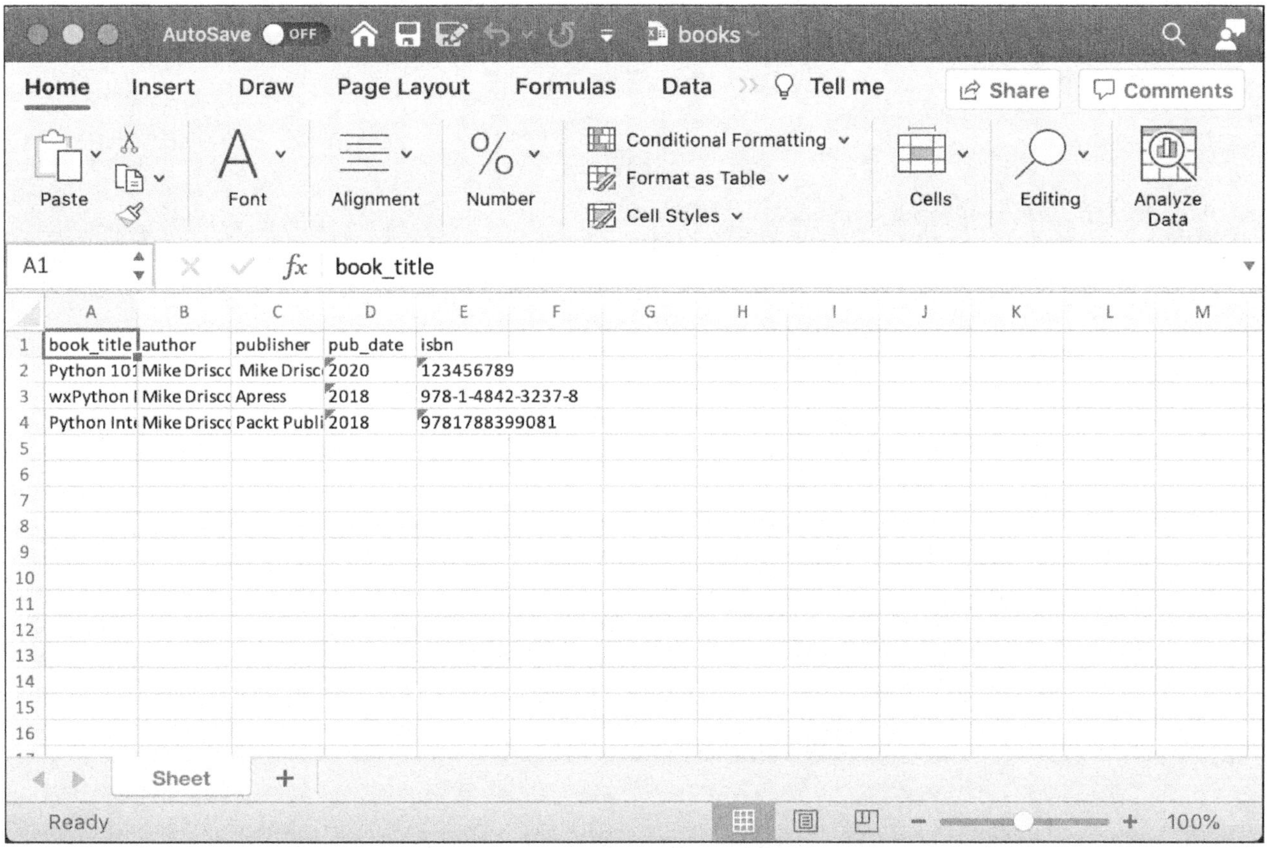

Fig. 8-1: Converted CSV to Excel Spreadsheet

You are now able to convert a CSV file to an Excel spreadsheet in less than twenty-five lines of code!

Now you are ready to learn how to convert an Excel spreadsheet to a CSV file!

Converting an Excel Spreadsheet to CSV

Converting an Excel spreadsheet to a CSV file can be useful if you need other processes to consume the data. Another potential need for a CSV file is when you need to share your Excel spreadsheet with someone who doesn't have a spreadsheet program to open it. While rare, this may happen.

You can convert an Excel spreadsheet to a CSV file using Python. Create a new file named `excel_-to_csv.py` and add the following code:

```
# excel_to_csv.py

import csv
import openpyxl

from openpyxl import load_workbook


def excel_to_csv(excel_file, csv_file):
    workbook = load_workbook(filename=excel_file)
    sheet = workbook.active
    csv_data = []

    # Read data from Excel
    for value in sheet.iter_rows(values_only=True):
        csv_data.append(list(value))

    # Write to CSV
    with open(csv_file, 'w') as csv_file_obj:
        writer = csv.writer(csv_file_obj, delimiter=',')
        for line in csv_data:
            writer.writerow(line)


if __name__ == "__main__":
    excel_to_csv("books.xlsx", "new_books.csv")
```

Once again you only need the `csv` and `openpyxl` modules to do the conversion. This time, you load the Excel spreadsheet first and iterate over the Worksheet using the `iter_rows` method. The `value` you receive in each iteration of `iter_tools` is a list of strings. You append the list of strings to `csv_data`.

The next step is to create a `csv.writer()`. Then you iterate over each list of strings in `csv_data` and call `writerow()` to add it to your CSV file.

Once your code finishes, you will have a brand new CSV file!

Wrapping Up

Converting a CSV file to an Excel spreadsheet is easy to do with Python. It's a useful tool that you can use to take in data from your clients or other data sources and transform it into something that you can present to your company.

You can apply cell styling to the data as you write it to your Worksheet too. By applying cell styling, you can make your data stand out with different fonts or background row colors.

Try this code out on your own Excel or CSV files and see what you can do.

Chapter 9 - Using Pandas with Excel

OpenPyXL is not the only tool you can use to read and write Excel spreadsheets. One popular package used by the scientific Python community that can read and write Excel spreadsheets is Pandas.

If you look in the Pandas documentation, you will discover that it is using the following Python packages for reading and writing Excel though:

- xlrd - Reading Excel
- xlwt - Writing Excel (xls)
- xlsxwriter - Writing Excel
- OpenPyXL - Reading and Writing (xlsx)
- pyxlsb - Reading xlsb files

Pandas doesn't have Excel file manipulation built-in. Instead, Pandas is off-loading that functionality to one or more external Python packages. When you search for reading and writing Excel files, you will discover that Pandas is a popular choice. The reason is that Pandas is incredibly popular for data analysis, and it provides a thin wrapper around other packages.

Pandas makes working with Excel easier for some developers because they already use Pandas and don't need to switch to another tool.

In this chapter, you will learn how to use Pandas to do the following:

- Read Excel spreadsheets
- Read multiple Excel worksheets
- Write DataFrames to Excel
- Convert CSV to Excel with Pandas

Your first step is to get Pandas installed so that you can start using it to read and write Excel!

Install Pandas and Dependencies

Installing Pandas is nice and easy with `pip`. All you need to do is the following:

```
python3 -m pip install pandas
```

If you are using Anaconda, you will want to use the `conda` package manager instead. Here is the proper `conda` command:

```
conda install pandas
```

Once you have Pandas installed, you should be good to go if you plan to work with the **xlsx** file type. You should already have OpenPyXL installed. If you do not have OpenPyXL installed, then the code in this chapter will not work. If you plan to work with the **xls** file type, you will need to install `xlrd` and `xlwt`. You can install these additional packages using `pip` or `conda`.

Now that you have everything you need, you can move on and learn how to read an Excel spreadsheet with Pandas!

Read Excel Spreadsheets

You will need an Excel spreadsheet so that you have something to read with Pandas. There is an Excel spredsheet provided on this book's GitHub code repository[18] called **books.xlsx**.

Now open up your Python editor and create a new file named **read_excel.py**. Then enter the following code:

```
# read_excel.py

import pandas as pd

df = pd.read_excel('books.xlsx')

print(df)
```

Here you import the `pandas` package as `pd` where `pd` is an alias for `pandas`. Then you call `read_excel()` and give it the path to your Excel file. The `read_excel()` function returns a `DataFrame`, which is a two-dimensional data structure for holding tabular data.

Finally, you print out the `DataFrame`. The following shows what the result of running this code displays:

```
           book_title          author  ... pub_date           isbn
0          Python 101  Mike Driscoll  ...     2020      123456789
1    wxPython Recipes  Mike Driscoll  ...     2018  978-1-4842-3237-8
2  Python Interviews  Mike Driscoll  ...     2018      9781788399081

[3 rows x 5 columns]
```

You can use Pandas to load up a data set that you have stored in an Excel spreadsheet. Once you convert the spreadsheet to a Pandas `DataFrame`, you can analyze the data.

Pandas will also let you choose which sheets to load. You will find out how to do load different sheets next!

[18]https://github.com/driscollis/automating_excel_with_python

Read Multiple Excel Worksheets

Pandas allows you to read an Excel file using `read_excel()`. By default, this function reads all the sheets in your Excel spreadsheet. In the previous example, you used an Excel spreadsheet that had one worksheet. You will use the **sample.xlsx** file from this book's GitHub code repository[19] as it has two worksheets in it.

Instead of reading the entire spreadsheet as you did in the last example, this time you will pass in the `sheet_name` as a parameter to `read_excel()`. The `sheet_name` can be used to specify which sheet you want to load, either by index or by sheet name.

To see how this works, create a new Python file named `read_excel_by_sheet.py`. Then enter this code:

```
# read_excel_by_sheet.py

import pandas as pd

sheet_one_data = pd.read_excel('sample.xlsx', sheet_name=0)
sheet_two_data = pd.read_excel('sample.xlsx', sheet_name="Sales")

print(sheet_one_data)
print(sheet_two_data)
```

In this first `read_excel()` example, you pass in the `sheet_name` by index. Here you use zero as the index. Zero, in this case, refers to sheet one. The second example passes in the `sheet_name` as a string. The string must match the sheet's actual name.

This code will print out two `DataFrames`, one for each sheet when you run this code. The output will look like this:

```
                Books      Unnamed: 1  ... Unnamed: 5 Unnamed: 6
0               Title          Author  ...        NaN        NaN
1          Python 101  Mike Driscoll  ...        NaN        NaN
2    wxPython Recipes  Mike Driscoll  ...        NaN        NaN
3  Python Interviews  Mike Driscoll  ...        NaN        NaN

[4 rows x 7 columns]
                Title  Amazon  Leanpub  Gumroad
0          Python 101     100      433       10
1    wxPython Recipes       5        0        0
2  Python Interviews      10        0        0
```

[19] https://github.com/driscollis/automating_excel_with_python

Now it's your turn! Try this code with your own Excel spreadsheets and modify it to work with your sheet names. You will quickly learn to use Pandas to read Excel files by testing this code yourself with your data.

You are now ready to learn how to turn Pandas DataFrames into an Excel spreadsheet!

Write DataFrames to Excel

When you are doing data analysis with Pandas, you will be working with `DataFrames`. However, when you finish your analysis, you may want to share the results with non-technical people. Pandas provides the `to_excel()` method for this purpose. You can convert your `DataFrames` to Excel!

Create a new file named `create_excel.py` and then enter the following code:

```
# create_excel.py

import pandas as pd

df = pd.DataFrame([[100, 433, 10], [34, 10, 0], [75, 125, 5]],
                  index=['Python 101', 'Python 201', 'wxPython'],
                  columns=['Amazon', 'Leanpub', 'Gumroad'])
df.to_excel('pandas_to_excel.xlsx', sheet_name='Books')
```

Here you create a Pandas `DataFrame`. The `index` parameter contains the first item in each row, starting in row two. The `columns` parameter contains the column labels, starting in column B. The other lists are mapped as rows in Excel when running the `to_excel()` method. You set the `sheet_name` yourself here, but the sheet name would default to `Sheet1` if you didn't.

When you run this code, you will get the following Excel spreadsheet:

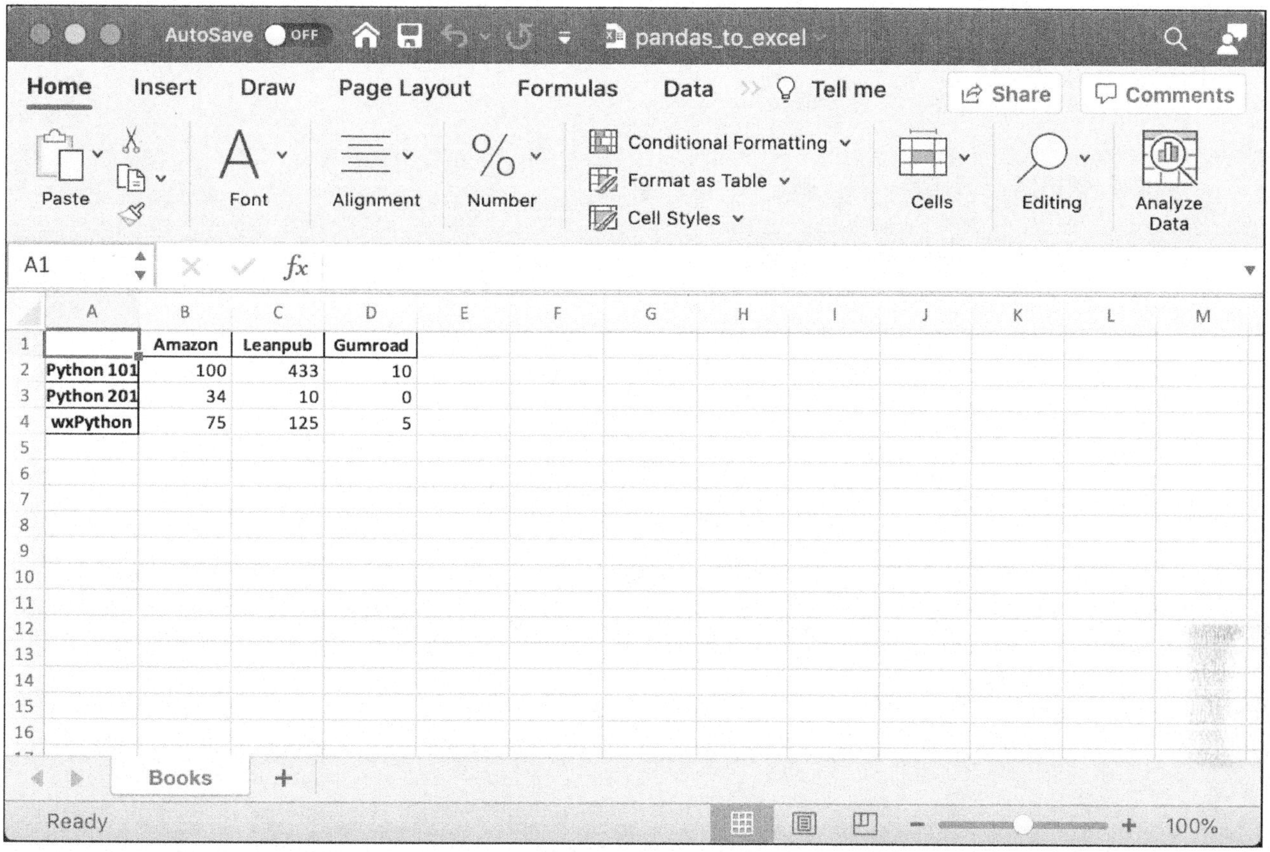

Fig. 9-1: Converted Pandas DataFrame to Excel Spreadsheet

If you have multiple `DataFrames` that you want to convert to Excel, Pandas provides the `ExcelWriter()` class. The `ExcelWriter()` provides an object that is accepted by the `to_excel()` method.

Open up a new Python file and name it `create_excel_sheets.py`, then add this code:

```
# create_excel_sheets.py

import pandas as pd


def create_multiple_sheets(path):
    df = pd.DataFrame(
        [[100, 433, 10], [34, 10, 0], [75, 125, 5]],
        index=["Python 101", "Python 201", "wxPython"],
        columns=["Amazon", "Leanpub", "Gumroad"],
    )
    df2 = pd.DataFrame(
        [[150, 233, 5], [5, 15, 0], [10, 120, 5]],
        index=[
```

```
            "Jupyter Notebook",
            "Python Interview",
            "Pillow: Image Processing with Python",
        ],
        columns=["Amazon", "Leanpub", "Gumroad"],
    )
    with pd.ExcelWriter(path) as writer:
        df.to_excel(writer, sheet_name="Books")
        df2.to_excel(writer, sheet_name="More Books")


if __name__ == "__main__":
    create_multiple_sheets("pandas_to_excel_sheets.xlsx")
```

In this example, you have two `DataFrames`. When you turn them into an Excel spreadsheet, you create an `ExcelWriter` object that you pass to each of the `DataFrame` instance's `to_excel()` method. You convert each `DataFrame` into a Worksheet in the Excel spreadsheet.

When you run this code, you will end up with a spreadsheet that contains two Worksheets and looks like this:

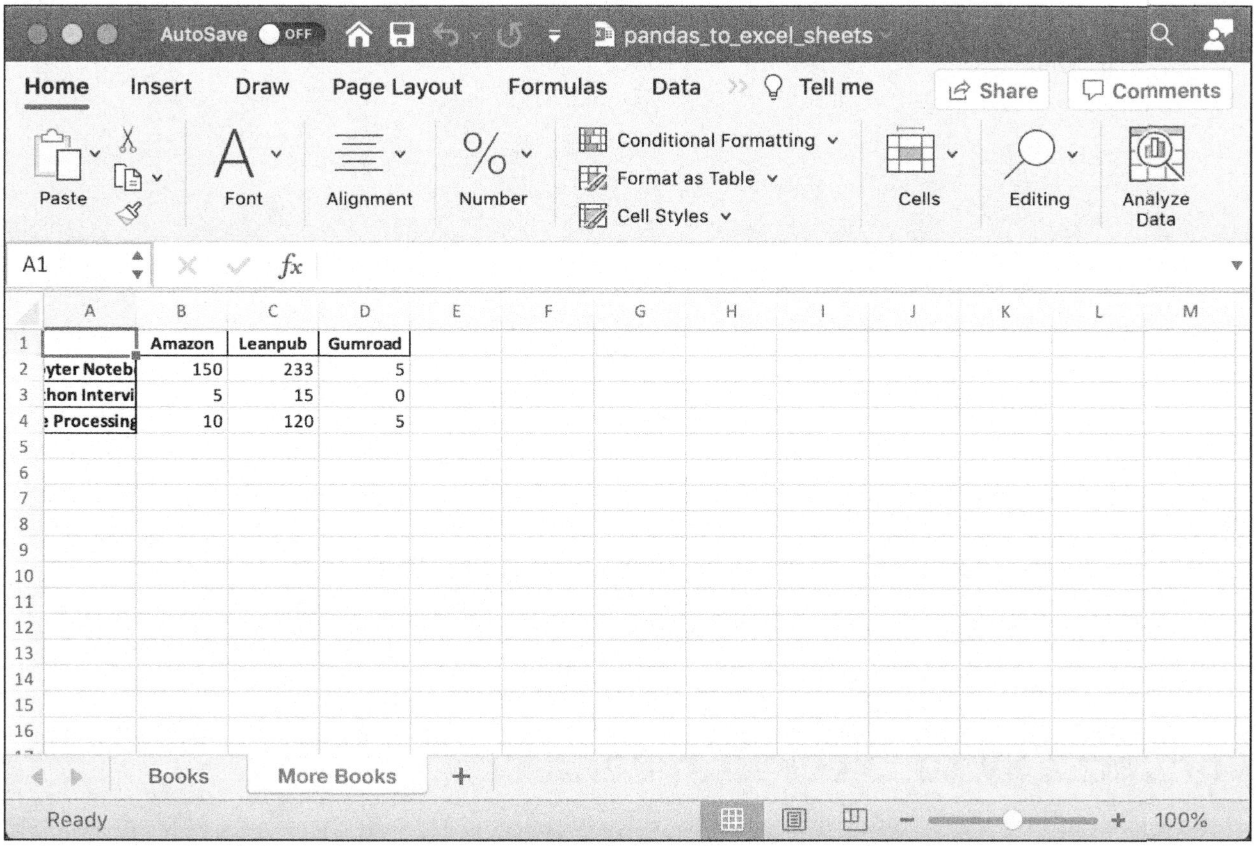

Fig. 9-2: Convert Multiple Pandas DataFrames to Excel

OpenPyXL has support for the Pandas `DataFrame` built-in. All you need to do is import `dataframe_to_rows` from `openpyxl.utils.dataframe` and it will convert a `DataFrame` to a row that is added to your OpenPyXL `Worksheet` object.

To see how that works, create a new file named `add_dataframes_to_excel.py` and enter the following code:

```
# add_dataframes_to_excel.py

import pandas as pd
import openpyxl
from openpyxl.utils.dataframe import dataframe_to_rows


def add_dataframes_to_excel(path):
    workbook = openpyxl.Workbook()
    sheet = workbook.active

    df = pd.DataFrame(
        [[100, 433, 10], [34, 10, 0], [75, 125, 5]],
```

```
        index=["Python 101", "Python 201", "wxPython"],
        columns=["Amazon", "Leanpub", "Gumroad"],
    )

    for row in dataframe_to_rows(df):
        sheet.append(row)
    workbook.save(path)


if __name__ == "__main__":
    add_dataframes_to_excel("df_to_excel.xlsx")
```

This code probably looks familiar. You create a `Workbook()` object and extract the active Worksheet. Then you have the Pandas `DataFrame` from earlier. The `for` loop is the new code where you convert the `DataFrame` to a series of rows that you can `append()` to your Worksheet.

Running this code will create an Excel spreadsheet that looks the same as the one you created at the beginning of this section.

Convert CSV to Excel with Pandas

The Pandas package can read CSV files in addition to Excel files. You can use this ability to convert CSV to Excel using Pandas.

To get started, create a new file named `csv_to_excel_pandas.py` and add the following code to it:

```
# csv_to_excel_pandas.py

import pandas as pd


def csv_to_excel(csv_file, excel_file, sheet_name):
    df = pd.read_csv(csv_file)
    df.to_excel(excel_file, sheet_name=sheet_name)


if __name__ == "__main__":
    csv_to_excel("books.csv", "pandas_csv_to_excel.xlsx", "Books")
```

Here you read in the CSV file using the `read_csv()` method, which takes the path to the CSV file (or a file-like object) and converts the file to a Pandas `DataFrame`. Next, you call `to_excel()` to convert the `DataFrame` to an Excel spreadsheet.

Your new Excel spreadsheet will look like this:

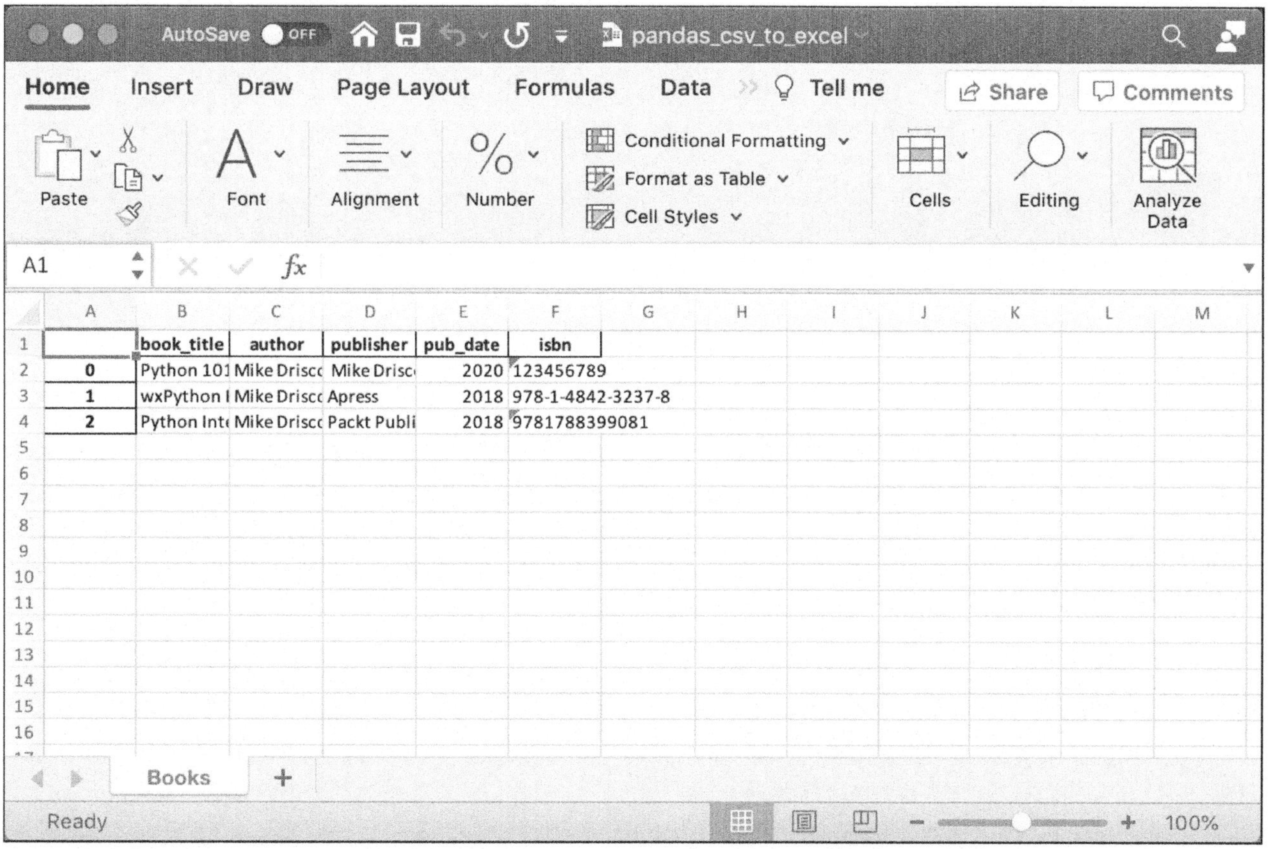

Fig. 9-3: Convert a CSV file to Excel with Pandas

Now you know how to use Pandas to convert a CSV file to an Excel spreadsheet!

Wrapping Up

Millions of users use Pandas to do data analysis and number crunching. This chapter doesn't even begin to scratch the surface of what you can do with Pandas. However, the purpose of this chapter is to teach you how to use Pandas to read and write Excel spreadsheets.

With that in mind, you learned how to do the following:

- Read Excel spreadsheets
- Read multiple Excel worksheets
- Write DataFrames to Excel
- Convert CSV to Excel with Pandas

Spend some time reading your spreadsheets with Pandas. If you are already familiar with Pandas and have some old code, try turning your existing `DataFrames` into Excel. Practicing with Pandas will help cement these ideas in your mind.

Chapter 10 - Python and Google Sheets

There are alternatives to using Microsoft Excel for managing your data in spreadsheets. One popular option is to use Google Sheets, which is an online option. Google Sheets provides many of the same features that Microsoft Excel does but is primarily only in the cloud. Microsoft has a cloud version of Excel in their Office 365 offering.

There are several different Python packages you can use to connect to Google Sheets. For this chapter, you will focus on one called `gspread`. You can learn more about `gspread` by checking out their GitHub repository[20].

In this chapter, you will learn how to do the following:

- Install `gspread`
- Create credentials with Google
- Create a new Google Sheet
- Read Google Sheets
- Update Google Sheets
- Delete Google Sheets

Now that you know what you will learn, it's time to get started!

Install gspread

The `gspread` package does not come with the Python programming language, so you need to install it yourself. You can do that using the `pip` utility.

Here is the command you need to run:

```
python3 -m pip install gspread
```

You also need to install the `oauth2client` package. You can use `pip` for that as well:

```
python3 -m pip install oauth2client
```

Now that you have `gspread` and `oauth2client` installed, you will need to set up your Google credentials and scopes so you can access Google Sheets with Python!

[20]https://github.com/burnash/gspread

Create Credentials with Google

There are lots of different directions on how to get set up from Google's side. You need to be able to access both **Google Sheets** and **Google Drive**. Here are some links that talk about how to get everything ready:

- https://docs.gspread.org/en/latest/oauth2.html
- https://developers.google.com/sheets/api/quickstart/python

You should follow the directions in the links above to make sure you have everything set up that you need before proceeding.

These are the primary steps that you need to go through. These steps may change, so refer to the links above if the following instructions don't work for you.

Your first step is to open up the Google Cloud Platform[21] (GCP) site, then create a new project. If you don't already have any projects of your own in GCP, it will look something like this:

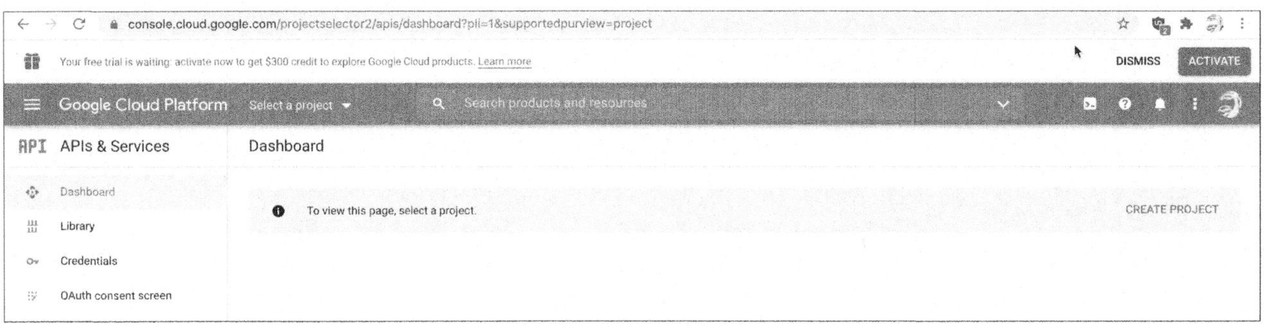

Fig. 10-1: Creating a New Project

If you do have other projects, your page may look much different than this initial page. You may need to click on the project combobox on the top left to find the "New Project" option.

After clicking **New Project**, you give it a name. For this tutorial, you can call it **PySpread**:

[21]https://console.cloud.google.com/

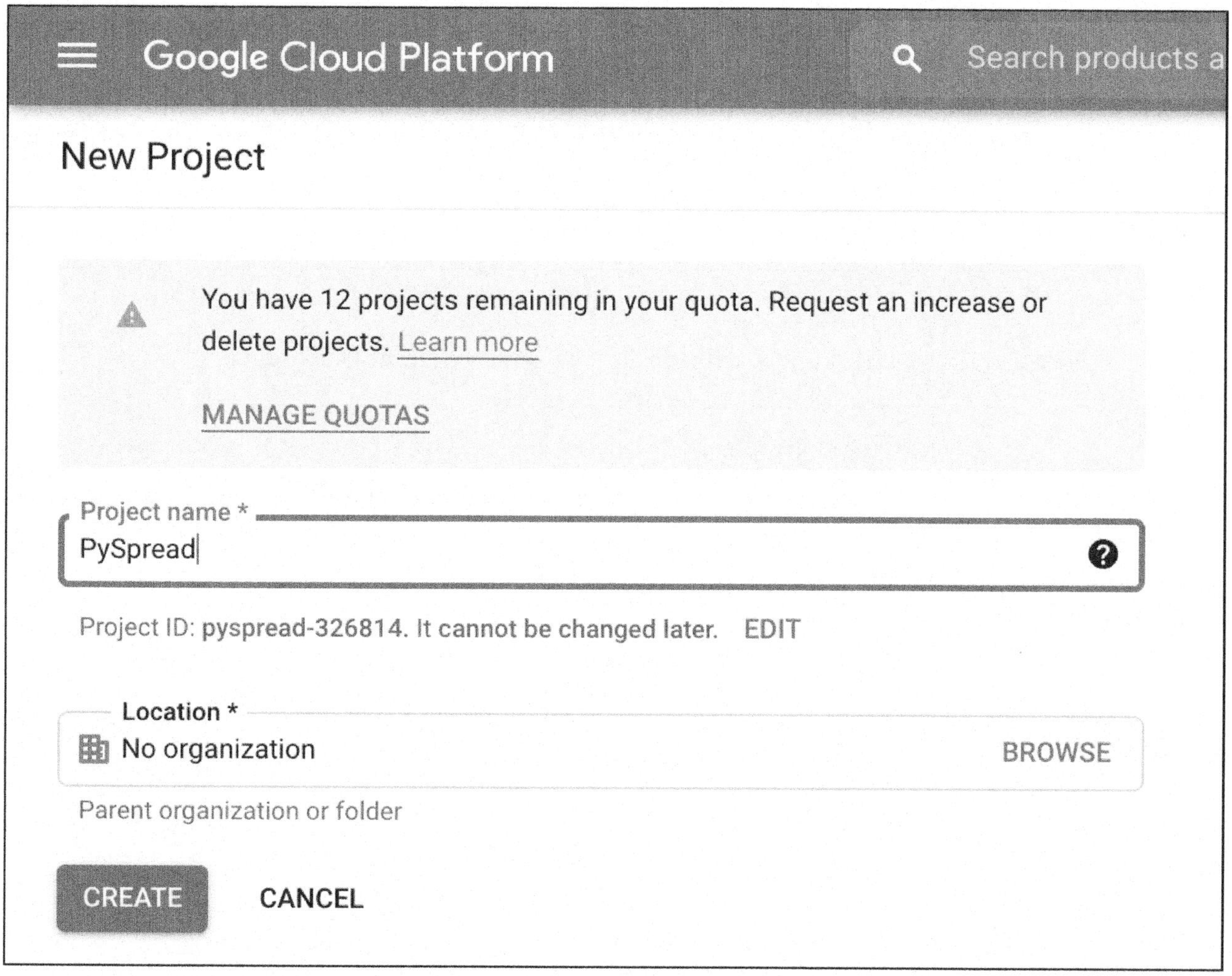

Fig. 10-2: Naming a New Project

Some of the websites that give instructions on this topic say that you should Enable APIs. Make sure that you have your new project selected so that you enable the APIs on the correct project.

Specifically, the APIs you would want to enable are Google Sheets and Google Drive. These steps seem to be optional, depending on how you plan to connect to Google Sheets. If you connect as a **Service Account**, this step is unnecessary. But it does appear to be required if you connect to Google without a Service Account.

For completeness, you will learn how to Enable APIs in Google. Click **Enable APIs and Services**:

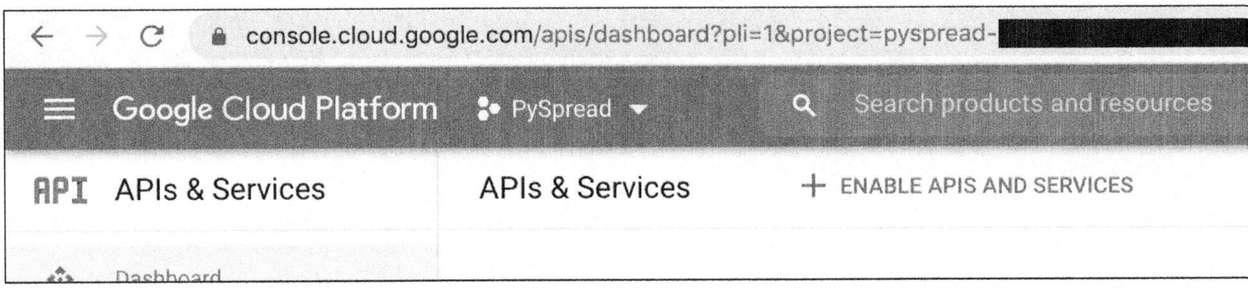

Fig. 10-3: Enabling APIs (Optional)

When you click that link / button, you will end up at a screen that looks like this:

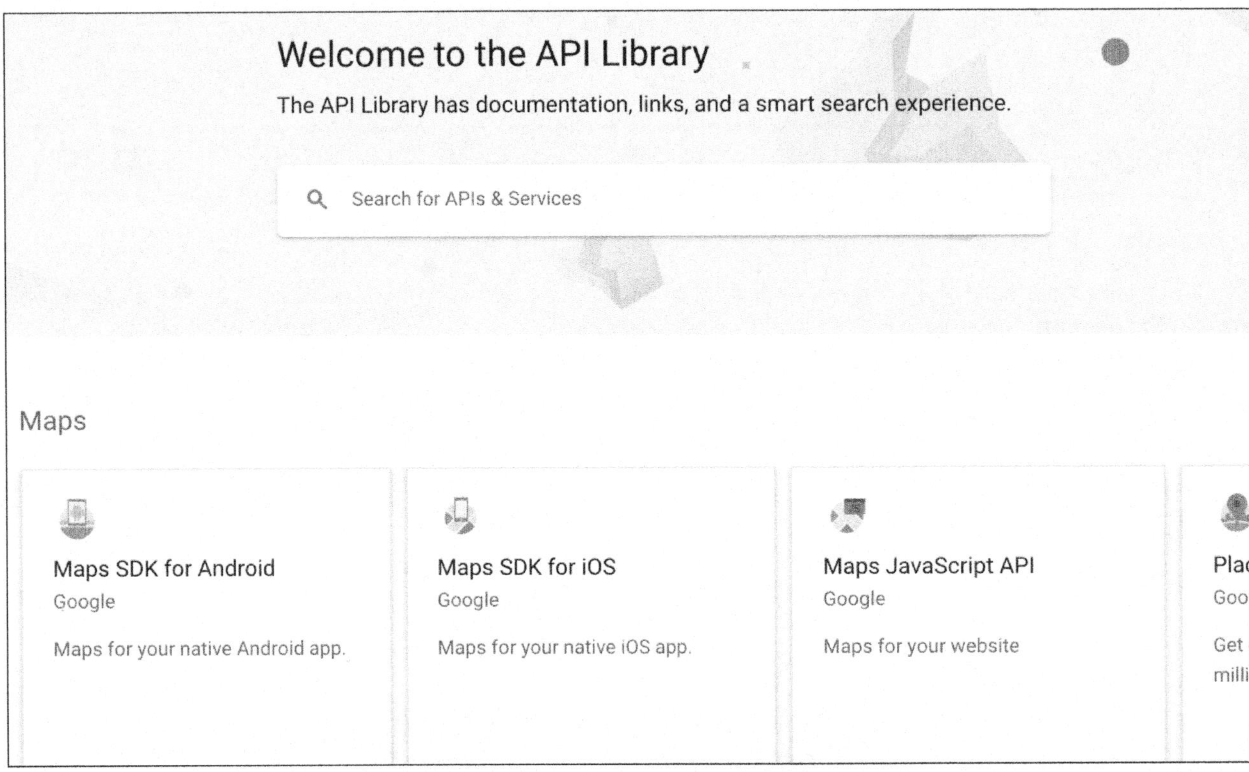

Fig. 10-4: Search APIs (Optional)

Search for Google Sheets, and you should be able to find it:

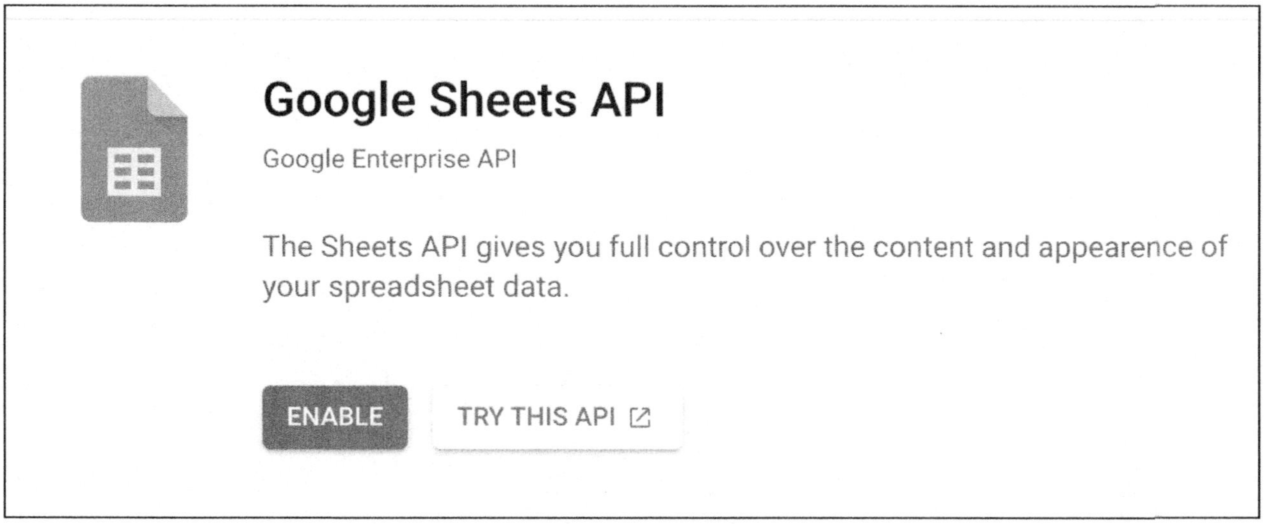

Fig. 10-5: Google Sheets (Optional)

)
After adding Google Sheets, go back and search for Google Drive:

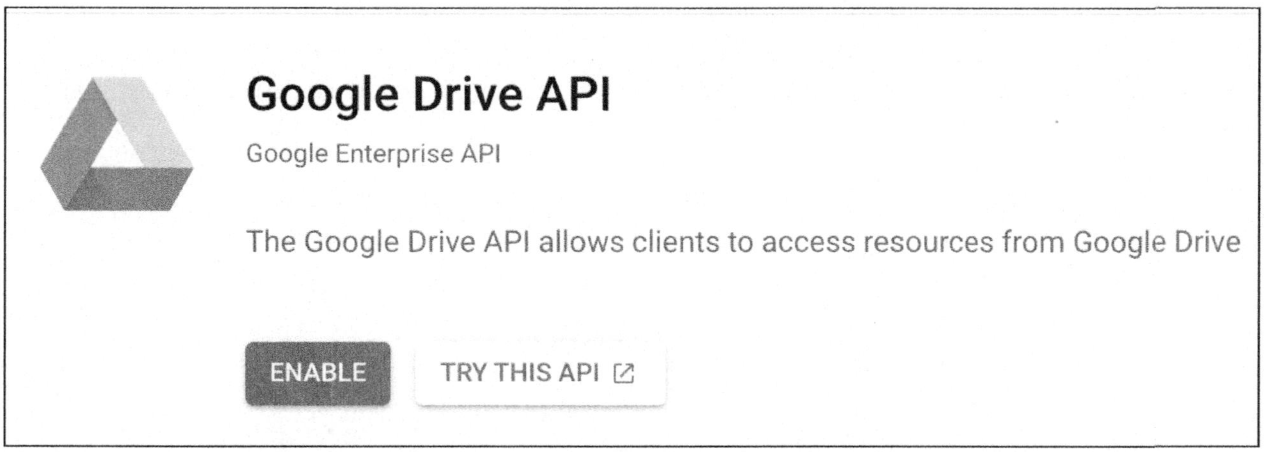

Fig. 10-6: Google Drive (Optional)

Now that you have the APIs you need for your application, you need to create credentials:

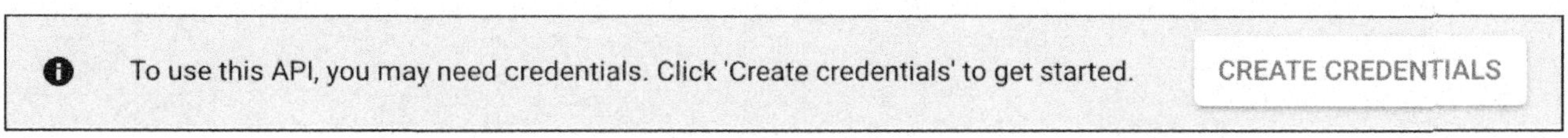

Fig. 10-7: Create Credentials

Creating credentials is required no matter which way you end up hooking into Google Sheets. For this tutorial, you will create a **Service Account**

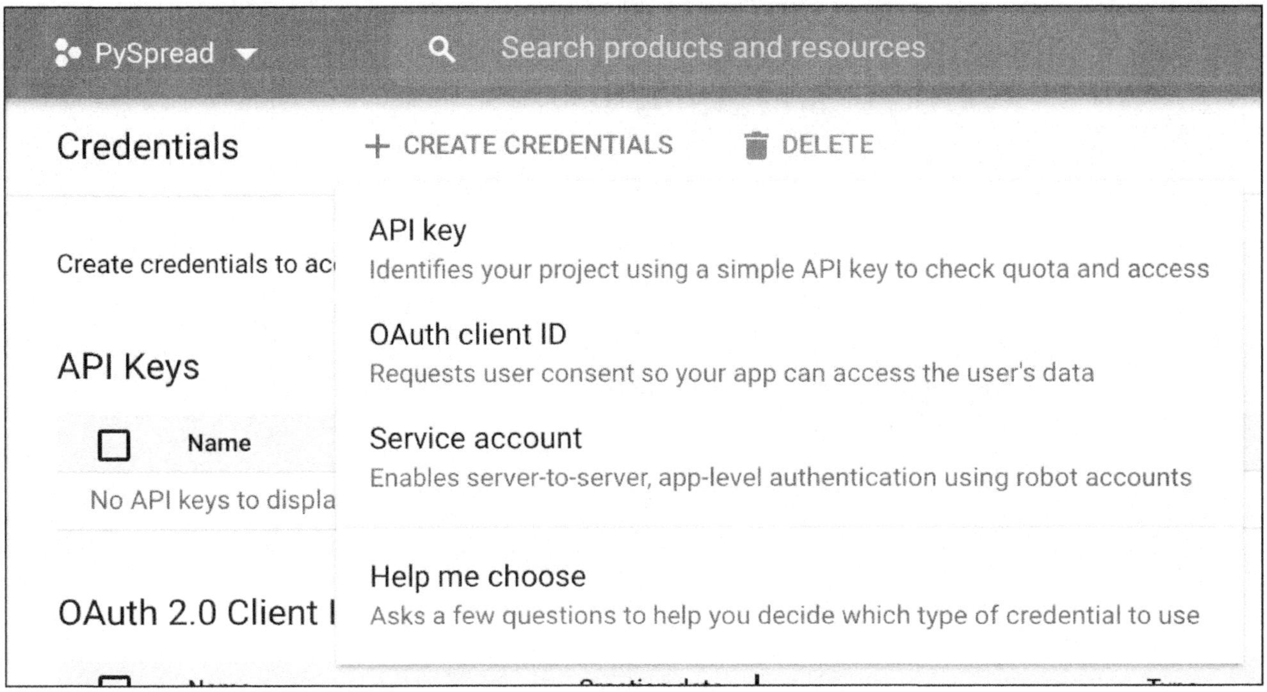

Fig. 10-8: Create Service Account Credentials

It would be best if you gave the Service Account a name as well. For consistency, you can name it **pyspread** in lowercase:

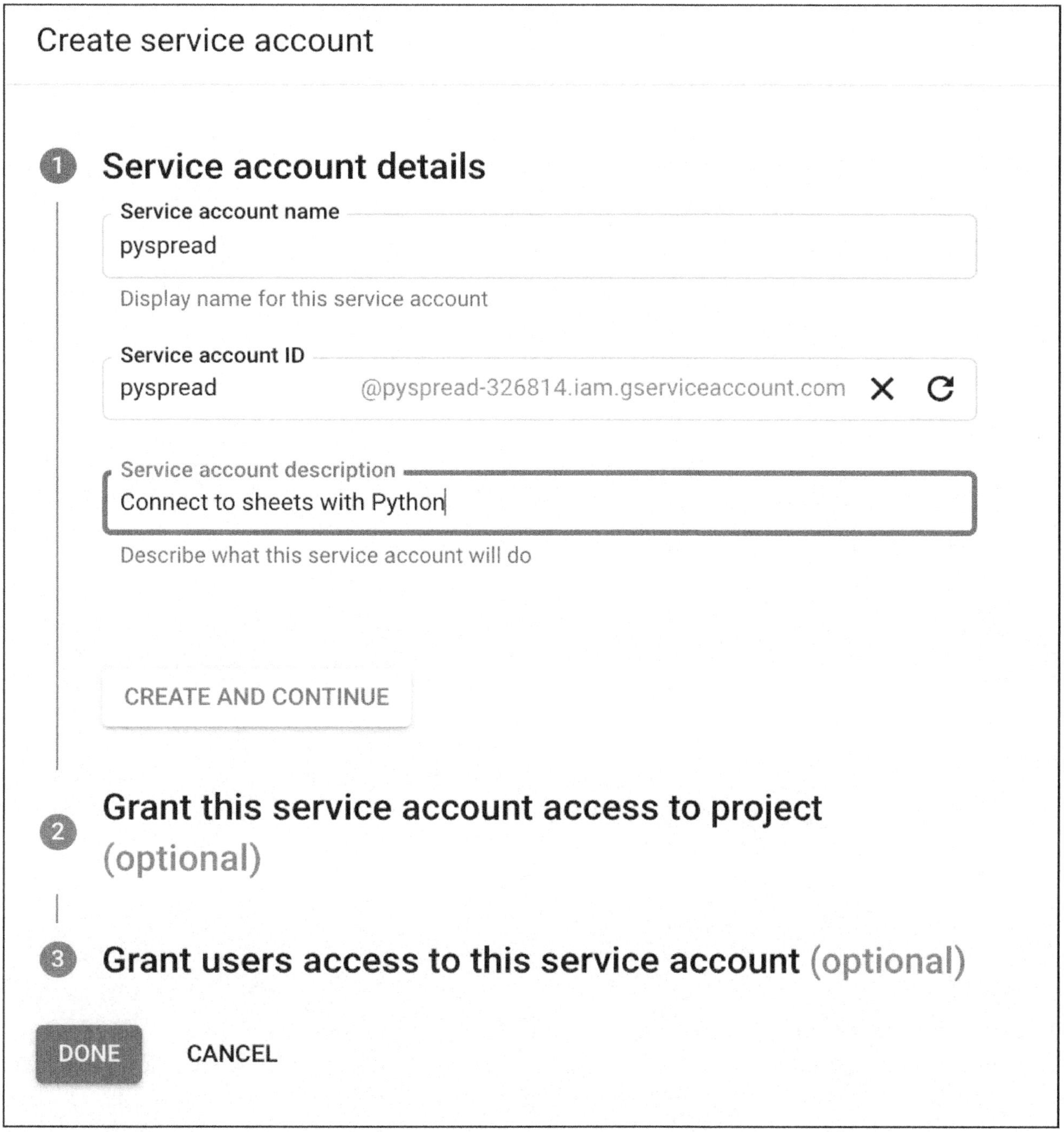

Fig. 10-9: Name Service Account Credentials

You can hit **Done** at this point as the other configuration steps here are optional.

You are almost done! However, you need to do one more step to make the Service Account work for you. Click on the little pencil-like icon on the far right. It will let you edit your Service Account:

Fig. 10-10: Modifying Your Service Account Credentials

Click on the **Keys** tab and then hit the **Add Key** button. This button will allow you to download the pyspread Service Account JSON file:

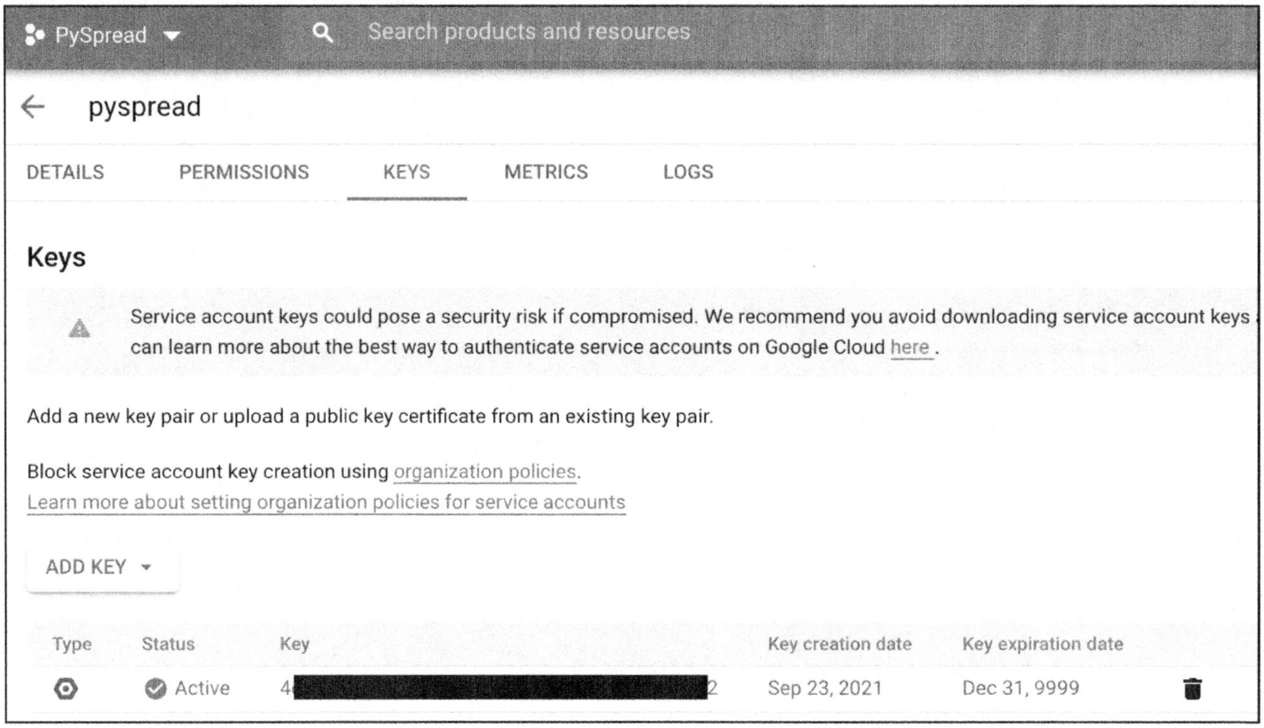

Fig. 10-11: Modifying Your Service Account Credentials

After downloading the file, you can place it in the same folder as your `gspread` application code will go in. Or you can remember to use the absolute path to the JSON file when you call your `gspread` application.

Note that Google does have a warning against using the JSON file for a Service Account as the credentials do not expire. Use at your own risk or go back to Google's site and learn how to connect to Google Sheets using a more complicated process.

Now you are ready to start working with Google Sheets using Python!

Create a New Google Sheet

Creating a new Google Sheet using Python isn't hard. You can create a Google Sheet in just over 30 lines of code!

Open up your Python editor of choice and create a new file named `hello_gsheet.py` to get started. Then enter the following code:

```
# hello_gsheet.py

import gspread
from oauth2client.service_account import ServiceAccountCredentials


def authenticate(credentials):
    """
    Authenticate with Google and get the client object
    """
    scope = [
        "https://www.googleapis.com/auth/spreadsheets",
        "https://www.googleapis.com/auth/drive.file",
        "https://www.googleapis.com/auth/drive",
    ]
    creds = ServiceAccountCredentials.from_json_keyfile_name(credentials, scope)
    client = gspread.authorize(creds)
    return client


def main():
    """
    Create a Google Sheet
    """
    # Pass in the file location for the JSON file you created
    client = authenticate("pyspread.json")
    try:
        workbook = client.open("test")
        print("Test Sheet opened")
    except:
        workbook = client.create("test")
        print("Test Sheet created")
    sheet = workbook.sheet1
    sheet.update("A1", [[1, 2], [3, 4]])
    workbook.share("YOUR_EMAIL_ADDRESS", perm_type="user", role="writer")


if __name__ == "__main__":
    main()
```

This code is split up into two functions:

- `authenticate()` - used to authenticate with Google
- `main()` - Run your program

In `authenticate()`, you specify what scopes you want your application to access when connecting to Google. Then you pass it your credentials JSON file that you downloaded from Google Cloud. Assuming you authenticate successfully, `authenticate()` will return a client object.

In `main()`, you attempt to open a Google Sheet named "test". If it already exists, the `client.open()` will return a Workbook object. In the case that "test" does not exist, you create the Google Sheet using `client.create()`.

Next, you add data to cells A1, A2, B1 and B2. You then use the `share()` method to send your email the "test" Google Sheet.

If you open your new Google Sheet, it will look like this:

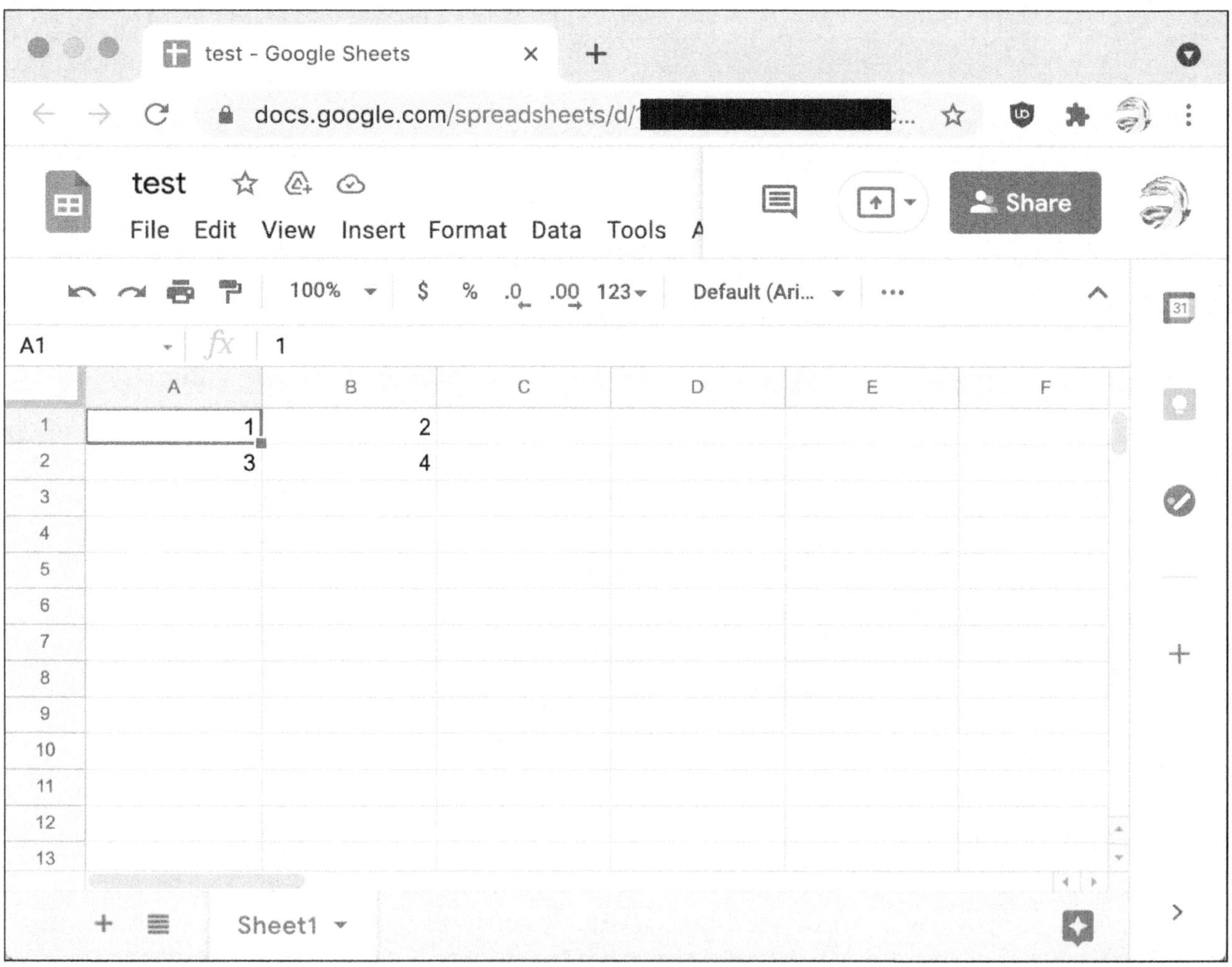

Fig. 10-12: A New Google Sheet

Now you know how to create a Google Sheet with Python! You are ready to learn how to read data from Google Sheets!

Read Google Sheets

Reading a Google Sheet requires you to use the same code you wrote in the previous section. Once you have the Google client object, you have three different options for opening the Google Sheet.

The most obvious is to use `open()`:

```
workbook = client.open("test")
```

You can also open a Google Sheet by key. The key comes from the URL, which you can extract yourself:

```
workbook = client.open_by_key("YOUR_HASHED_GOOGLE_KEY")
```

The last option is to simply use the URL itself:

```
workbook = client.open_by_url('https://docs.google.com/spreadsheet/ccc?key=0Bm...END\
_OF_KEY')
```

For this tutorial, you will use `open()` since you already know the name of the Google Sheet that you wish to read. Open up your Python editor and create a new file named `read_gsheet.py`. Then enter the following code:

```
# read_gsheet.py

import gspread
from oauth2client.service_account import ServiceAccountCredentials


def authenticate(credentials):
    scope = [
        "https://www.googleapis.com/auth/spreadsheets",
        "https://www.googleapis.com/auth/drive.file",
        "https://www.googleapis.com/auth/drive",
    ]
    creds = ServiceAccountCredentials.from_json_keyfile_name(credentials, scope)
    client = gspread.authorize(creds)
    return client
```

```
def main():
    client = authenticate("pyspread.json")
    try:
        workbook = client.open("test")
        print("Test Sheet opened")
    except Exception:
        print("Error opening test spreadsheet")
        return
    sheet = workbook.sheet1
    print("Worksheets: " + str(workbook.worksheets()))
    print(f"All values on row 1: {sheet.row_values(1)}")
    print(f"All values in column 1: {sheet.col_values(1)}")
    print(f"All values in worksheet: {sheet.get_all_values()}")
    # Get all values from worksheet as a list of dictionaries
    values = sheet.get_all_records()
    print(f"All records: {values=}")


if __name__ == "__main__":
    main()
```

This code may look a little familiar. The `authenticate()` function remains the same, but you did update your `main()` function. In this example, you attempt to open the "test" Google Sheet. If not found, you print an error and exit the program.

If the worksheet is found, then you extract data from it. You use the following methods:

- `worksheets()` - Returns a list of Worksheet objects
- `row_values()` - Returns a list of the values in the row specified
- `col_values()` - Returns a list of values in the column specified
- `get_all_values()` - Returns a list of lists of the values found. Each nested list represents a row
- `get_all_records()` - Returns a list of dictionaries

When you run this code, you will see the following output:

```
Test Sheet opened
Worksheets: [<Worksheet 'Sheet1' id:0>]
All values on row 1: ['1', '2']
All values in column 1: ['1', '3']
All values in worksheet: [['1', '2'], ['3', '4']]
All records: values=[{'1': 3, '2': 4}]
```

You can also tell `gspread` to get specific values from your Google Sheet. For example, here's how you would get the value of "B1":

```
value = sheet.acell('B1').value
```

Alternatively, you can also get the value by using row and column coordinates:

```
# Get value from row 1, column 2
value = sheet.cell(1, 2).value
```

If the cell contains a formula that you want to extract, you would do one of the following:

```
# Using cell name
formula = sheet.acell('B1', value_render_option='FORMULA').value

# Using cell coordinates
formula = sheet.cell(1, 2, value_render_option='FORMULA').value
```

Now that you have a good foundation in reading Google Sheets, you are ready to learn about updating their data!

Update Google Sheets

There are three ways you can update a Google Sheet's cell using `gspread`. You will go over each method.

The first method uses the `update()` method. You pass in the name of the cell and its new value:

```
sheet.update('B1', 'Python Rocks!')
```

You can also use row and column coordinates to set a cell's value using the `update_cell()` method:

```
sheet.update_cell(1, 2, 'Python Rocks!')
```

`Gspread` also supports updating a range of cells using the `update()` method:

```
sheet.update('A1:B2', [[1, 2], [3, 4]])
```

Now you are ready to learn how to delete a Google Sheet!

Delete Google Sheets

You can automate the deletion of Google Sheets with `gspread` as well. All you need is the `del_worksheet()` method which you use from your Workbook object.

Here is an example where the `main()` function is updated:

```
def main():
    client = authenticate("pyspread.json")
    try:
        workbook = client.open("test")
        print("Test Sheet opened")
    except:
        workbook = client.create("test")
        print("Test Sheet created")
    sheet = workbook.sheet1
    workbook.del_worksheet(sheet)
```

To delete a worksheet from your Workbook, you need to have the worksheet object. Then you pass the worksheet to `del_worksheet()` to remove it from your Google documents.

Sometimes you may only need to clear the worksheet of its data. In that case, you can use the worksheet's `clear()` method:

```
sheet.clear()
```

The `clear()` method will clear the entire worksheet.

If you only need to clear one cell or a range of cells, you can use `batch_clear()`. The `batch_clear()` method takes a list of strings that specify a cell, a range of cells or multiple ranges to clear:

```
sheet.batch_clear(["A1:B1", "C2:E2"])
```

Now you know the basics of deleting and clearing a Google Sheet!

Wrapping Up

This chapter taught you how to connect Python to Google Sheets using the `gspread` package. Specifically, you learned about the following:

- Install `gspread`
- Create credentials with Google
- Create a new Google Sheet
- Read Google Sheets
- Update Google Sheets
- Delete Google Sheets

This chapter does not cover everything that you can do with `gspread`. The `gspread` package allows you to search for cells as well as format the cells. There is also integration support for `NumPy` and `Pandas` in `gspread`. See the `gspread` documentation[22] for more details.

In the meantime, practice what you have learned in this chapter and see how well you can automate Google Sheets with Python!

[22]https://docs.gspread.org

Chapter 11 - XlsxWriter

OpenPyXL isn't the only Python package for Excel. There are many others. One of the best, most full-featured alternatives to OpenPyXL is XlsxWriter. This chapter aims to give you an overview of what you can do with XlsxWriter. However, it will not be exhaustive because XlsxWriter has many of the same features plus a few different ones that OpenPyXL does not.

XlsxWriter is for creating Excel spreadsheets only. You cannot use XlsxWriter to read an Excel spreadsheet!

In this chapter, you will focus on the following:

- Creating an Excel spreadsheet
- Formatting cells
- Adding a chart
- Creating Sparklines
- Data validation

Before you can start using XlsxWriter, you need to install it.

Installation

XlsxWriter doesn't come with Python, so you will need to install it. You can use Python's `pip` utility to get XlsxWriter on your system by using the following command:

```
python3 -m pip install XlsxWriter
```

Now you have XlsxWriter installed on your computer. You are ready to get started by creating your first spreadsheet with XlsxWriter!

Creating an Excel Spreadsheet

Creating an Excel Spreadsheet with XlsxWriter can be done with only a few lines of code. To see how this works, you will need to open your Python editor and create a new file named `create_-spreadsheet.py`.

Then enter the following code:

```python
# create_spreadsheet.py

import xlsxwriter


def create_workbook(path):
    workbook = xlsxwriter.Workbook(path)
    sheet = workbook.add_worksheet(name="Hello")
    data = [["Python 101", 1000],
            ["Jupyter Notebook 101", 400],
            ["ReportLab: PDF Processing", 250]
    ]

    row = 0
    col = 0
    for book, sales in data:
        sheet.write(row, col, book)
        sheet.write(row, col + 1, sales)
        row += 1

    sheet2 = workbook.add_worksheet(name="World")
    workbook.close()


if __name__ == "__main__":
    create_workbook("hello.xlsx")
```

The first step in writing your new code is to import `xlsxwriter` itself. Then you create a `xlsxwriter.Workbook()` object, which takes the file path of the Excel spreadsheet that you plan to save.

You then call `add_worksheet()` with the name of the worksheet that you are adding. The call to `add_worksheet()` returns a Worksheet object. Since an empty spreadsheet is boring, you create some data and then loop over it. In each iteration, you `write()` a row of data to the Worksheet object (`sheet`).

At the end of your code, you create a second blank worksheet and then save the workbook.

When you run this code, you will create an Excel spreadsheet named `hello.xlsx`. If you open the spreadsheet, it will look like this:

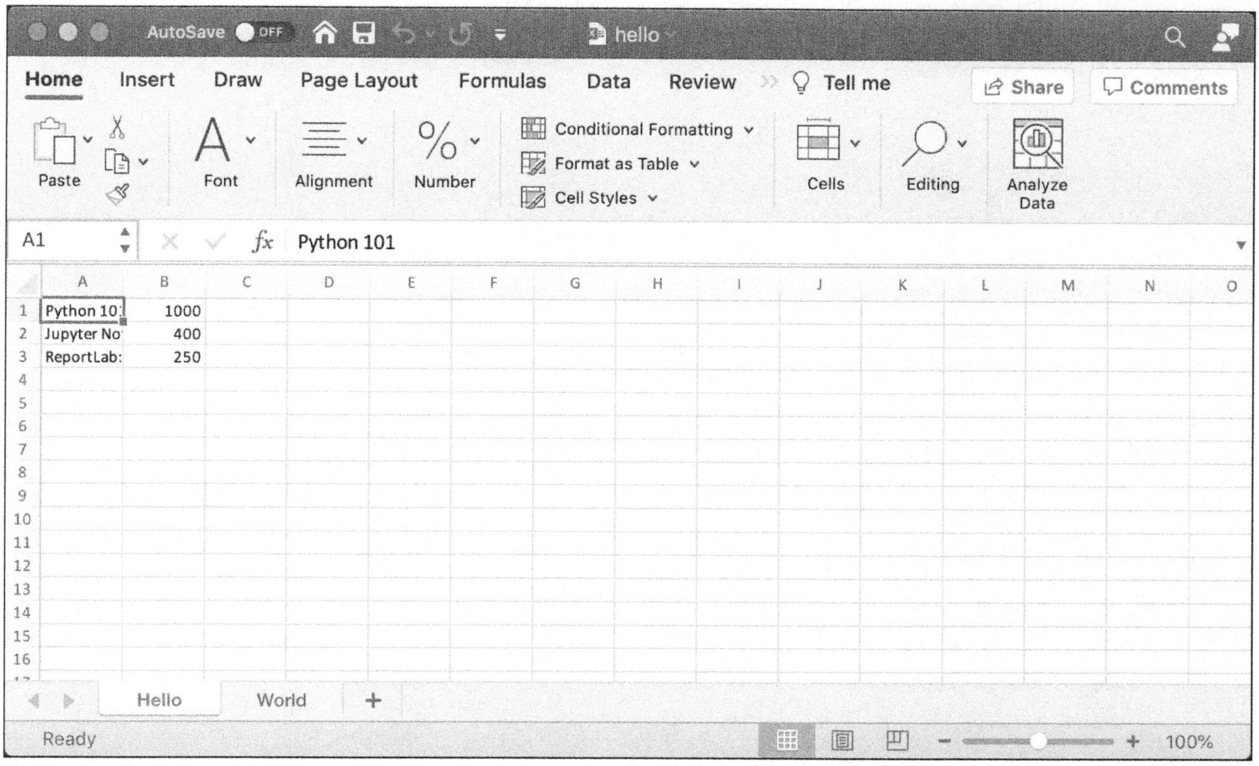

Fig. 11-1: Creating an Excel Spreadsheet with XlsxWriter

Isn't that a lovely spreadsheet? Good job! Now you're ready to learn how to add some formatting to your cells!

Formatting Cells

Excel lets you format every cell in your spreadsheet differently. The XlsxWriter package also gives you the ability to programmatically format each cell differently. You can make your spreadsheet more attractive looking by adding formatting to your cells.

In this example, you will learn to make text bold and apply some number formatting to your cells. To get started, create a new file named `formatting_spreadsheet.py` and then add this code to it:

```
# formatting_spreadsheet.py

import xlsxwriter


def format_data(path):
    workbook = xlsxwriter.Workbook(path)
    sheet = workbook.add_worksheet(name="Hello")
    data = [["Python 101", 1000, 9.99],
```

```
            ["Jupyter Notebook 101", 400, 14.99],
            ["ReportLab: PDF Processing", 250, 24.99]
    ]

    # Add formatting objects
    bold = workbook.add_format({'bold': True})
    money = workbook.add_format({'num_format': '$#,##0.00'})

    # Add headers
    sheet.write("A1", "Book Title", bold)
    sheet.write("B1", "Copies Sold", bold)
    sheet.write("C1", "Book Price", bold)

    row = 1
    col = 0
    for book, sales, amount in data:
        sheet.write(row, col, book)
        sheet.write(row, col + 1, sales)
        sheet.write(row, col + 2, amount, money)
        row += 1

    workbook.close()


if __name__ == "__main__":
    format_data("formatting.xlsx")
```

This code starts out much like the last example. But this time around, you add one additional piece of data per row, namely the "Book Price".

Then you add two formatting objects:

- bold - For making the text bold in a cell
- money - For formatting a float or integer in a cell

The next step is to add header columns that describe what is in the following rows. For the header columns, you apply the `bold` formatting to make them stand out. Then you look over the data you created and add each row to the worksheet. The last `write()` call that you make in this code uses the `money` formatting object to apply formatting to the "Book Price" to have a decimal place and a dollar sign.

Try running this code and then open the Excel spreadsheet that it generates. Your new spreadsheet will look like this:

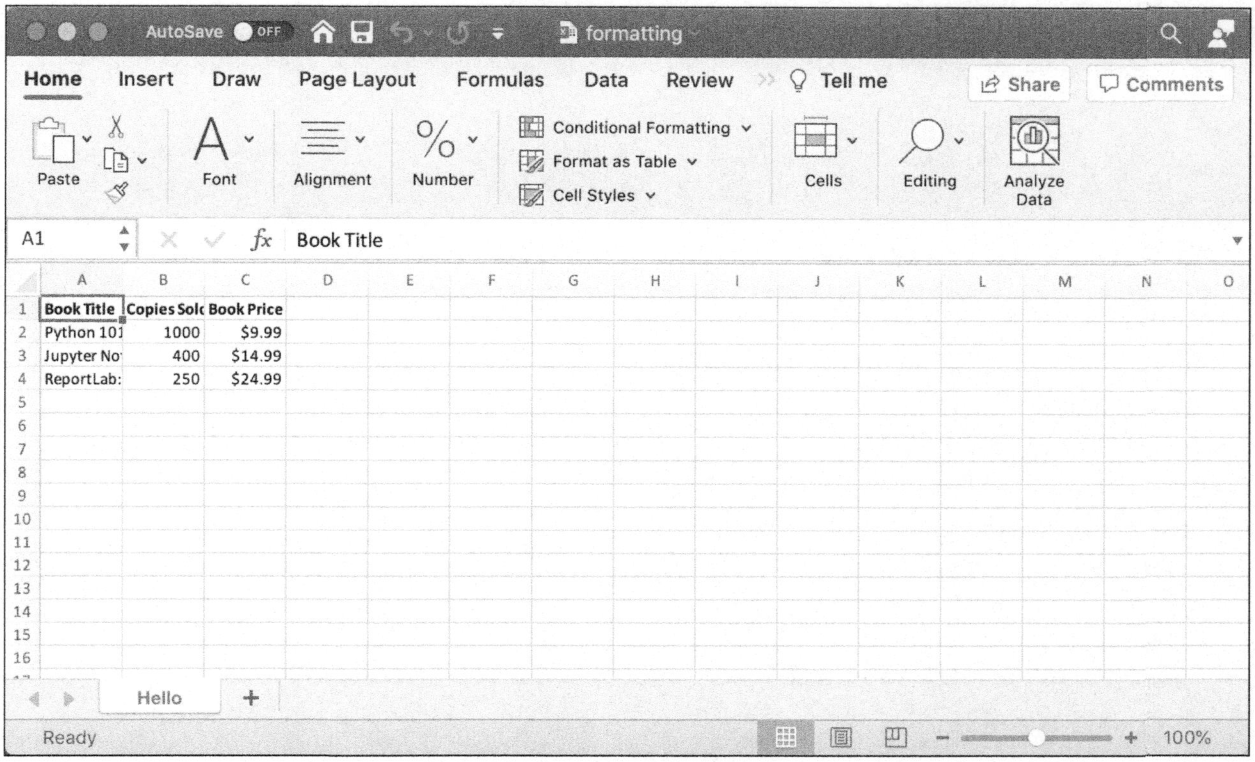

Fig. 11-2: Cell Formatting with XslxWriter

This spreadsheet looks nice and professional now. You should try to figure out how to create a totals field and add that to your spreadsheet.

Now you are ready to learn how to add a chart using XlsxWriter!

Adding a Chart

Creating a chart is a good way to visualize your data using Microsoft Excel. The XlsxWriter package can create charts for you as well. For this example, you will create a line chart.

To get started, you will need to create a new Python file named `line_chart.py`. Then enter the following code:

```python
# line_chart.py

import xlsxwriter


def chart(path):
    workbook = xlsxwriter.Workbook(path)
    sheet = workbook.add_worksheet(name="Hello")

    data = [15, 65, 50, 20, 5, 50]
    sheet.write_column("A1", data)

    # Create the chart object
    chart = workbook.add_chart({"type": "line"})
    chart.add_series({"values": "=Hello!$A$1:$A$6"})

    # Add the chart to the spreadsheet
    sheet.insert_chart("C1", chart)
    workbook.close()


if __name__ == "__main__":
    chart("line_chart.xlsx")
```

In this example, you create the `Workbook` and worksheet objects the same way you did in the previous examples. Then you add some data using the `write_column()` method. The `write_column()` method allows you to write out data using "A1" (or named cell) syntax.

Next, you call the worksheet's `add_chart()` method and pass in a dictionary that tells XlsxWriter that you want to create a line chart. To add values to your chart, you use the `add_series()` method, where you tell it which cells in the Excel spreadsheet to use to generate the chart. You use Excel's cell reference syntax (i.e. "=Hello!$A$1:$A$6") to tell Excel that the data it needs to create the chart is in cells **A1:A6**.

Finally, you pass the chart location and the chart object to `insert_chart()`.

When you run this code and open the Excel spreadsheet, you will see the following:

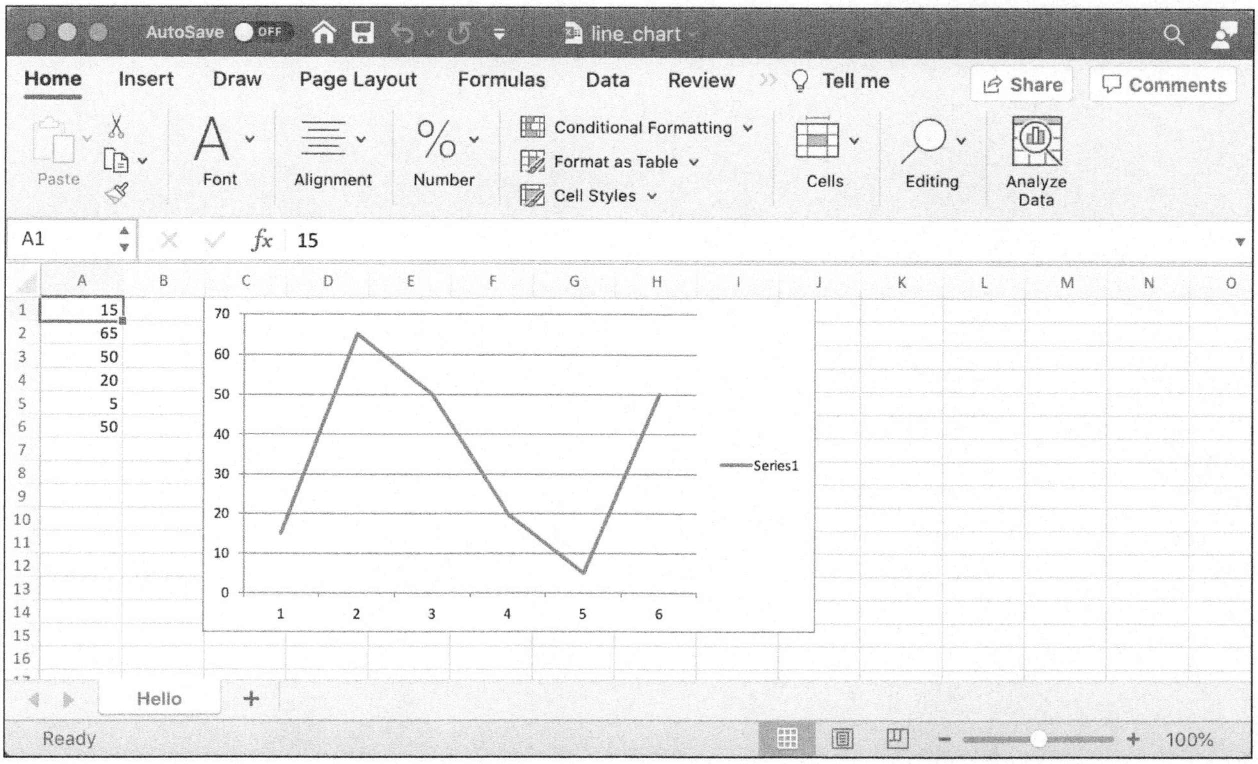

Fig. 11-3: Adding a Line Chart with XslxWriter

That's a nice-looking chart for a minimal amount of code. If you'd like to learn more about charts in XlsxWriter, you should read the chart documentation[23].

Now you're ready to learn about Sparklines!

Creating Sparklines

A Sparkline is a small chart that fits into a single cell. In contrast, regular charts are placed over multiple cells. You can add a Sparkline by using the worksheet's `add_sparkline()` method. Sparklines were added to Microsoft Excel in the 2010 edition.

To see how this works, create a new Python file named `sparklines.py` and enter this code:

[23]https://xlsxwriter.readthedocs.io/working_with_charts.html

```python
# sparklines.py

import xlsxwriter


def sparklines(path):
    workbook = xlsxwriter.Workbook(path)
    sheet = workbook.add_worksheet(name="Sparky")
    spark_styles = [{'range': 'Sparky!A1:E1',
                     'markers': True},
                    {'range': 'Sparky!A2:E2',
                    'type': 'column',
                    'style': 12},
                    {'range': 'Sparky!A3:E3',
                     'type': 'win_loss',
                     'negative_points': True}
                    ]

    data = [[-5, 5, 3, -2, 0,],
            [50, 40, 44, 20, 35],
            [0, 1, -1, 0, 1]]
    for row in range(len(data)):
        sheet.write_row(f"A{row+1}", data[row])
        # Add sparklines
        sheet.add_sparkline(f"F{row+1}", spark_styles[row])

    workbook.close()


if __name__ == "__main__":
    sparklines("sparklines.xlsx")
```

This code shows you how to create three different types of Sparklines. The first Sparkline uses markers. The second uses style 12 and is of type "column". The third is of type "win_loss" and you also turn on `negative_points`.

To add the Sparklines to your spreadsheet, you loop over a nested list of lists and add each row to the spreadsheet. You also add a Sparkline and specify which spark style to use.

When your code finishes, you should end up with a spreadsheet that looks something like this:

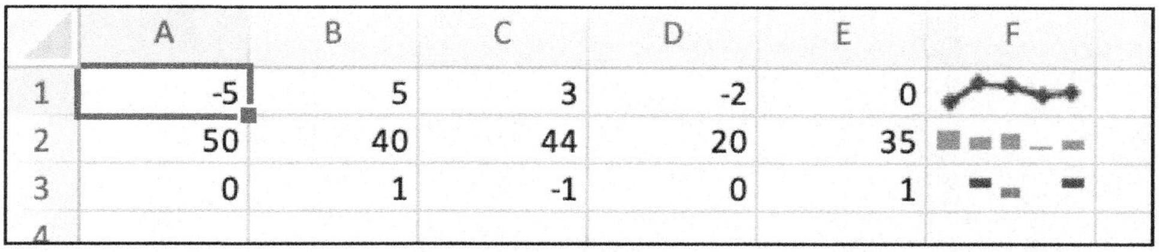

Fig. 11-4: Adding Sparklines with XslxWriter

Sparklines are an interesting feature, but they do not convey as much information as a regular chart. The Sparkline does add a little something extra to your data though.

The next topic for you to learn about is data validation!

Data Validation

XslxWriter has decent documentation[24] for their data validation support. You can use data validation to validate that the data the user enters is correct.

For this example, you will create a cell that only accepts integers between the values of 1 and 15. Create a new file named `data_validation.py` and enter the following code:

```
# data_validation.py

import xlsxwriter


def validate(path):
    workbook = xlsxwriter.Workbook(path)
    sheet = workbook.add_worksheet()

    sheet.set_column('A:A', 34)
    sheet.set_column('B:B', 15)

    header_format = workbook.add_format(
        {
            "border": 1,
            "bg_color": "#33f3ff",
            "bold": True,
            "text_wrap": True,
            "valign": "vcenter",
            "indent": 1,
        }
```

[24]https://xlsxwriter.readthedocs.io/working_with_data_validation.html

```
    )

    sheet.write("A1", "Data Validation Example", header_format)
    sheet.write("B1", "Enter Values Here", header_format)

    sheet.write("A3", "Enter an integer between 1 and 15")
    sheet.data_validation(
        "B3",
        {"validate": "integer", "criteria": "between",
         "minimum": 1, "maximum": 15},
    )
    workbook.close()

if __name__ == "__main__":
    validate("validation.xlsx")
```

The first new piece of code here is the `set_column()` method. You can use `set_column()` to set a column's width. In this example, you set the A and B column's to different widths.

Next, you create a special format called `header_format`:

```
header_format = workbook.add_format(
    {
        "border": 1,
        "bg_color": "#33f3ff",
        "bold": True,
        "text_wrap": True,
        "valign": "vcenter",
        "indent": 1,
    }
)
```

This code allows you to add a border, set the background color, bold the text, and more. Study this dictionary carefully to see what all it does for you. After you define this code, you apply it to cells A1 and B1.

To add data validation to a cell, you call the `data_validation()` method. In this example, `data_validation()` takes in the named cell ("B3") that you want to add validation to as well as the type of validation you wish to apply. The validation specifications are a dictionary. In this case, you set B3 up to validate that integers are entered and that they are between 1 and 15.

When you run this code, your spreadsheet will look like this:

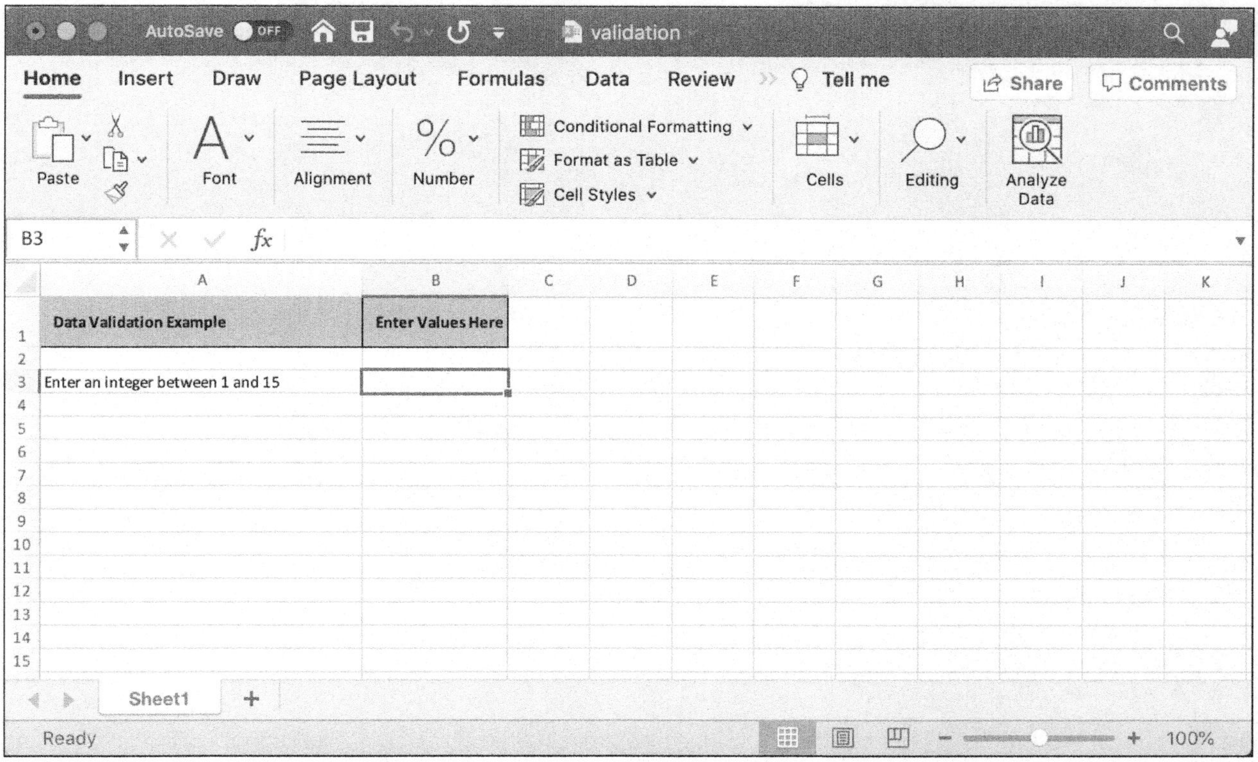

Fig. 11-5: Adding Data Validation with XslxWriter

Try entering an integer that is outside the range of 1-15. Here is what happens when you enter 18:

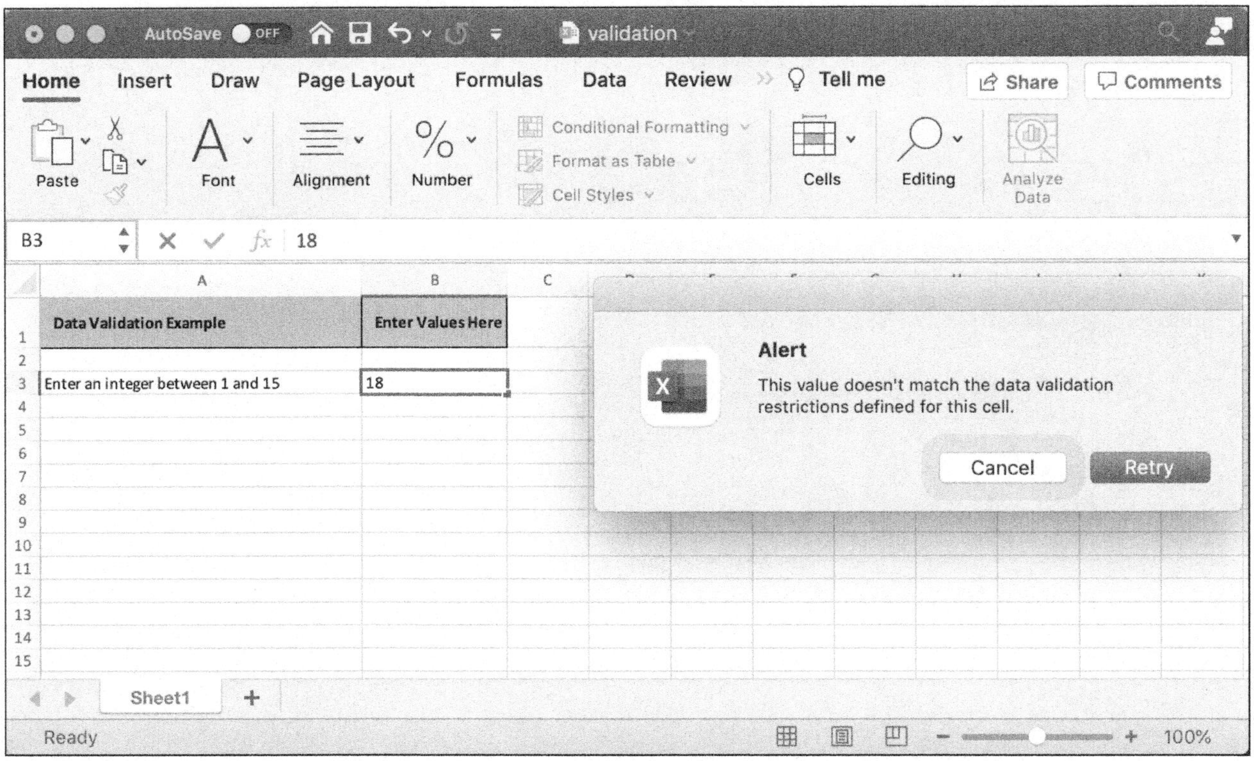

Fig. 11-6: Data Validation Alert Message

You get an alert message telling you that you can't do that! Check out XlsxWriter's documentation for many other examples of data validation.

Wrapping Up

The XlsxWriter package is very versatile. XlsxWriter is a great way to generate Microsoft Excel spreadsheets in Python. The only downside is that XlsxWriter does not support reading Excel spreadsheets.

In this chapter, you learned about the following topics:

- Creating an Excel spreadsheet
- Formatting cells
- Adding a chart
- Creating Sparklines
- Data validation

XlsxWriter can do much more than what is covered here. For example, you can add filters, cell comments, conditional formatting, worksheet tables, and much more. Check this package out, and try creating your spreadsheets today!

Appendix A - Cell Comments

Microsoft Excel can add comments to each cell in your spreadsheet. A company may use comments to give feedback about how the spreadsheet works or add documentation about complex formulas in the spreadsheet.

In this appendix, you will learn about the following topics:

- Adding comments with Excel
- Adding comments to cells with OpenPyXL
- Loading comments from a workbook

According to the OpenPyXL documentation[25], OpenPyXL only supports the reading and writing of comments. All formatting is lost. Comment dimensions are lost when reading but can be maintained when saving. Comments are not currently supported if `read_only=True`.

Note: In Office 365, Microsoft added threaded-comments and renamed the old comment functionality "notes".

You will start by learning how to add comments and view them solely with Microsoft Excel. Then you will learn how to use OpenPyXL and Python to work with cell comments.

Adding Comments with Excel

If you are not a power user of Microsoft Excel, you may not have realized that this commenting feature was present in Excel. Microsoft has made it fairly easy to add comments to the cells in your spreadsheet. This section of the appendix assumes you have Microsoft Excel installed.

Open up a new Excel spreadsheet. Then right-click on a cell. For this example, use **A1**. You should see the following context menu:

[25]https://openpyxl.readthedocs.io/en/stable/comments.html

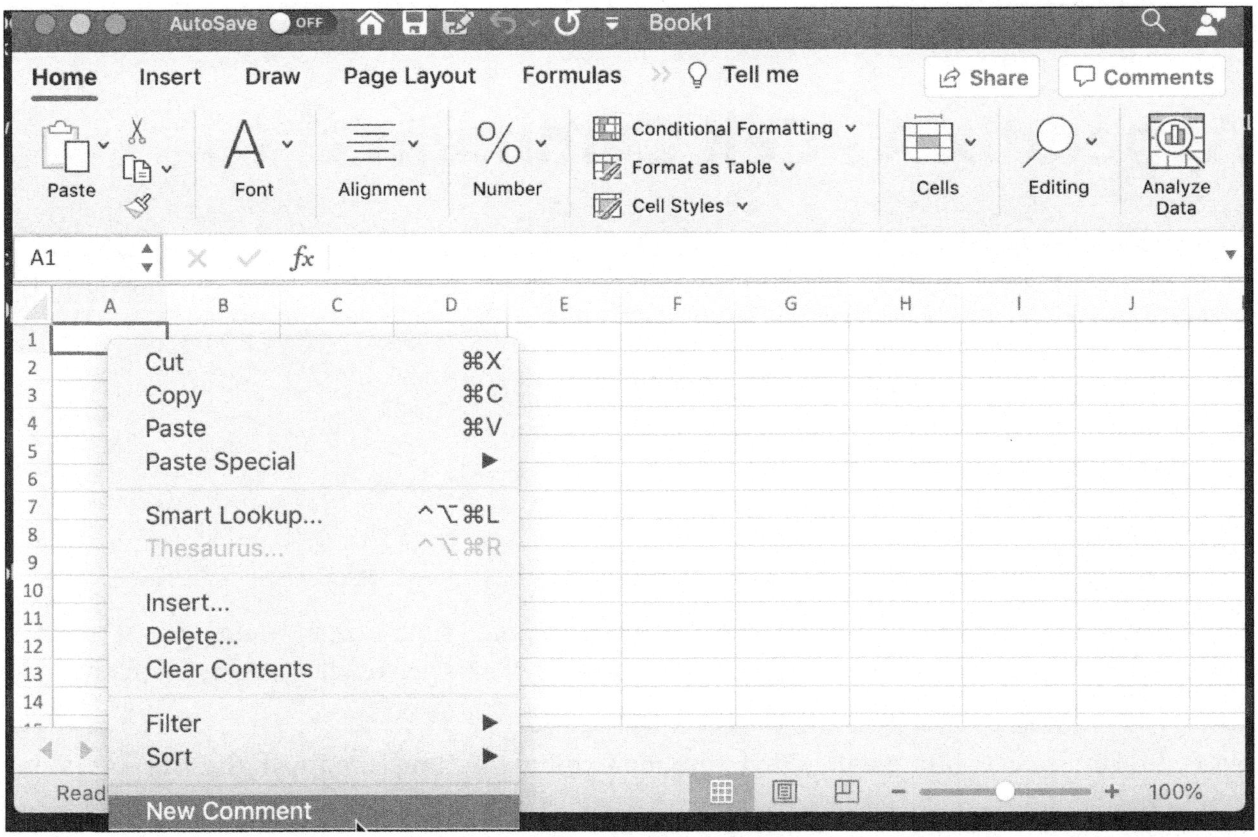

Fig. Appendix A-1: Right-Clicking and Adding a Comment

Choose **New Comment** from the context menu. It's quite a ways down the list of menu options, but you'll find it. After selecting **New Comment**, you will see the following dialog:

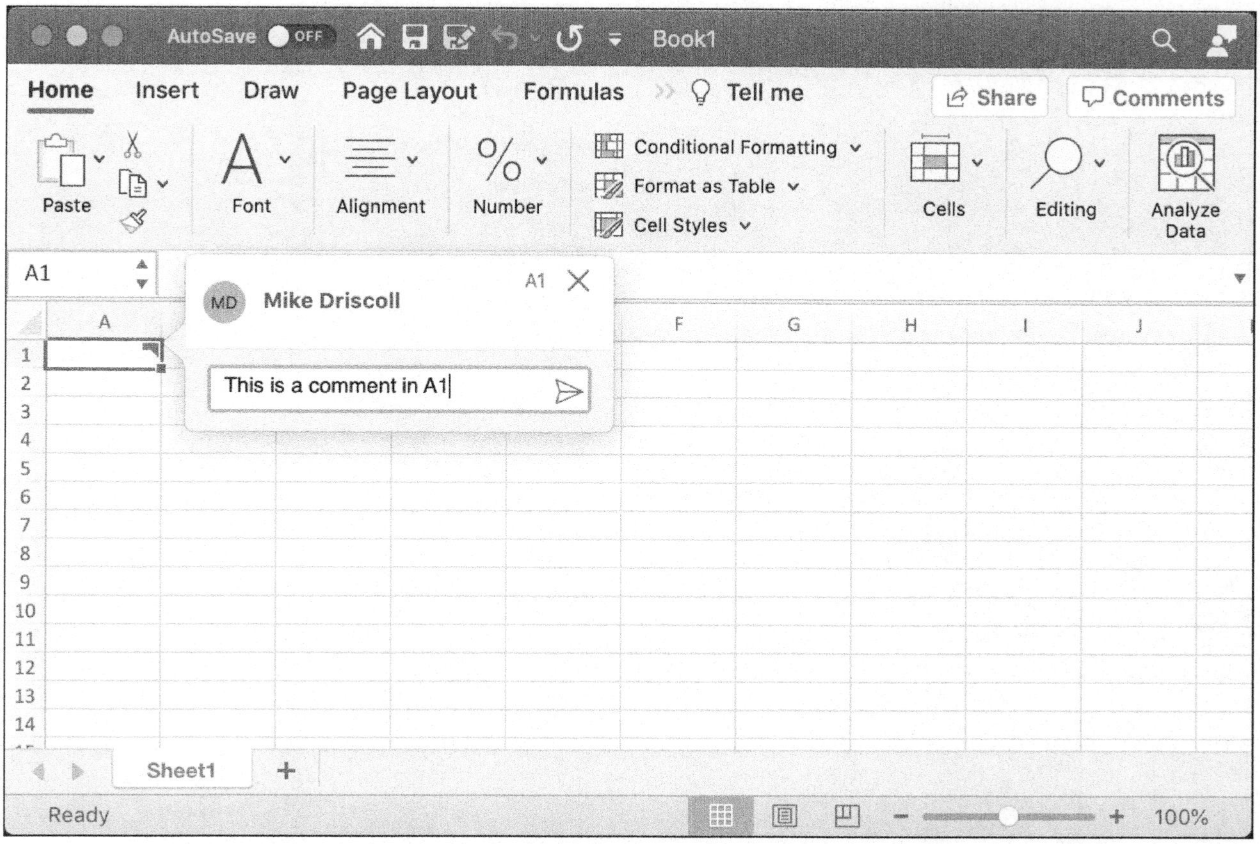

Fig. Appendix A-2: Adding Content to Comment Dialog

This screenshot shows you where you write your comment. In this example, the text "This is a comment in A1" was used. When you are ready to save the comment, click the large arrow / paper airplane symbol at the bottom right of the dialog.

Your comment will save with a timestamp and appear like this:

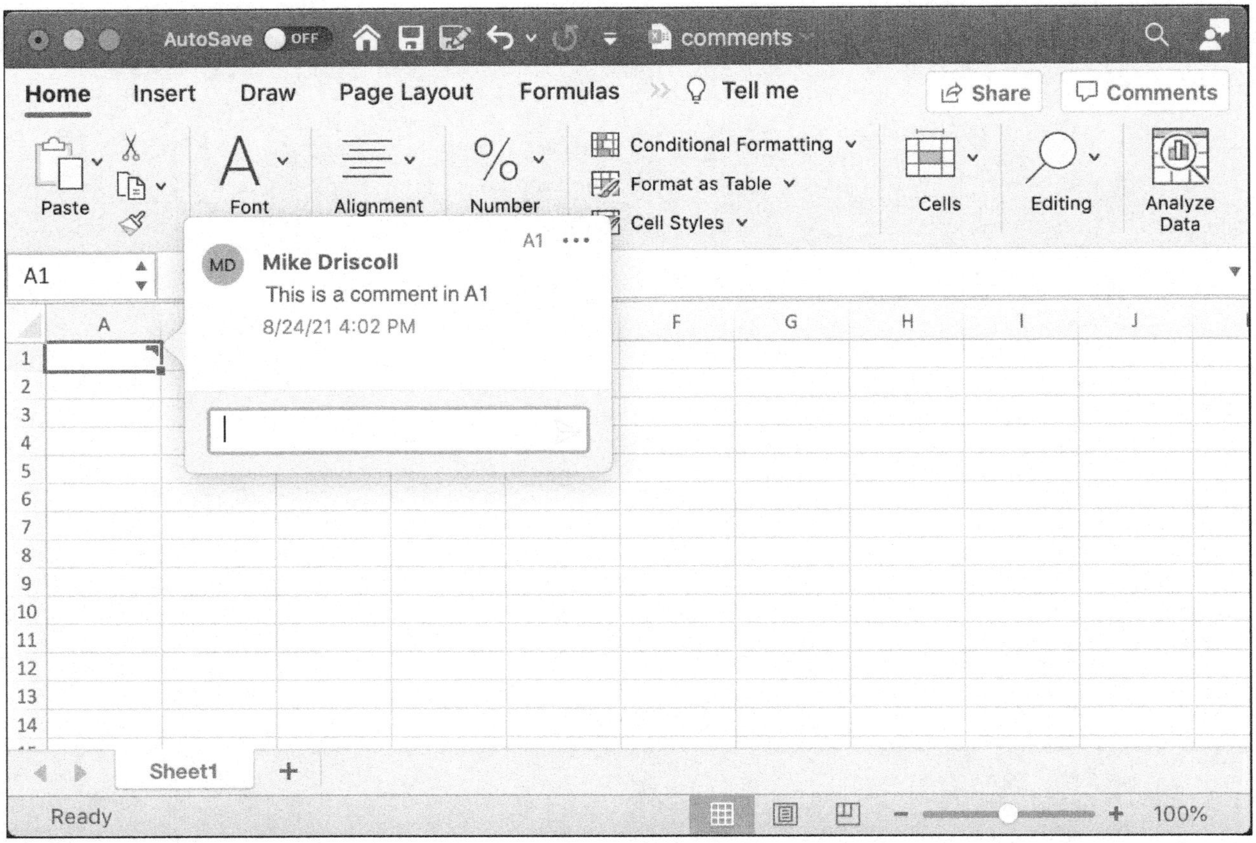

Fig. Appendix A-3: Comment Posted

Microsoft allows you to add another comment at this time if you want to do so. When there are multiple comments on a single cell, they are called *threaded comments*.

Save your Excel spreadsheet with the name **comments.xlsx**. If you don't have Microsoft Excel yourself, you can download the **comments.xlsx** file from this book's source repository on GitHub[26].

Now you are ready to learn about adding comments using OpenPyXL!

Adding Comments to Cells with OpenPyXL

The documentation[27] for OpenPyXL on comments claims you can add and save comments to an Excel spreadsheet. Depending on the version of Excel that you have, when you follow the documentation, you may end up saving a **note**, not a **comment**. Microsoft changes the terminology depending on whether or not you are using a standalone Excel version versus Office 365.

Regardless, you will use their currently documented method for adding comments, and perhaps it will work the way it should at some point. Go ahead and create a file named `creating_comments.py`. Then enter the following code:

[26]https://github.com/driscollis/automating_excel_with_python
[27]https://openpyxl.readthedocs.io/en/stable/comments.html

```python
# creating_comments.py

from openpyxl import Workbook
from openpyxl.comments import Comment


def main(filename, cell):
    workbook = Workbook()
    sheet = workbook.active

    comment = Comment(text="Comment written by OpenPyXL",
                      author="OpenPyXL")
    sheet[cell].comment = comment
    comment.width = 300
    comment.height = 30

    print(comment.text)
    print(f"Comment author: {comment.author}")
    workbook.save(filename)


if __name__ == "__main__":
    main("automated_comments.xlsx", "B1")
```

You will need to import the `Comment` class from `openpyxl.comments` to use it. The `Comment` takes four parameters:

- `text` - The comment text (required)
- `author` - The name of the author (required)
- `height` - The comment box height, default is 79
- `width` - The comment box width, default is 144

In your code, you set the `text` and `author` parameters explicitly. Then you modify the `width` and `height` by setting them using the comment's attributes. Finally, you print out the object's `text` and `author` and save the Excel spreadsheet.

If you open the Excel file and mouse over **B1**, you will see that the comment doesn't pop up. Instead, you'll see a different kind of box:

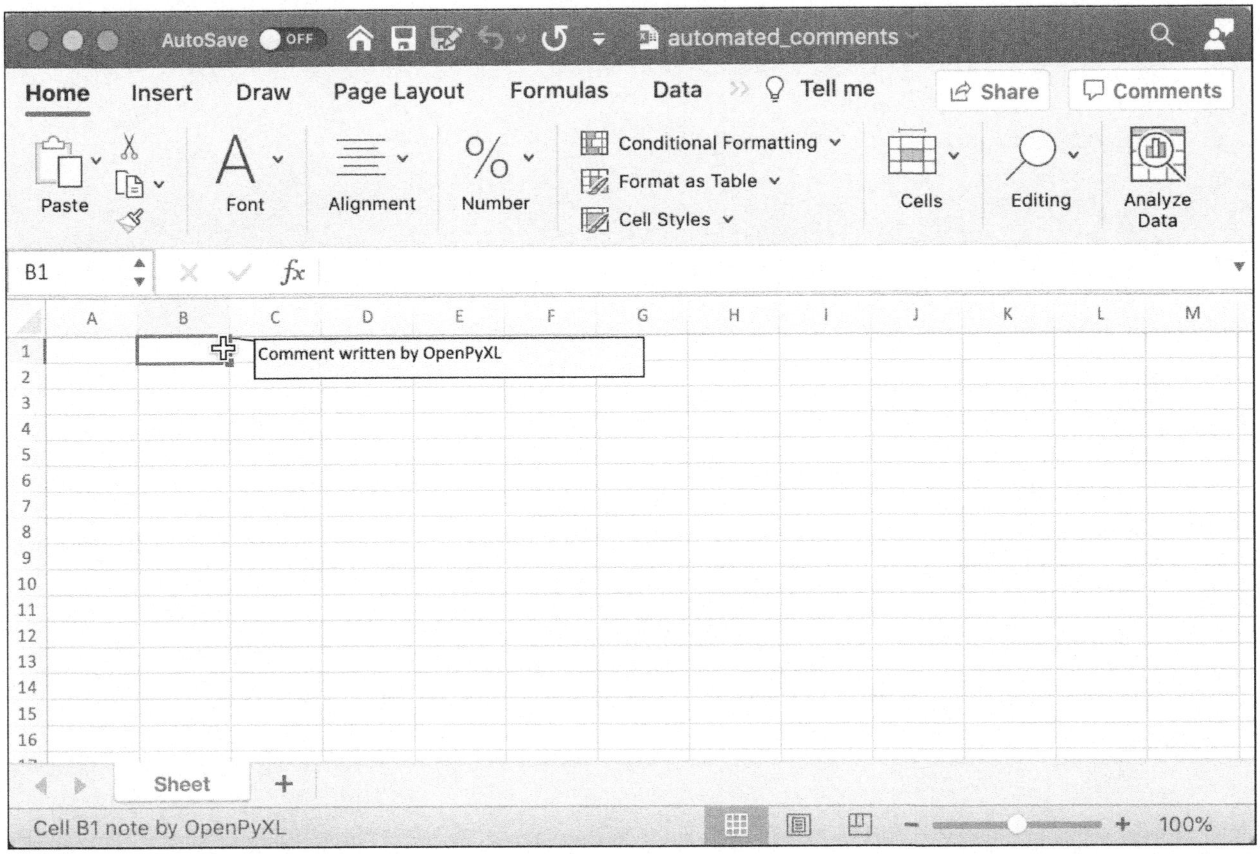

Fig. Appendix A-4: Note

This spreadsheet shows a note, not a comment. You can confirm that it is a note by right-clicking on the cell, and you will see options for edit the note or removing the note.

The next topic you will explore is how well OpenPyXL loads a comment from a workbook.

Loading Comments from a Workbook

You can use OpenPyXL to read comments out of your Excel document. To be effective, you should pass in which cells have comments. Otherwise, you would need to loop over the rows and columns and find the comments, if any.

You will be using the former approach where you pass in the cell(s) that you know have comments. Create a new file named `reading_comments.py`. Then enter the following code:

```python
# reading_comments.py

from openpyxl import load_workbook
from openpyxl.comments import Comment


def main(filename, cell):
    workbook = load_workbook(filename=filename)
    sheet = workbook.active
    comment = sheet[cell].comment
    print(comment)


if __name__ == "__main__":
    main("comments.xlsx", "A1")
```

Here you create a `main()` function that takes in the name of the Excel file and from which `cell` to load a comment. You use the `comments.xlsx` file that you created in the first section. If you don't have that file handy, you can download it from GitHub[28]. Next, you use `sheet[cell].comment` to extract the comment from the cell.

When you print the comment, you will see something like this:

```
Comment: [Threaded comment]

Your version of Excel allows you to read this threaded comment; however, any edits
to it will get removed if the file is opened in a newer version of Excel.
Learn more: https://go.microsoft.com/fwlink/?linkid=870924

Comment:
    This is a comment in A1 by tc={36BFDB51-47A0-8346-936E-835C6F72E94D}
```

Loading the comment appears to work correctly in this case. Although the author appears to saved as a hash that OpenPyXL can't read.

Wrapping Up

OpenPyXL allows you to read comments in Excel easily. In this appendix, you learned about the following:

- Adding comments with Excel

28 https://github.com/driscollis/automating_excel_with_python

- Adding comments to cells with OpenPyXL
- Loading comments from a workbook

If you can't get comments to work correctly, you may be using a version of Excel that doesn't call them "Notes" or you may be using LibreOffice or something similar. That's okay. The functionality is very similar.

Appendix B - Print Settings Basics

OpenPyXL gives you the ability to set up your spreadsheet's print settings. Their documentation[29], such as it is, claims near-full support. The only exception mentioned is that OpenPyXL may have only partial support for nested headers and footers.

Unfortunately, much of OpenPyXL's print setting support is undocumented. For example, the `addHeader` attribute is not actually in the `Worksheet` code, and the attribute gets injected into the object at runtime. If you dig in the source code, you will eventually discover that `addHeader` is an instance of `HeaderFooter` from the `header_footer` module.

With that said, this chapter will look at the documented features, which are:

- Centering your data
- Adding headers
- Adding print titles
- Specifying a print area

You will get started by learning how to set horizontal and vertical centering.

Centering Your Data

OpenPyXL lets you enable horizontal and vertical centering of your data when printing it. That means that if your spreadsheet has data in it, that data will be centered at print time if both are enabled.

To see how this works, create a new file named `print_options_center.py` and enter the following code:

```
# print_options_center.py

from openpyxl import Workbook


def center_data(path):
    workbook = Workbook()
    sheet = workbook.active
    sheet["A1"] = "Hello"
```

[29]https://openpyxl.readthedocs.io/en/stable/print_settings.html

```
    sheet["A2"] = "from"
    sheet["A3"] = "OpenPyXL"

    sheet.print_options.horizontalCentered = True
    sheet.print_options.verticalCentered = True

    workbook.save(path)


if __name__ == "__main__":
    center_data("print_options_center.xlsx")
```

You can tell OpenPyXL to center your data horizondally when printing by setting the following:

- `print_options.horizontalCentered = True`

If you wanted to center vertically, you would do this instead:

- `sheet.print_options.verticalCentered = True`

In this example, you set both to `True`, which will center the data on the page. You can confirm this by opening up the print dialog by pressing **CTRL+P** or by going to the **File** menu and choosing the **Print** option. Either way, you will see the following dialog:

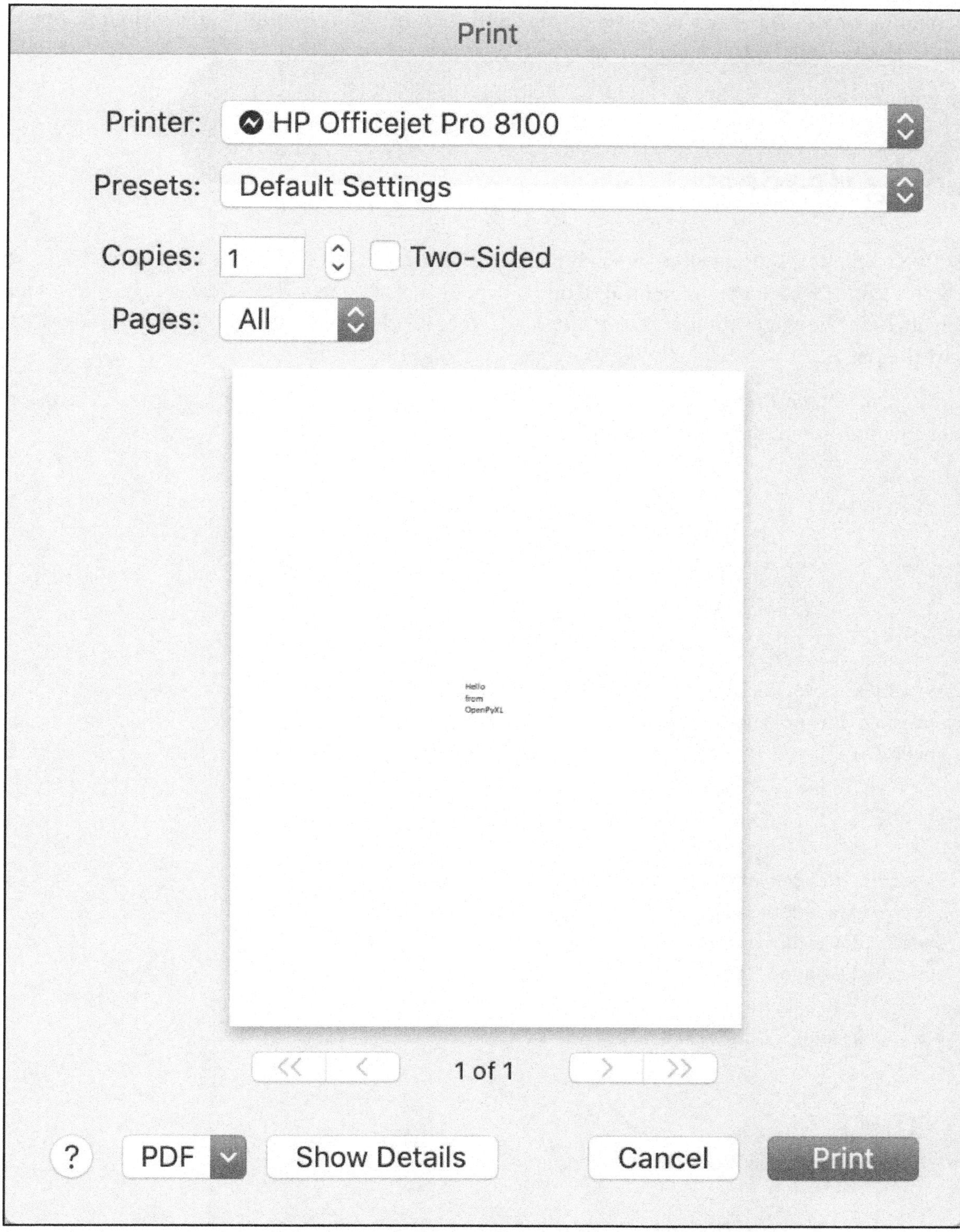

Fig. Appendix B-1: Centering Data Horizontally and Vertically

This dialog gives you a preview of how your printed sheet will appear on paper. As you can see, your data is centered on the page.

Try enabling one or the other of these settings and then re-run the code. You can then re-open the **Print** dialog and see how the document layout changes.

Now you are ready to move on and learn about adding page headers.

Adding Headers

OpenPyXL lets you set a header for each page that you print. If you have a large spreadsheet with many rows in it, then it can be helpful to add a header to each page. The header is especially helpful if you include the page numbers, so if the large document were to get dropped, you could easily re-sort the pages.

You will need to create a new Python file to see how this works. Name your new file `print_options_header.py` and then enter the following code:

```
# print_options_header.py

from openpyxl import Workbook


def add_header(path):
    workbook = Workbook()
    sheet = workbook.active
    sheet["A1"] = "Hello"
    sheet["A2"] = "from"
    sheet["A3"] = "OpenPyXL"

    sheet.oddHeader.left.text = "Page &[Page] of &N"
    sheet.oddHeader.left.size = 14
    sheet.oddHeader.left.font = "Tahoma,Bold"
    sheet.oddHeader.left.color = "CC3366"

    workbook.save(path)


if __name__ == "__main__":
    add_header("print_options.xlsx")
```

This code shows some of the undocumented functionality that OpenPyXL can deliver. For example, the documentation (at the time this book was written) does not explain what this code does:

```
sheet.oddHeader.left.text = "Page &[Page] of &N"
```

Fortunately, it will print out the current page and the total number of pages in this format: "Page 1 of N". However, you don't have any way of knowing if there is a way to change this. For example, some companies don't print a page number on the first page. There is no way of knowing if that is supported programmatically here.

The rest of the code in this example sets the font face, its size, and its color.

When you run this code and open up the **Print** dialog, you will see the following:

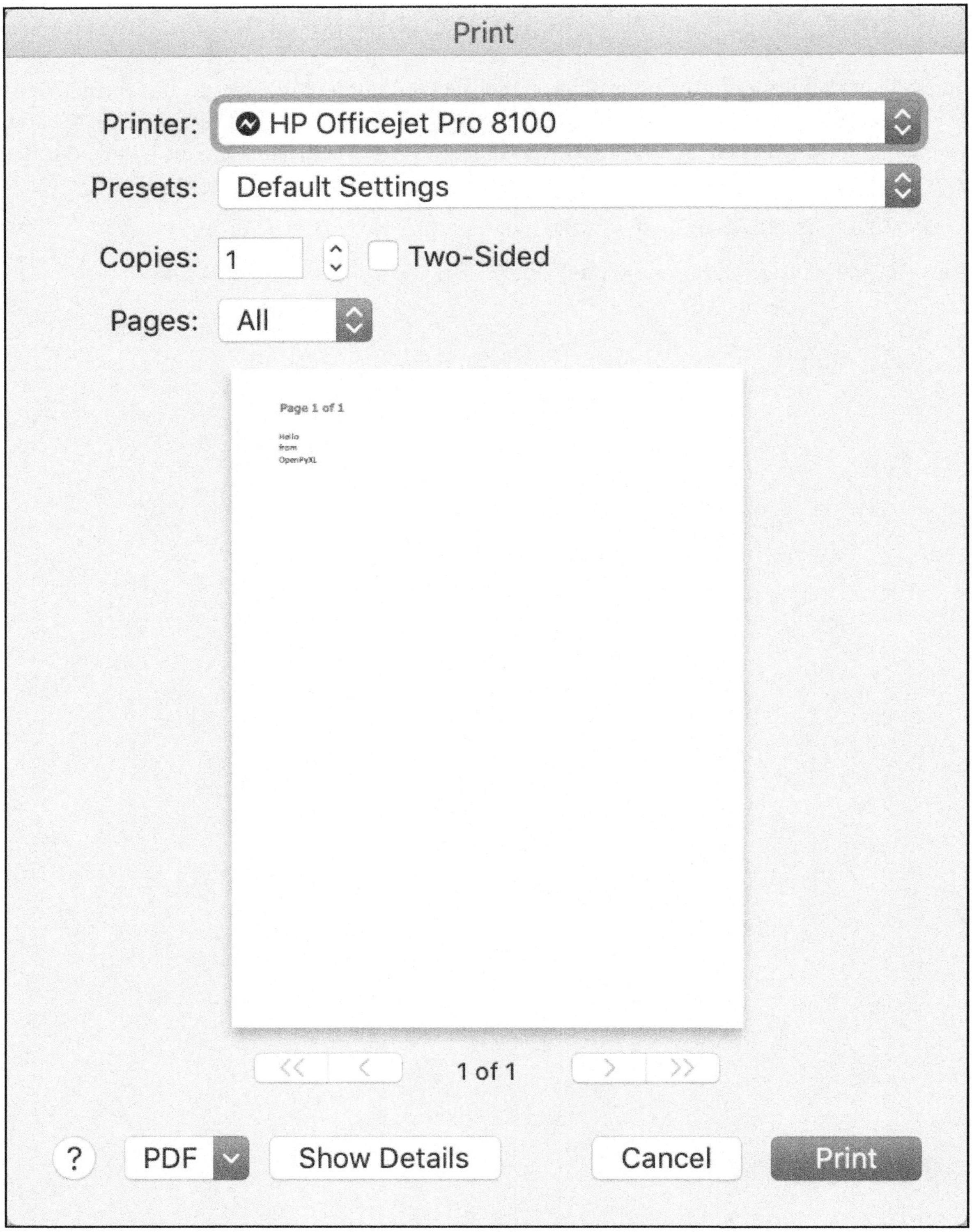

Fig. Appendix B-2: Print Dialog with Header

This code doesn't say if you can set the header to be in the center or on the right. However, you can replace `left` with `center` or `right`, and the header will be shifted accordingly on the page.

Here is how your spreadsheet would look if saved to PDF:

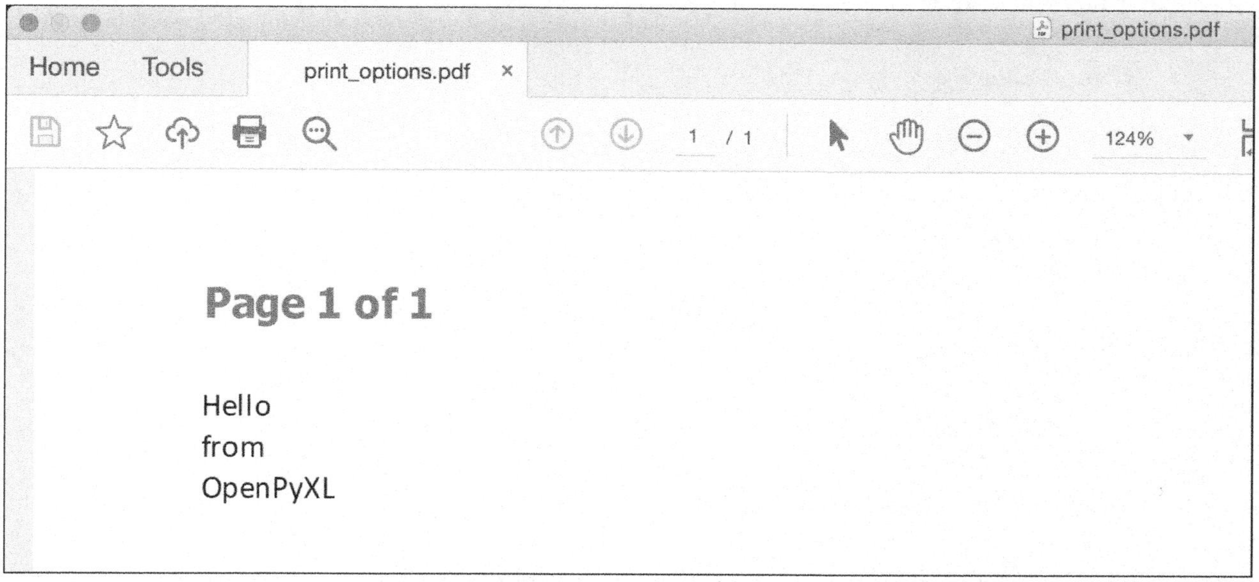

Fig. Appendix B-3: Header in PDF

This screenshot makes it a little easier to see the formatting of your data on the page. Go ahead and experiment, and you'll discover some of the subtleties of print option formatting in OpenPyXL.

Now you can move on and learn about adding titles to the data.

Adding Print Titles

Microsoft Excel allows you to freeze frames in Excel always to have a certain row shown while you scroll. Normally, the row chosen is the header row so that you always know what each column represents.

You can do something similar when you go to print your data. You want to be able to always show a particular set of columns and rows on every page. OpenPyXL lets you set this programmatically.

Create a new file named `print_titles.py` and enter the following:

```
# print_titles.py

from openpyxl import Workbook


def print_titles(path):
    workbook = Workbook()
    sheet = workbook.active
```

```
    # Add 101 rows of data
    sheet.append(["Book", "Kindle", "Paperback"])
    for row in range(100):
        sheet.append(["Python 101", 9.99, 15.99])

    # Set the first three columns as the title columns
    sheet.print_title_cols = "A:C"
    # Set the first row as the title row
    sheet.print_title_rows = "1:1"

    workbook.save(path)


if __name__ == "__main__":
    print_titles("print_titles.xlsx")
```

Here you use the `sheet` object's `print_title_cols` to set which columns you print on each page. Then you use the `sheet` object's `print_title_rows` attribute to set which rows you want to print first on each page. In this case, you set the columns to **A**:**C** and the first row.

When you run this code and open the **Print** dialog, you can see that when you go to print, it has three pages:

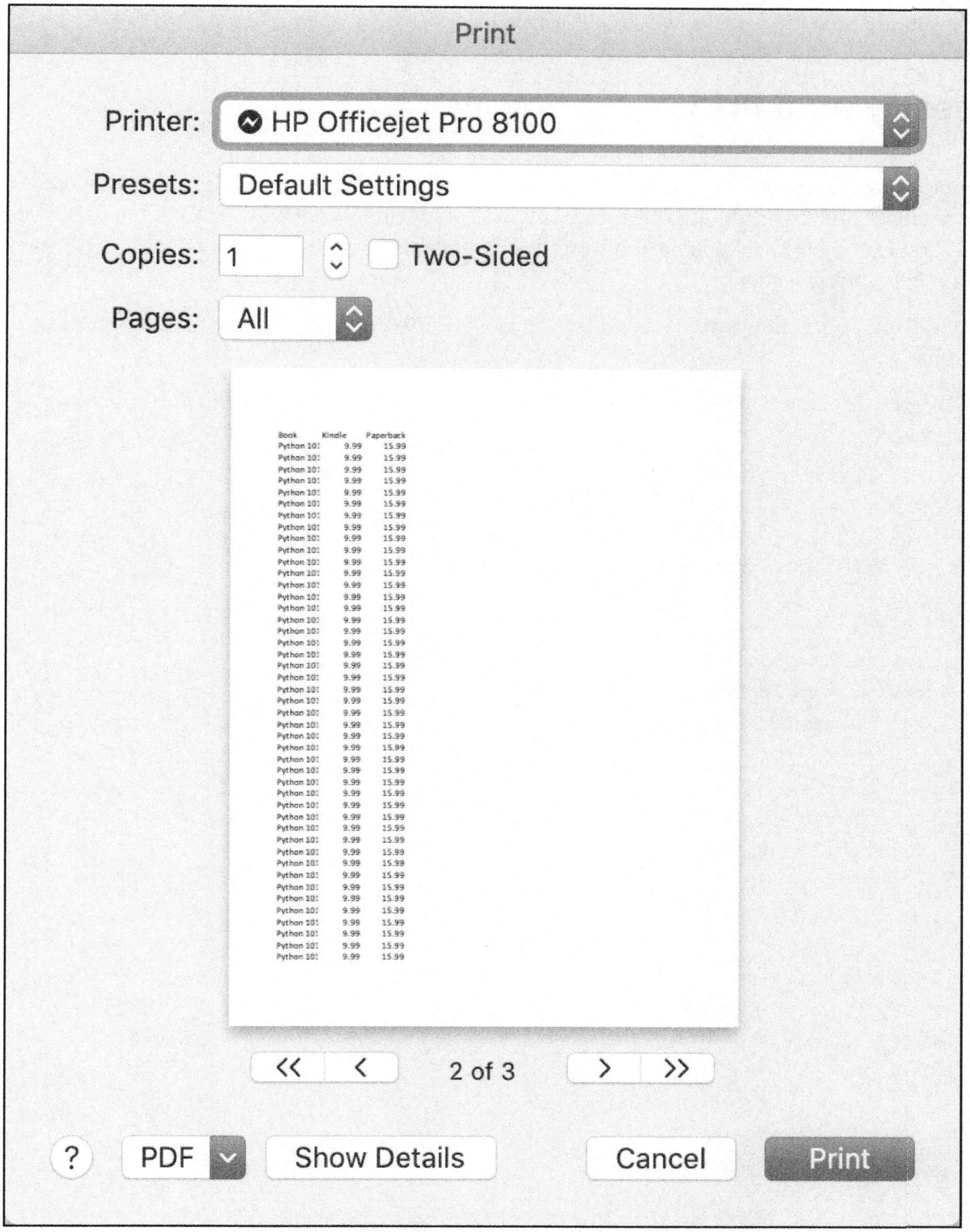

Fig. Appendix B-4: Adding Titles in Print Dialog

It's hard to see in this screenshot, but if you click through each page in the print preview, you can see that the first row is the same in all of them.

Now you are ready to learn how to set a print area!

Specifying a Print Area

The print area is the set of data that you print. By default, when you go to print your spreadsheet, Excel will attempt to print out everything. You may not want to print all your data, but only a subset of it. You can select the columns and rows that you want manually to print or set it up in the **File** menu, **Print Area** section.

If you'd like to set the print area with Python, you must modify the `sheet` object's `print_area` attribute.

You can see this in action by writing some code! Create a new file and name it `print_area.py`. Then enter this code:

```
# print_area.py

from openpyxl import Workbook


def print_area(path):
    workbook = Workbook()
    sheet = workbook.active

    # Add 101 rows of data
    sheet.append(["Book", "Kindle", "Paperback"])
    for row in range(100):
        sheet.append(["Python 101", 9.99, 15.99])

    # Only print the data in A1 - B20
    sheet.print_area = "A1:B20"

    workbook.save(path)


if __name__ == "__main__":
    print_area("print_area.xlsx")
```

Here you set the `print_area` to **A1:B20**. That will print the first 20 rows, but only the data in columns **A** and **B**.

If you run this code and open up the **Print** dialog, you will the following:

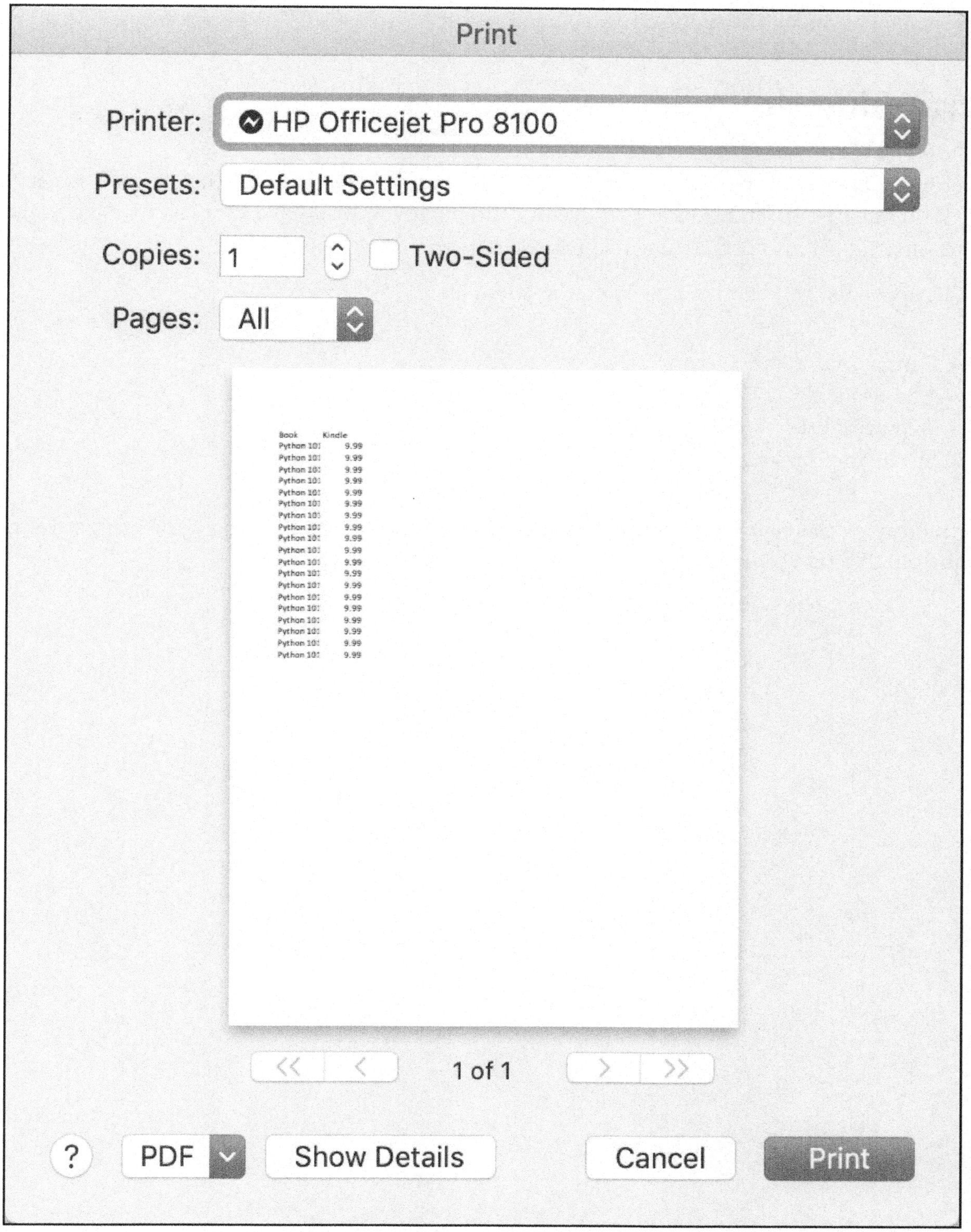

Fig. Appendix B-5: Specifying the Print Area in Print Dialog

This screenshot shows that you are only printing one page, and that page isn't going to be full of data either because it is only twenty rows worth of data! Try modifying the print area range yourself and see how it changes for yourself!

Wrapping Up

OpenPyXL provides a fairly robust API for modifying the print settings in Microsoft Excel. You should set any print settings that you need to, although you may have to resort to some trial and error since the API is not fully documented.

In this appendix, you learned how to do the following:

- Center your data
- Add headers
- Add print titles
- Specify a print area

Try modifying the code examples in this appendix. You can learn a lot about the print settings by trying out different settings.

Appendix C - Formulas

Microsoft Excel supports many different types of formulas that you may choose to use on your data. There are several support documents on this topic on the Microsoft website. Here are just a couple of samples:

- Overview of formulas in Excel[30]
- Create a simple formula in Excel[31]

In this appendix, you will learn about the following topics:

- The parts of an Excel formula
- Adding a formula in Excel
- Adding a formula with OpenPyXL

You will start by learning about the parts of an Excel formula!

The Parts of an Excel Formula

There are multiple parts to an equation or formula in Microsoft Excel. An Excel formula can contain any or all of the following: **functions**, **references**, **operators**, and **constants**. The best way to learn what they are is to look at a formula and then go over the components that make it up.

For this example, you will use Excel's `PI()` function, which returns the value of pi (3.14159...):

```
=PI() * B12 ^ 2
```

Here are the parts that make up an Excel formula:

- `PI()` - A **function** that you call in Excel (`SUM()` is another popular function).
- `B12` - A **reference** to a cell. In this case, B12 returns the value found in the cell, B12.
- `2` - The number "2" in the above formula is called a **constant**. A number or text value in a formula is a constant.
- `*` and `^` - The asterisk and caret symbols in this example are **operators**. The asterisk is for multiplication while the caret raises a number to a power.

Now that you know what makes up a formula, you are ready to write your own!

[30]https://support.microsoft.com/en-us/office/overview-of-formulas-in-excel-ecfdc708-9162-49e8-b993-c311f47ca173
[31]https://support.microsoft.com/en-us/office/create-a-simple-formula-in-excel-11a5f0e5-38a3-4115-85bc-f4a465f64a8a

Adding a Formula in Excel

To add a formula to a cell, you need to pick a cell. Then you are required to type the equals (=) sign, followed by the formula name, some references, constants, and/or operators.

For example, if you wanted to find the sum of the first 12 rows in column "B" in Excel, you could type this into cell "B13":

```
=SUM(B1:B12)
```

The formula above tells Microsoft Excel to add up all the numeric data in cells B1 through B12.

Adding a Formula with OpenPyXL

OpenPyXL has limited support for Microsoft Excel formulas. To see what formulas OpenPyXL supports creating, you can import `FORMULAE` from `openpyxl.utils`.

Here's how you do it:

```
>>> from openpyxl.utils import FORMULAE
>>> FORMULAE
frozenset({'ABS',
           'ACCRINT',
           'ACCRINTM',
           'ACOS',
           'ACOSH',
           'AMORDEGRC',
           'AMORLINC',
           'AND',
           ...,
           'XIRR',
           'XNPV',
           'YEAR',
           'YEARFRAC',
           'YIELD',
           'YIELDDISC',
           'YIELDMAT',
           'ZTEST'})
>>> len(FORMULAE)
352
```

This code shows you that OpenPyXL supports 352 formulas in Excel. Now that you know what formulas you can create, it would be great to use that knowledge.

Create a new file named `summing.py` and enter the following code:

```python
# summing.py

from openpyxl import Workbook


def main(filename):
    workbook = Workbook()
    sheet = workbook.active

    # Add data to spreadsheet
    data_rows = [
        ["Book", "Kindle", "Paperback"],
        [1, 9.99, 15.99],
        [2, 9.99, 25.99],
        [3, 9.99, 25.99],
        [4, 4.99, 29.99],
        [5, 14.99, 39.99],
    ]

    for row in data_rows:
        sheet.append(row)

    # Sum up columns
    sheet["A7"] = "Totals"
    sheet["B7"] = "=SUM(B2:B6)"
    sheet["C7"] = "=SUM(C2:C6)"
    workbook.save(filename)


if __name__ == "__main__":
    main("summing.xlsx")
```

Here you create an Excel file with five lines of raw sales data. The last row is for totals. You can total up those rows using Excel's `SUM()` function.

When you run this code, the output will look like this:

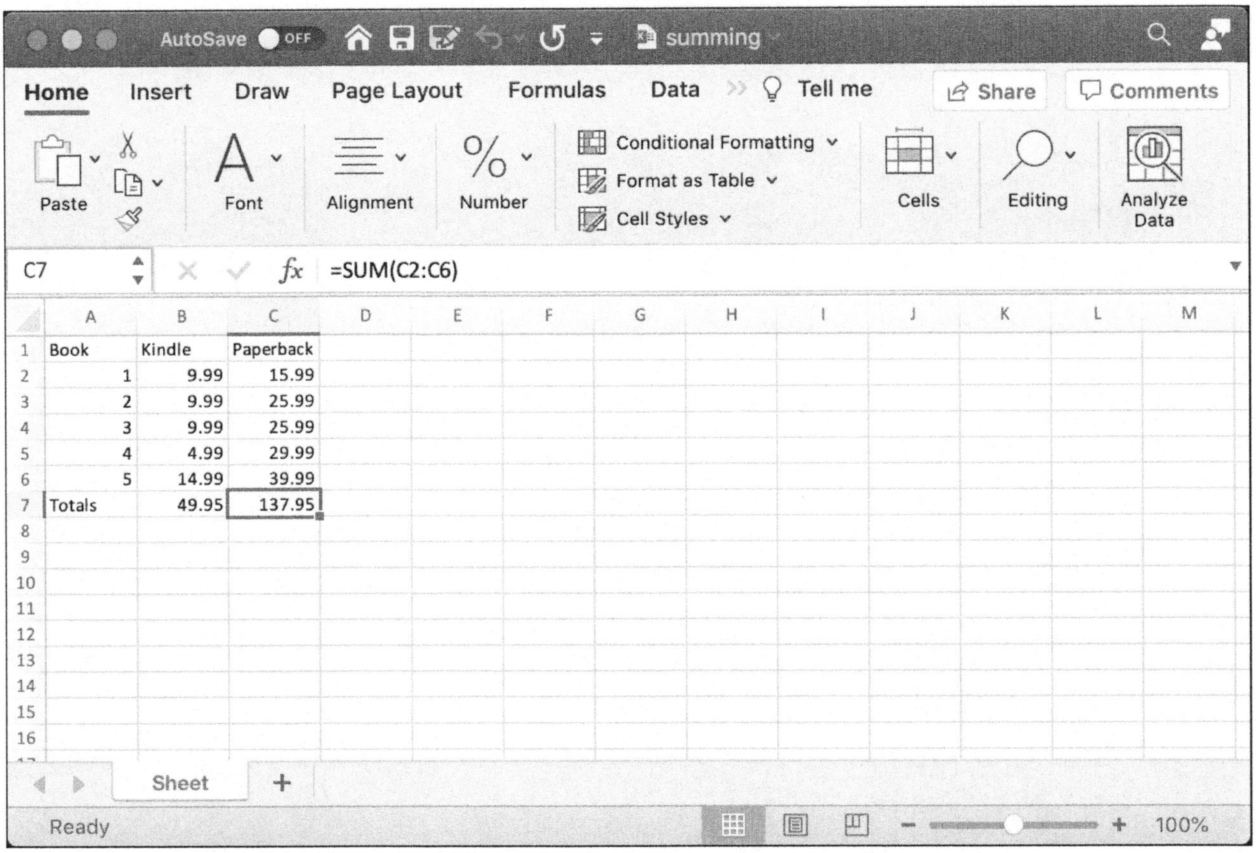

Fig. Appendix C-1: Summing Columns

You successfully applied the `SUM()` function on the data in the "B" and "C" columns of your Excel spreadsheet. Try applying an average or one of the other useful formulas that are in that list. You can use this technique to add any of those formulas to the spreadsheet.

If you combine this knowledge with the cell styling chapter, you can highlight certain pieces of your data very well.

Wrapping Up

OpenPyXL is a very flexible package. OpenPyXL can create over 350 different Excel formulas!

In this appendix, you learned about the following:

- The parts of an Excel formula
- Adding a formula in Excel
- Adding a formula with OpenPyXL

You can take this knowledge and combine it with many of the other tricks in this book to create unique spreadsheets of your own.

Afterword

For the second time as an author, I started working on this book with only a handful of knowledge of the package I was writing about. Fortunately, OpenPyXL is put together well and I was able to figure out everything I needed to from their documentation, the package itself, or from examples I found online.

OpenPyXL is one of the most robust Python packages for reading and writing Microsoft Excel spreadsheets. While there are some rough spots in the documentation that make it hard to follow at the time I wrote this book, I still feel like OpenPyXL is one of the best packages for processing Excel spreadsheets.

My technical reviewer, Ethan, was very helpful in correcting some of my ideas about charts. You can thank him for making that chapter much better than it would have been without his help.

I sincerely hope you find this book valuable for expanding your knowledge of Python and for helping you to automate the processing of Excel spreadsheets!

Thank you for reading this book.

Mike

Printed in Great Britain
by Amazon

10124778R00129